# The Golden Age of Zen

# The Golden Age of Zen
## JOHN C. H. WU

WITH AN INTRODUCTION BY
## THOMAS MERTON

IMAGE BOOKS
DOUBLEDAY
New York  London  Toronto  Sydney  Auckland

AN IMAGE BOOK

PUBLISHED BY DOUBLEDAY

a division of Bantam Doubleday Dell Publishing Group, Inc.

1540 Broadway, New York, New York 10036

IMAGE, DOUBLEDAY, and the portrayal of a deer drinking
from a stream are trademarks of Doubleday, a division of
Bantam Doubleday Dell Publishing Group, Inc.

First Image Books edition published January 1996

Library of Congress Cataloging-in-Publication Data
Wu, Ching-hsiung, 1899–
    The golden age of Zen / John C. H. Wu; with
an introduction by Thomas Merton. – 1st Image
Books ed.
        p.      cm.
    Includes index.
    1. Zen Buddhism—China—History.    2. Priests,
Zen—China.    I. Title.
BQ9562.5.W8    1996              95-17230
294.3'927'0951—dc20              CIP

ISBN 0-385-47993-X

# Contents

# Preface

By the "Golden Age of Zen" I mean the Zen as experienced and taught by the great Zen masters of the T'ang period (618–906). Although the school of Zen had its origins in the sixth century with the coming of Bodhidharma, its solid foundations were actually laid by Hui-neng in the seventh century. The whole movement flowered forth magnificently in the hands of such vigorous spirits as Ma-tsu, Shih-t'ou, Nan-ch'üan, Pai-chang, Huang-po, and Chao-chou. In the ninth century, it began to ramify into different branches. Inevitably the sap of Zen ran thin in the course of the succeeding generations, but with the founders of the "houses" there is still no sign of abatement of the original vigor.

In the epilogue I have drawn mainly upon the Zen literature after T'ang. Those little sparks of Zen will serve to indicate that although the school of Zen has long since passed its zenith, the spirit of Zen never dies.

Father Thomas Merton's introduction to this book presents an illuminating picture of the nature of Zen. Here as in his other writings he goes to the bottom of things, and he finds that at bottom humanity is one, and one with its Divine Source. I suggest that the reader should first study his introduction before he proceeds to take up the body of the book. In a real sense this book may be regarded as a long footnote to the profound insights embodied in his introduction.

I am grateful to Father Merton not only for the invaluable introduction he has contributed, but even more for his generous cooperation in the making of the book itself. There is no telling how much the friendship of this *true man* has meant to me during all these lonely years of my life.

The story of my friendship with the late Daisetz Suzuki is told in the appendix to this book. It is touching to think that he spent a great part of his last months perusing and enjoying the manuscript of this book.

Finally, this book would not have seen the light so soon were it not for the encouragement of my friend Dr. Chang Chi-yun, the founder and the head of the College of Chinese Culture. He is a humanist in the full sense of the word, for to him nothing human is alien. At his request I had the pleasure of offering a special seminar on Zen Buddhism at his college, and I have not only enjoyed but profited by the class discussions. I had taught the same subject at Seton Hall University. It is delightful to compare the reactions from students of entirely different backgrounds and to find that ultimately the diversity of views points up the selfsame mysterious Whole.

In this book I have used "Zen" and "Ch'an" interchangeably. With this exception, I have followed the Wade-Giles system of romanizing the Chinese words.

John C. H. Wu
(Wu Ching-hsiung)

August 22, 1967
Taipei, Taiwan, China

# Preface to the
# Second Edition

The first edition of this book, published in 1967, has been out of print for some time. I am, therefore, happy to accede to the earnest request of United Publishing Center to publish the present edition in order to answer the growing demands for the book. As the first edition is fraught with misprints, I have taken this occasion for correcting all the mistakes to the best of my ability. In this I am indebted to the kind cooperation of my friends Dr. Wei Tat and Mr. Liu Chih-hsiang.

The reader will be interested to know that a Chinese translation of this book was made by the able hands of Dr. Wu Yi and published by the Taiwan Commercial Press in 1969. This excellent translation has since passed through five editions. I am deeply consoled to learn that the message of this book is so well received among the younger generation of Chinese intellectuals.

Finally, let me offer this edition to the blessed memory of Thomas Merton, one of my dearest friends.

John C. H. Wu

August 4, 1975
91 Yang Ming Road,
Yangmingshan, Taipei,
Taiwan, Republic of China

# A Christian Looks at Zen

## BY THOMAS MERTON

Here is a book that will do much to clarify the still very confused western idea of Zen Buddhism. It is not an apologia, not a criticism, not a purely academic history, not a romantic exercise of imaginative concordism. It looks at the great Chinese Zen masters of the seventh to tenth centuries A.D., and portrays them in their "Five Houses." It enables us to situate their teaching and to enjoy it in its context.

Dr. John C. H. Wu is in a uniquely favorable position to carry out this task. An eminent jurist and diplomat, a Chinese convert to Catholicism, a scholar but also a man of profoundly humorous simplicity and spiritual freedom, he is able to write of Buddhism not from hearsay or study alone, but from within. Dr. Wu is not afraid to admit that he brought Zen, Taoism, and Confucianism with him into Christianity. In fact in his well-known Chinese translation of the New Testament he opens the Gospel of St. John with the words "In the beginning was the Tao."

He nowhere feels himself obliged to pretend that Zen causes him to have dizzy spells or palpitations of the heart. Nor does he attempt the complex and frustrating task of trying to conciliate Zen insights with Christian doctrine. He simply takes hold of Zen and presents it without comment. Anyone who has any familiarity with Zen will immediately admit that this is the only way to talk about it. To approach the subject with an intellectual or theological chip on the shoulder would end only in confusion. The truth of the matter is that you can hardly set Christianity and Zen side by side and compare them. This would almost be like trying to compare mathematics and tennis. And if you are writing a book on tennis, which might conceivably be read by many mathematicians, there is little point in bringing mathematics into the discussion: best to stick to the tennis. That is what Dr. Wu has done with Zen.

On the other hand, Zen is deliberately cryptic and disconcerting. It seems to say the most outrageous things about the life of the spirit. It seeks to jolt even the Buddhist mind out of its familiar thought routines and devout imaginings, and no doubt it will be even more shocking to those whose religious outlook is remote from Buddhism. Zen can sound, at times, frankly and avowedly irreligious. And it is, in the sense that it makes a direct attack on formalism and myth and regards conventional religiosity as a hindrance to mature spiritual development. On the other hand, in what sense is Zen, as such, religious at all? Yet where do we ever find "pure Zen" dissociated from a religious and cultural matrix of some sort? Some of the Zen masters were iconoclasts. But the life of an ordinary Zen temple is full of Buddhist piety and ritual, and some Zen literature abounds in devotionalism and in conventional Buddhist religious concepts. The Zen of D. T. Suzuki is completely free from all this. But can it be called typical? One of the advantages of Dr. Wu's Christian treatment is that he too is able to see Zen apart from this accidental setting. It is like seeing the mystical doctrine of St. John of the Cross apart from the somewhat irrelevant backdrop of Spanish baroque. However the whole study of Zen can bristle with questions like these, and when the well-meaning inquirer receives answers to his questions, then hundreds of other questions arise to take the place of the two or three that have been answered.

Though much has been said, written, and published in the West about Zen, the general reader is probably not much the wiser for most of it. And unless he has some idea of what Zen is all about he may be mystified by this book, which is full of the classic Zen material: curious anecdotes, strange happenings, cryptic declarations, explosions of illogical humor, not to mention contradictions, inconsistencies, eccentric and even absurd behavior, and all for what? For some apparently esoteric purpose which is never made clear to the satisfaction of the logical western mind. This being the case, it becomes the difficult task of the writer of an introduction to actually introduce the western reader to Zen: that is, to try to get the reader to properly identify what he is about to encounter and not think of it as something entirely other than it is.

Now the reader with a Judeo-Christian background of some sort (and who in the West does not still have some such background?) will naturally be predisposed to misinterpret Zen because he will instinctively take up the position of one who is confronting a "rival system of thought" of a "competing ideology" or an "alien worldview" or more simply "a false religion." Anyone who adopts such a position makes it impossible for himself to see what Zen is, because he assumes in advance that it must be something that it expressly refuses to be. Zen is not a systematic explanation of life, it is not an ideology, it is not a worldview, it is not a theology of revelation and salvation, it is not a mystique, it is not a way of ascetic perfection, it is not mysticism as this is understood in the West, in fact it fits no convenient category of ours. Hence all our attempts to tag it and dispose of it with labels like "pantheism," "quietism," "illuminism," "pelagianism" must be completely incongruous, and proceed from a naive assumption that Zen pretends to justify the ways of God to man and to do so falsely. Zen is not concerned with God in the way Christianity is, though one is entitled to discover sophisticated analogies between the Zen experience of the Void (śūnyatā) and the experience of God in the "unknowing" of apophatic Christian mysticism. However, Zen cannot be properly judged as a mere doctrine, for though there are in it implicit doctrinal elements, they are entirely secondary to the inexpressible Zen experience.

True, we cannot really understand Chinese Zen if we do not grasp the implicit Buddhist metaphysic which it so to speak acts out. But the Buddhist metaphysic itself is hardly doctrinal in our elaborate philosophical and theological sense: Buddhist philosophy is an interpretation of ordinary human experience, but an interpretation which is not revealed by God nor discovered in the access of inspiration nor seen in a mystical light. Basically, Buddhist metaphysics is a very simple and natural elaboration of the implications of Buddha's own experience of enlightenment. Buddhism does not seek primarily to understand or to "believe in" the enlightenment of Buddha as the solution to all human problems, but seeks an existential and empirical participation in that enlightenment experience. It is conceivable that one might have the "enlightenment" without being aware of any discursive philosophical implications at all. These implications are not seen as having any theological bearing whatever, and they point only to the ordinary natural condition of man. It is true that they arrive at certain fundamental deductions, which were in the course of time elaborated into complex religious and philosophical systems. But the chief characteristic of Zen is that it rejects all these systematic elaborations in order to get back, as far as possible, to the pure unarticulated and unexplained ground of direct experience. The direct experience of what? Life itself. What it means that I exist, that I live: who is this "I" that exists and lives? What is the difference between the authentic and an illusory awareness of the self that exists and lives? What are and are not the basic facts of existence?

When we in the West speak of "basic facts of existence" we tend immediately to conceive these facts as reducible to certain austere and foolproof propositions—logical statements that are guaranteed to have meaning because they are empirically verifiable. These are what Bertrand Russell called "atomic facts." Now for Zen it is inconceivable that the basic facts of existence should be able to be stated in any proposition however atomic. For Zen, from the moment fact is transferred to a statement it is falsified. One ceases to grasp the naked reality of experience, and one grasps a form of words instead. The verification which Zen seeks is not to be found in a dialectical transaction involving the reduction of fact to logical statement and the reflective verification of statement by fact. It may be said that long before Bertrand Russell spoke of "atomic facts" Zen had split the atom and made its own kind of statement in the explosion of logic into *satori* (enlightenment). The whole aim of Zen is not to make foolproof statements about experience, but to come to direct grips with reality without the mediation of logical verbalizing.

But what reality? There is certainly a kind of living and nonverbal dialectic in Zen between the ordinary everyday experience of the senses (which is by no means arbitrarily repudiated) and the experience of enlightenment. Zen is not an idealistic rejection of sense and matter in order to ascend to a supposedly invisible reality which alone is real. The Zen experience is a direct grasp of the unity of the invisible and the visible, the noumenal and the phenomenal, or if you prefer an experiential realization that any such division is bound to be pure imagination. As D. T. Suzuki states,

Tasting, seeing, experiencing, living—all these demonstrate that there is something common to enlightenment-experience and our sense-experience; the one takes place in our innermost being, the other on the periphery of our consciousness. Personal experience thus seems to be the foundation of Buddhist philosophy. In this sense Buddhism is radical empiricism or experientialism, whatever dialectic later developed to probe the meaning of the enlightenment experience.[1]

Now the great obstacle to mutual understanding between Christianity and Buddhism lies in the western tendency to focus not on the Buddhist experience which is essential, but on the explanation which is accidental and which indeed Zen often regards as completely trivial and even misleading.

Buddhist meditation, but above all that of Zen, seeks not to explain but to pay attention, to become aware, to be mindful, in other words to develop a certain kind of consciousness that is above and beyond deception by verbal formulas. Deception in what? Deception in its grasp of itself as it really is. Deception due to diversion and distraction from what is right there—consciousness itself.

Zen, then, aims at a kind of certainty: but it is not the logical certainty of philosophical proof, still less the religious certainty that comes with the acceptance of the word of God by obedience of faith. It is rather the certainty that goes with an authentic metaphysical intuition, which is also existential and empirical. The purpose of all Buddhism is to refine the consciousness until this kind of insight is attained and the religious implications of the insight are then variously worked out and applied to life in the different Buddhist traditions.

In the Mahāyāna tradition, which includes Zen, the chief implication of this insight into the human condition is karuṇā (compassion) which leads to a paradoxical reversal of what the insight itself might seem to imply. Instead of rejoicing in his escape from the phenomenal world of suffering, the bodhisattva elects to remain in it and finds in it his nirvāṇa, by reason not only of the metaphysic which identifies the phenomenal and the noumenal, but also of the compassionate love which identifies all the sufferers in the round of birth and death with the Buddha whose enlightenment they potentially share. Though there are a heaven and a hell for Buddhists, these are not ultimate, and in fact it would be entirely ambiguous to assume that Buddha is regarded as a savior who leads his faithful disciples to Nirvāṇa as to a kind of negative heaven. (Pure Land Buddhism or Amidism is however distinctly a salvation religion.)

It cannot be repeated too often: in understanding Buddhism it would be a great mistake to concentrate on the "doctrine," the formulated philosophy of life, and to neglect the experience which is absolutely essential, the very heart of Buddhism. This is in a sense the exact opposite of the situation in Christianity. For Christianity begins with revelation. Though it would be misleading to classify this revelation simply as a doctrine and an explanation (it is far more than that—the revelation of God himself in the mystery of Christ), it is nevertheless communicated to us in words, in statements, and everything depends on the believer accepting the truth of these statements.

Therefore Christianity has always been profoundly concerned with these statements: with the accuracy of their transmission from the original sources, with the precise understanding of their exact meaning, with the elimination and indeed the condemnation of false interpretations. At times this concern has been exaggerated almost to the point of an obsession, accompanied by arbitrary and fanatical insistence on hairsplitting distinctions and the purest niceties of theological detail.

This obsession with doctrinal formulas, juridical order, and ritual exactitude has often made people forget that the heart of Catholicism too is a living experience of unity in Christ which far transcends all conceptual formulations. What too often has been overlooked, in consequence, is that Catholicism is the taste and experience of eternal life: "We announce to you the eternal life which was with the Father and has appeared to us. What we have seen and have heard we announce to you, in order that you also may have fellowship with us and that our fellowship may be with the Father and with his Son Jesus Christ" (1 John 1:2–3). Too often the Catholic has imagined himself obliged to stop short at a mere correct and external belief expressed in good moral behavior, instead of entering fully into the life of hope and love consummated by union with the invisible God "in Christ and in the Spirit, thus fully sharing in the Divine Nature" (Eph. 2:18; 2 Pet. 1:4; Col. 1:9–17; 1 John 4:12).

The Second Vatican Council has (we hope) happily put an end to this obsessive tendency in Catholic theological investigation. But the fact remains that for Christianity, a religion of the Word, the understanding of the statements which embody God's revelation of himself remains a primary concern. Christian experience is a fruit of this understanding, a development of it, a deepening of it.

At the same time, Christian experience itself will be profoundly affected by the idea of revelation, which the Christian himself will entertain. For example, if revelation is regarded simply as a system of truths about God and an explanation of how the universe came into existence, what will eventually happen to it, what is the purpose of Christian life, what are its moral norms, what will be the rewards of the virtuous and so on, then Christianity is in effect reduced to a worldview, at times a religious philosophy and little more, sustained by a more or less elaborate cult, by a moral discipline, and a strict code of law. "Experience" of the inner meaning of Christian revelation will necessarily be distorted and diminished in such a theological setting. What will such experience be? Not so much a living theological experience of the presence of God in the world and in mankind through the mystery of Christ, but rather a sense of security in one's own correctness: a feeling of confidence that one has been saved, a confidence which is based on the reflex awareness that one holds the correct view of the creation and purpose of the world and that one's behavior is of a kind to be rewarded in the next life. Or, perhaps, since few can attain this level of self-assurance, then the Christian experience becomes one of anxious hope—a struggle with occasional doubt of the "right answers," a painful and constant effort to meet the severe demands of morality and law, and a somewhat desperate recourse to the sacraments, which are there to help the weak who must constantly fall and rise again.

This of course is a sadly deficient account of true Christian experience, based on a distortion of the true import of Christian revelation. Yet it is the impression non-Christians often get of Christianity from the outside, and when one proceeds to compare, say, Zen experience in its purity with this diminished and distorted type of Christian experience then one's comparison is just as meaningless and misleading as a comparison between Christian philosophy and theology on their highest and most sophisticated level with the myths of a popular and decadent Buddhism.

When we set Christianity and Buddhism side by side, we must try to find the points where a genuinely common ground between the two exists. At the present moment, this is no easy task. In fact it is still practically impossible, as suggested above, to really find any such common ground except in a very schematic and artificial way. After all, what do we mean by Christianity, and what do we mean by Buddhism? Is Christianity Christian theology? ethics? mysticism? worship? Is our idea of Christianity to be taken without further qualification as the Roman Catholic church? Or does it include Protestant Christianity? The Protestantism of Luther or that of Bonhoeffer? The Protestantism of the God-is-dead school? The Catholicism of St. Thomas? Of St. Augustine and the Western church fathers? A supposedly "pure" Christianity of the Gospels? A demythologized Christianity? A social gospel? And what do we mean by Buddhism? The Theravada Buddhism of Ceylon, or that of Burma? Tibetan Buddhism? Tantric Buddhism? Pure Land Buddhism? Speculative and scholastic Indian Buddhism of the Middle Ages? Or Zen?

The immense variety of forms taken by thought, experience, worship, moral practice in both Buddhism and Christianity makes all comparisons haphazard, and in the end when someone like the late Dr. Suzuki published *Mysticism: Christian and Buddhist*, it turned out to be, rather practically in fact, a comparison between Meister Eckhart and Zen. To narrow the field in this way is at least relevant, though to take Meister Eckhart as representative of Christian mysticism is hazardous. At the same time we must remark that Dr. Suzuki was much too convinced that Eckhart was unusual in his time and that his statements must have shocked most of his contemporaries. Eckhart's condemnation was in fact due in some measure to rivalry between Dominicans and Franciscans and his teaching, bold and in some points unable to avoid condemnation, was nevertheless based on St. Thomas to a great extent and belonged to a mystical tradition that was very much alive and was, in fact, the most vital religious force in the Catholicism of his time. Yet to identify Christianity with Eckhart would be completely misleading. That was not what Suzuki intended. He was not comparing the mystical theology of Eckhart with the Buddhist philosophy of the Zen masters, but the experience of Eckhart, ontologically and psychologically, with the experience of the Zen masters. This is a reasonable enterprise, offering some small hope of interesting and valid results.

But can one distill from religious or mystical experience certain pure elements which are common everywhere in all religions? Or is the basic understanding of the nature and meaning of experience so determined by the variety of doctrines that a comparison of experiences involves us inevitably in a comparison of metaphysical or religious beliefs? This is no easy question either. If a Christian mystic has an experience which can be phenomenologically compared with a Zen experience, does it matter that the Christian in fact believes he is personally united with God and the Zen man interprets his experience as śūnyatā or the Void being aware of itself? In what sense can these two experiences be called mystical? Suppose that the Zen masters forcefully repudiate any attempt on the part of Christians to grace them with the title of mystics.

It must certainly be said that a certain type of concordist thought today too easily assumes as a basic dogma that "the mystics" in all religions are all experiencing the same thing and are all alike united in their liberation from the various doctrines, explanations, and creeds of their less fortunate coreligionists. All religions thus "meet at the top" and their various theologies and philosophies become irrelevant when we see that they were merely means for arriving at the same end and all means are alike efficacious. This has never been demonstrated with any kind of rigor and though it has been persuasively advanced by talented and experienced minds, we must say that a great deal of study and investigation must be done before much can be said on this very complex question, which once again seems to imply a purely formalistic view of theological and philosophical doctrines, as if a fundamental belief were something that a mystic could throw off like a suit of clothes and as if his very experience itself were not in some sense modified by the fact that he held this belief.

At the same time, since the personal experience of the mystic remains inaccessible to us and can only be evaluated indirectly through texts and other testimonials—perhaps written and given by others—it is never easy to say with any security that what a Christian mystic, a Sufi, and a Zen master experience is really "the same thing." What does such a claim really mean? Can it be made at all, without implying (quite falsely) that these higher experiences are experiences of something? It therefore remains a very serious problem to distinguish, in all these higher forms of religious and metaphysical consciousness, what is "pure experience" and what is to some extent determined by language, symbol, or indeed by the "grace of a sacrament." We have hardly reached the point where we know enough about these different states of consciousness and about their metaphysical implication to compare them in accurate detail. But there are nevertheless certain analogies and correspondence which are evident even now and which may perhaps point out the way to a better mutual understanding. Let us not rashly take them as proofs but only as significant clues.

Is it therefore possible to say that both Christians and Buddhists can equally well practice Zen? Yes, if by Zen we mean precisely the quest for direct and pure experience on a metaphysical level, liberated from verbal formulas and linguistic preconceptions. On the theological level the question becomes more complex. It will be touched on at the end of this introduction.

The best we can say is that in certain religions, Buddhism for instance, the philosophical or religious framework is of a kind that can more easily be discarded because it has in itself a built-in ejector, so to speak, by which the meditator is at a certain point flung out from the conceptual apparatus into the Void. It is possible for a Zen master to say nonchalantly to his disciple, "If you meet the Buddha, kill him!" But in Christian mysticism the question whether or not the mystic can get along without the human "form" (gestalt) or the sacred humanity of Christ is still hotly debated, with the majority opinion definitely maintaining the necessity for the Christ of faith to be present as icon at the center of Christian contemplation. Here again, the question is confused by the failure to distinguish between the objective theology of Christian experience and the actual psychological facts of Christian mysticism in certain cases. And then one must ask, at what point do the abstract demands of theory take precedence over the psychological facts of experience? Or, to what extent does the theology of a theologian without experience claim to interpret correctly the "experienced theology" of the mystic who is perhaps not able to articulate the meaning of his experience in a satisfactory way?

We keep returning to one central question in two forms: the relation of objective doctrine to subjective mystic (or metaphysical) experience and the difference between this relationship in Christianity and in Zen. In Christianity the objective doctrine retains priority both in time and in eminence. In Zen the experience is always prior, not in time but in importance. This is because Christianity is based on supernatural revelation, and Zen, discarding all idea of any revelation and even taking a very independent view of sacred tradition (at least written), seeks to penetrate the natural ontological ground of being. Christianity is a religion of grace and divine gift, hence of total dependence on God. Zen is not easily classified as a religion (it is in fact easily separable from any religious matrix and can supposedly flourish in the soil either of non-Buddhist religions or no religion at all), and in any event it strives, like all Buddhism, to make man completely free and independent even in his striving for salvation and enlightenment. Independent of what? Of merely external supports and authorities which keep him from having access to and making use of the deep resources in his own nature and psyche. (Both Chinese and Japanese Zen flourished in extremely disciplined and authoritarian cultures. Hence their emphasis on "autonomy" meant in fact an ultimate and humble discovery of inner freedom after one had exhausted all the possibilities on an intensely strict and austere authoritarian training as the methods of the Zen masters make abundantly clear!)

On the other hand, let us repeat that we must not neglect the great importance of experience in Christianity. But Christian experience always has a special modality, due to the fact that it is inseparable from the mystery of Christ and the collective life of the Church, the Body of Christ. To experience the mystery of Christ mystically or otherwise is always to transcend the merely individual psychological level and to "experience theologically with the Church" (sentire cum ecclesia). In other words, this experience must always be in some way reducible to a theological form that can be shared by the rest of the Church or that shows that it is a sharing of what the rest of the Church experiences. Therefore in the recording of Christian experiences, there is a natural tendency to set them down in language and symbols that are easily accessible to other Christians. This may perhaps sometimes mean an unconscious translation of the inexpressible into familiar symbols that are always at hand ready for immediate use.

Zen, however, resolutely resists any temptation to be easily communicable, and a great deal of the paradox and violence of Zen teaching and practice is aimed at blasting the foundation of ready explanation and comforting symbol out from under the disciple's supposed "experience." The Christian experience is acceptable in so far as it accords with an established theological and symbolic pattern. The Zen experience is only acceptable on the basis of its absolute singularity: and yet it must be in some way communicable. How?

We cannot begin to understand how the Zen experience is manifested and communicated between master and disciple unless we realize what is communicated. If we do not know what is supposed to be signified, the strange method of signification will leave us totally disconcerted and more in the dark than we were when we started. In Zen what is communicated is not a message. It is not simply a "word," even though it might be the "word of the Lord." It is not a "what." It does not bring "news" which the receiver did not already have, about something the one informed did not yet know. What Zen communicates is an awareness that is potentially already there but is not conscious of itself. Zen is then not kerygma but realization, not revelation but consciousness, not news from the Father who sends his Son into this world, but awareness of the ontological ground of our own being here and now, right in the midst of the world. We will see later that the supernatural kerygma and the metaphysical intuition of the ground of being are far from being incompatible. One may be said to prepare the way for the other. They can well complement each other, and for this reason Zen is perfectly compatible with Christian belief and indeed with Christian mysticism (if we understand Zen in its pure state, as metaphysical intuition).

If this is true, then we must recognize that it is perfectly logical to admit, with the Zen masters, that "Zen teaches nothing." One of the greatest of the Chinese Zen masters, the last accepted patriarch, Hui-neng (seventh century A.D.), was asked a leading question by a disciple: "Who has inherited the spirit of the Fifth Patriarch?" (i.e., who is Patriarch now?)

Hui-neng replied: "One who understands Buddhism."

The monk pressed his point: "Have you then inherited it?"

Hui-neng said: "No."

"Why not?" asked the monk.

"Because I do not understand Buddhism."

This story is meant precisely to illustrate the fact that Hui-neng *had* inherited the role of patriarch, or the charisma of teaching the purest Zen. He was qualified to transmit the enlightenment of the Buddha himself to disciples. If he had laid claim to an authoritative teaching that made this enlightenment understandable to those who did not possess it, then he would have been teaching something else, that is to say a doctrine about enlightenment. He would be disseminating the message of his own understanding of Zen, and in that case he would not be awakening others to

Zen in themselves, but imposing on them the imprint of his own understanding and teaching. Zen does not tolerate this kind of thing, since this
would be incompatible with the true purpose of Zen: awakening a deep
ontological awareness, a wisdom-intuition (prajñā) in the ground of the
being of the one awakened. And in fact the pure consciousness of prajñā
would not be pure and immediate if it were a consciousness that one
understands prajñā.

The language used by Zen is therefore in some sense an antilanguage,
and the "logic" of Zen is a radical reversal of philosophical logic. The
human dilemma of communication is that we cannot communicate ordinarily without words and signs, but even ordinary experience tends to be
falsified by our habits of verbalization and rationalization. The convenient
tools of language enable us to decide beforehand what we think things
mean and tempt us all too easily to see things only in a way that fits our
logical preconceptions and our verbal formulas. Instead of seeing things
and facts as they are, we see them as reflections and verifications of the
sentences we have previously made up in our minds. We quickly forget
how to simply see things and substitute our words and our formulas for
the things themselves, manipulating facts so that we see only what fits our
convenient prejudices. Zen uses language against itself to blast out these
preconceptions and to destroy the specious "reality" in our minds so that
we can *see directly*. Zen is saying, as Wittgenstein said: "Don't think: Look!"

Since the Zen intuition seeks to awaken a direct metaphysical consciousness beyond the empirical, reflecting, knowing, willing, and talking
ego, this awareness must be immediately present to itself and not medi-
ated by either conceptual, reflexive, or imaginative knowledge. And yet
far from being mere negation, Zen is also entirely positive. As D. T.
Suzuki wrote, "Zen always aims at grasping the central fact of life, which
can never be brought to the dissecting table of the intellect. To grasp the
central fact of life, Zen is forced to propose a series of negations. Mere
negation however is not the spirit of Zen." He also stated that Zen masters neither affirm nor negate, they simply act or speak in such a way that
the action or speech itself is a plain fact bursting with Zen.

When the spirit of Zen is grasped in its purity, it will be seen what a
real thing that [in this case a slap] is. For here is no negation, no
affirmation, but a plain fact, a pure experience, the very foundation of

our being and thought. All the quietness and emptiness one might desire in the midst of most active mentation lies therein. Do not be carried away by anything outward or conventional. Zen must be seized with bare hands, with no gloves on.[2]

It is in this sense that "Zen teaches nothing," it merely enables us to wake up and become aware. It does not teach, it points.[3] The acts and gestures of a Zen master are no more statements than is the ringing of an alarm clock.

All the words and actions of the Zen masters and of their disciples are to be understood in this context. Usually the master is simply "producing facts" which the disciple either sees or does not see.

Many of the Zen stories, which are almost always incomprehensible in rational terms, are simply the ringing of an alarm clock, and the reaction of the sleeper. Usually the misguided sleeper makes a response which in effect turns off the alarm so that he can go back to sleep. Sometimes he jumps out of bed with a shout of astonishment that it is so late. Sometimes he just sleeps and does not hear the alarm at all!

In so far as the disciple takes the fact to be a sign of something else, he is misled by it. The master may (by means of some other fact) try to make him aware of this. Often it is precisely at the point where the disciple realizes himself to be utterly misled that he also realizes everything else along with it: chiefly, of course, that there was nothing to realize in the first place except the fact. What fact? If you know the answer you are awake. You hear the alarm!

But we in the West, living in a tradition of stubborn ego-centered practicality and geared entirely for the use and manipulation of everything, always pass from one thing to another, from cause to effect, from the first to the next and to the last and then back to the first. Everything always points to something else and hence we never stop anywhere because we cannot: as soon as we pause, the escalator reaches the end of the ride and we have to get off and find another one. Nothing is allowed just to be and to mean itself: everything has to mysteriously signify something else. Zen is especially designed to frustrate the mind that thinks in such terms. The Zen "fact" whatever it may be always lands across our road like a falling tree beyond which we cannot pass.

Nor are such facts lacking in Christianity—the Cross for example. Just

as the Buddha's "Fire Sermon" radically transforms the Buddhist's awareness of all that is around him, so the "word of the Cross" in very much the
same way gives the Christian a radically new consciousness of the meaning of his life and of his relationship with other men and with the world
around him.

In both cases, the "facts" are not merely impersonal and objective, but
facts of personal experience. Both Buddhism and Christianity are alike in
making use of ordinary everyday human existence as material for a radical
transformation of consciousness. Since ordinary everyday human existence is full of confusion and suffering, then obviously one will make
good use of both of these in order to transform one's awareness and one's
understanding and to go beyond both to attain "wisdom" in love. It would
be a grave error to suppose that Buddhism and Christianity merely offer
various explanations of suffering—or justifications and mystifications built
on this ineluctable fact. On the contrary both show that suffering remains
inexplicable most of all for the man who attempts to explain it in order to
evade it—or who thinks explanation itself is an escape. Suffering is not a
"problem" as if it were something we could stand outside and control.
Suffering, as both Christianity and Buddhism see, each in its own way, is
part of our very ego-identity and empirical existence, and the only thing
to do about it is to plunge right into the middle of contradiction and
confusion in order to be transformed by what Zen calls the "great death"
and Christianity calls "dying and rising with Christ."

Let us now return to the obscure and tantalizing facts in which Zen
deals. In the relation between Zen master and disciple, the most usually
encountered fact is the disciple's frustration, his inability to get somewhere by the use of his own will and his own reasoning. Most sayings of
the Zen masters deal with this situation and try to convey to the disciple
that he has a fundamentally misleading experience of himself and of his
capacities.

"When the cart stops," said Huai-jang, the master of Ma-tsu, "do you
whip the cart or whip the ox?"[4] And he added, "If one sees the Tao from
the standpoint of making and unmaking, or gathering and scattering, one
does not really see the Tao."[5]

If this remark about whipping the cart or the ox is obscure, perhaps
another *mondō* (question and answer) will suggest the same fact in a different way.

A monk asks Pai-chang, "Who is the Buddha?"

Pai-chang answers: "Who are you?"[6]

A monk wants to know what prajñā (the metaphysical wisdom-intuition of Zen) is. Not only that, but *Mahāprajñā*, great or Absolute Wisdom. The whole works. The master answers without concern:

"The snow is falling fast and all is enveloped in mist."

The monk remains silent.

The master asks: "Do you understand?"

"No, Master, I do not."

Thereupon the master composed a verse for him:

> *Mahāprajñā*
> *It is neither taking in nor giving up.*
> *If one understands it not,*
> *The wind is cold, the snow is falling.*[7]

The monk is trying to understand when in fact he ought to try to *look*. The apparently mysterious and cryptic sayings of Zen become much simpler when we see them in the whole context of Buddhist "mindfulness" or awareness, which in its most elementary form consists in that "bare attention" which simply *sees* what is right there and does not add any comment, any interpretation, any judgment, any conclusion. It just *sees*. Learning to see in this manner is the basic and fundamental exercise of Buddhist meditation.[8]

If one reaches the point where understanding fails, this is not a tragedy: it is simply a reminder to stop thinking and start looking. Perhaps there is nothing to figure out after all: perhaps we only need to wake up.

A monk said: "I have been with you [Master], for a long time, and yet I am unable to understand your way. How is this?"

The master said: "Where you do not understand, there is the point for your understanding."

"How is understanding possible when it is impossible?"

The master said: "The cow gives birth to a baby elephant; clouds of dust rise over the ocean."[9]

In more technical language, and therefore perhaps more comprehensibly for us, Suzuki says: "Prajñā is pure act, pure experience . . . it has a distinct noetic quality . . . but it is not rationalistic . . . it is characterized by immediacy . . . it must not be identified with ordinary intuition . . . for in the case of prajñā intuition there is no definable object to be intuited . . . In prajñā intuition the object of intuition is never a concept postulated by an elaborate process of reasoning; it is never 'this' or 'that'; it does not want to attach itself to one particular object."[10] For this reason, Suzuki concludes that prajñā intuition is different from "the kind of intuition we have generally in religious and philosophical discourses" in which God or the Absolute are objects of intuition and "the act of intuition is considered complete when a state of identification takes place between the object and the subject."[11]

This is not the place to discuss the very interesting and complex question raised here. Let us only say that it is by no means certain that the religious, or at any rate mystical, intuition always sees God "as object." And in fact at the end of this introduction we shall see Suzuki qualifies this opinion quite radically by admitting that the mystical intuition of Eckhart is the same as prajñā.

Leaving this question aside, it must be said here that if anyone tries to spell out a philosophical or doctrinal interpretation for the Zen sayings like those we have quoted above, he is mistaken. If he seeks to argue that when Pai-chang points to the falling snow as answer to a question about the Absolute, as though to say that the falling snow were identified with the Absolute, in other words that this intuition was a reflexive pantheistic awareness of the Absolute as object, seen in the falling snow, then he has entirely missed the point of Zen. To imagine that Zen is teaching pantheism is to imagine that it is trying to explain something. We repeat, Zen explains nothing. It just sees. Sees what? Not an Absolute Object but Absolute Seeing.

Though this may seem very remote from Christianity, which is definitely a message, we must nevertheless remember the importance of direct experience in the Bible. All forms of knowing especially in the religious sphere, and especially where God is concerned, are valid in proportion as they are a matter of experience and of intimate contact. We are all familiar with the Biblical expression "to know" in the sense of to possess in the act of love. This is not the place to examine the possible Zen-like analogies in the experiences of the Old Testament prophets. They were certainly as factual, as existential, and as disconcerting as any fact of Zen!

Nor can we more than indicate briefly here the well-known importance of direct experience in the New Testament. This is of course to be sought above all in the revelation of the Holy Spirit, the mysterious gift in which God becomes one with the believer in order to know and love himself in the believer.

In the first two chapters of the first Epistle to the Corinthians, St. Paul distinguishes between two kinds of wisdom: one which consists in the knowledge of words and statements, a rational, dialectical wisdom, and another which is at once a matter of paradox and of experience and goes beyond the reach of reason. To attain to this spiritual wisdom, one must first be liberated from servile dependence on the "wisdom of speech" (1 Cor. 1:17). This liberation is effected by the word of the Cross which makes no sense to those who cling to their own familiar views and habits of thought and is a means by which God "destroys the wisdom of the wise" (1 Cor. 1:18–23). The word of the Cross is in fact completely baffling and disconcerting both to the Greeks with their philosophy and to the Jews with their well-interpreted Law. But when one has been freed from dependence on verbal formulas and conceptual structures, the Cross becomes a source of "power." This power emanates from the "foolishness of God" and it also makes use of "foolish instruments," the Apostles (1 Cor. 1:27ff.). On the other hand, he who can accept this paradoxical "foolishness" experiences in himself a secret and mysterious power, which is the power of Christ living in him as the ground of a totally new life and a new being (1 Cor. 2:1–4; Eph. 1:18–23; Gal. 6:14–16).

Here it is essential to remember that for a Christian the word of the Cross is nothing theoretical, but a stark and existential experience of union with Christ in his death in order to share in his resurrection. To fully hear and receive the word of the Cross means much more than simple assent to the dogmatic proposition that Christ died for our sins. It means to be "nailed to the Cross with Christ" so that the ego-self is no longer the principle of our deepest actions which now proceed from Christ living in us. "I live, now not I, but Christ lives in me" (Gal. 2:19–20; see also Rom. 8:5–17). To receive the word of the Cross means the acceptance of a complete self-emptying, a *kenosis*, in union with the self-emptying of Christ "obedient unto death" (Phil. 2:5–11). It is essential to true Christianity that this experience of the Cross and of self-emptying be central in the life of the Christian so that he may fully receive the Holy

Spirit and know (again by experience) all the riches of God in and through Christ (John 14:16–17, 26; 15:26–27; 16:7–15).

When Gabriel Marcel says, "There are thresholds which thought alone, left to itself, can never permit us to cross. An experience is required —an experience of poverty and sickness,"[12] he is stating a simple Christian truth in terms familiar to Zen.

We must never forget that Christianity is much more than the intellectual acceptance of a religious message by a blind and submissive faith which never understands what the message means except in terms of authoritative interpretations handed down externally by experts in the name of the Church. On the contrary, faith is the door to the full inner life of the Church, a life which includes not only access to an authoritative teaching but above all to a deep personal experience which is at once unique and yet shared by the whole Body of Christ, in the Spirit of Christ. St. Paul compares this knowledge of God, in the Spirit, to the subjective knowledge that a man has of himself. Just as no one can know my inner self except my own "spirit," so no one can know God except God's Spirit; yet this Holy Spirit is given to us in such a way that God knows himself in us, and this experience is utterly real, though it cannot be communicated in terms understandable to those who do not share it (see 1 Cor. 2:7–15). Consequently, St. Paul concludes, "We have the mind of Christ" (ibid., 16).

Now when we see that for Buddhism prajñā is describable as "having the Buddha mind," we understand that there must surely be some possibility of finding an analogy somewhere between Buddhist and Christian experience, though we are now speaking more in terms of doctrine than of pure experience. Yet the doctrine is about the experience. We cannot push our investigation further here, but it is significant that Suzuki, reading the following lines from Eckhart (which are perfectly orthodox and traditional Catholic theology), said they were "the same as prajñā intuition."[13] "In giving us His love God has given us the Holy Ghost so that we can love Him with the love wherewith He loves Himself." The Son who, in us, loves the Father, in the Spirit, is translated thus by Suzuki into Zen terms: "one mirror reflecting another with no shadow between them."[14] Suzuki also frequently quotes a sentence of Eckhart's: "The eye wherein I see God is the same eye wherein God sees me"[15] as an exact expression of what Zen means by prajñā.

Whether or not Dr. Suzuki's interpretation of the text in Zen terms is theologically perfect in every way remains to be seen; though at first sight there seems to be no reason why it should not be thoroughly acceptable. What is important for us here is that the interpretation is highly suggestive and interesting in itself, reflecting a kind of intuitive affinity for Christian mysticism. Furthermore it is highly significant that a Japanese thinker schooled in Zen should be so open to what is basically the most obscure and difficult mystery of Christian theology: the dogma of the Trinity and of the mission of the Divine Persons in the Christian and in the Church. This would seem to indicate that the real area for investigation of analogies and correspondences between Christianity and Zen might after all be theology rather than psychology or asceticism. At least theology is not excluded but it must be theology as experienced in Christian contemplation, not the speculative theology of text books and disputations.

The few words that have been written in this introduction, and the brief, bare suggestions it contains, are by no means intended as an adequate "comparison" between Christian experience and Zen experience. Obviously, we have done little more than express a pious hope that a common ground can someday be found. But at least this should make the western and Christian reader more ready to enter this book with an open mind and perhaps help him to suspend judgment for a while, and not decide immediately that Zen is so esoteric and so outlandish that it has no interest or importance for us. On the contrary, Zen has much to teach the West, and recently Dom Aelred Graham, in a book which became deservedly popular,[16] pointed out that there was not a little in Zen that was pertinent to our own ascetic and religious practice. It is quite possible for Zen to be adapted and used to clear the air of ascetic irrelevancies and help us to regain a healthy natural balance in our understanding of the spiritual life.

But Zen must be grasped in its simple reality, not rationalized or imagined in terms of some fantastic and esoteric interpretation of human existence.

Though few westerners will ever actually come to a real understanding of Zen, it is still worth their while to be exposed to its brisk and heady atmosphere. This book will be a good place to make the acquaintance of

*Splashy cold water.*

what can be called the very quintessence of Buddhist wisdom, in the golden age of Chinese Zen.

July 1966
Abbey of Gethsemani

## NOTES

1. D. T. Suzuki, *Mysticism: Christian and Buddhist* (New York, 1957) 48.
2. D. T. Suzuki, *Introduction to Zen Buddhism* (London, 1960) 51.
3. Ibid., 38.
4. See below, Chapter 5, p. 92.
5. Ibid., 93.
6. See below, Chapter 6, p. 115.
7. Suzuki, *Introduction*, 99–100.
8. See Nyanaponika Thera-Colombo, *The Heart of Buddhist Meditation* (Ceylon, 1956).
9. Suzuki, *Introduction*, 116.
10. Suzuki, *Studies in Zen* (London, 1957) 87–89.
11. Ibid., 89.
12. Quoted by A. Gelin in *Les Pauvres de Yahve* (Paris, 1954) 57.
13. *Mysticism*, p. 40. The quotation is from Evans' translation of Eckhart, London, 1924, 147.
14. Ibid., 41.
15. Ibid., 50.
16. Dom Aelred Graham, *Zen Catholicism* (New York, 1963).

# The Genealogy of
# THE FIVE HOUSES
# OF CH'AN

The Sixth Patriarch Hui-neng
(638 – 713)

Ch'ing-yüan Hsing-ssu
(d. 740)

Nan-yüeh Huai-jang
(677 – 744)

Shih-t'ou Hsi-ch'ien
(700 – 790)

Ma-tsu Tao-i
(709 – 788)

T'ien-huang
Tao-wu
(748 – 807)

Yüeh-shan
Wei-yen
(751 – 834)

Pai-chang
Huai-hai
(720 – 814)

Nan-ch'üan
P'u-yüan
(748 – 834)

Lung-t'an
Ch'ung-hsin
(d. 838)

Yün-yen
T'an-ch'eng
(782 – 841)

Chao-chou
Ts'ung-shen
(778 – 897)

Te-shan
Hsüan-chien
(780 – 865)

Tung-shan
Liang-chieh
(807 – 869)

Kuei-shan
Ling-yu
(771 – 853)

Huang-po'
Hsi-yün
(d. 850)

Hsüeh-feng
I-ts'un
(822 – 908)

Ts'ao-shan
Pen-chi
(840 – 901)

Yang-shan
Hui-chi
(814 – 890)

Lin-chi
I-hsüan
(d. 867)

Yün-men
Wen-yen
(d. 949)

Hsüan-sha
Shih-pei
(835 – 908)

Lo-han
Kuei-ch'en
(867 – 928)

Fa-yen Wen-i
(885 – 958)

CHAPTER I

# Zen: Its Origin and Its Significance

## 1. ZEN AND TAO

Like all vital traditions, the origins of the school of Zen are shrouded in myth and legend. The whole movement is alleged to have taken its start from Śākyamuni Buddha himself. Once upon a time, Śākyamuni was lecturing to a great multitude gathered on Lin-shan or Spirit Mountain. After his lecture he picked up a flower and held it before his audience without speaking a word. Quite mystified, the whole assembly remained silent, pondering as to what Śākyamuni wished to convey by this unexpected action. Only the Venerable Kāśyapa broke into an understanding smile. Śākyamuni was pleased and declared, "I have the secret of the right Dharma Eye, the ineffably subtle insight into Nirvāṇa—which opens the door of mystic vision of the Formless Form, not depending upon words and letters, but transmitted outside of all scriptures. I hereby entrust this secret to the great Kāśyapa."

It is fitting that Zen should have begun with a flower and a smile. This episode, you may say, is too beautiful to be true. Yet it is too beautiful not to be true. The life of Zen does not depend upon historical truth. Whoever has invented the story has caught the very spirit of Zen—a flower that smiles evoking a smile that flowers.

Kāśyapa is said to be the First Indian Patriarch of the school of Zen. After him there came in succession twenty-seven patriarchs, of whom Bodhidharma was the twenty-eighth and the last patriarch of Zen in India. When he came to China, he became the First Patriarch of Zen in

China. Thus, Bodhidharma may be regarded as the bridge between India and China in the history of Zen.

It is almost certain that the genealogy of Indian patriarchs was a later make-up. There is no record in Sanskrit to show that there was an Indian school of Zen as such. Although the word Zen (Ch'an in Chinese) was a transliteration of *dhyāna*, there can be no greater difference in meaning between two terms than the Indian dhyāna and the Chinese Ch'an. Dhyāna signifies a concentrated and methodical meditation, while Zen, as the founding fathers of the Chinese school understood it, has for its essence a sudden flash of insight into reality, or a direct intuitive perception of the Self-nature. Time and again they have warned their disciples that to meditate or reflect is to miss it altogether.

The late Dr. Hu Shih went to the extent of saying, "Chinese Zennism arose not out of Indian yoga or Dhyāna but as a revolt against it." Perhaps it was not so much a deliberate revolt as an unconscious transformation of dhyāna. But whether we call it a revolt or a transformation, one thing is certain, and that is that Zen is different from dhyāna. In the words of D. T. Suzuki, "Zen as such did not exist in India—that is, in the form as we have it today." He considers Zen as "the Chinese interpretation of the doctrine of enlightenment." At the same time, he does not fail to add that the interpretation was a creative one, for the Chinese upholders of the doctrine of enlightenment did not wish to swallow Indian Buddhism undigested. "The practical imagination of the Chinese people came thus to create Zen, and developed it to the best of their abilities to suit their own religious requirements."

In my view, the school of Zen derived its original impetus from the generous impulse of Mahāyāna Buddhism. Without this, such a vigorous and dynamic spiritual movement could not have been started even by revival of the original Taoism of Lao-tzu and Chuang-tzu. Paradoxical as it may sound, it was the Mahāyāna impulse that gave rise to a real revival and development of the original insights of Lao and Chuang, in the form of Zen. As Thomas Merton, with his piercing insight, has truly observed, "The true inheritors of the thought and spirit of Chuang-tzu are the Chinese Zen Buddhists of the T'ang period."

It is not too much to say that the fundamental insights of Zen masters are identical with those of Lao-tzu and Chuang-tzu. The first and second chapters of the *Tao-te ching* constitute the metaphysical background of

Zen. The relation between Zen and Chuang-tzu has been presented by Suzuki with the utmost fairness and clarity: "The most distinctively characteristic hallmark of Zen is its insistence on the awakening of *pratyatmajñā*, [which] is an inner perception deeply reaching the core of one's being." "This," he proceeds to say, "corresponds to Chuang-tzu's 'mind-fasting' or 'mind-forgetting' or 'clear as the morning.' " If this is true—and no one with an unbiased mind can think otherwise—it means that Chuang-tzu's essential insight constitutes the very core of Zen. And the only difference is that while with Chuang-tzu it remained a pure insight, it has become the "most essential discipline" in Zen. And it is in the development of this discipline that modern Japanese Zen has made its signal contribution.

It will contribute greatly toward the understanding of the essential nature of Zen to have a clear grasp of what Chuang-tzu meant by "mind-fasting," "mind-forgetting," and "clear as the morning." Let me give an account of them in that order.

*Mind-fasting.* This is found in Chuang-tzu's essay "The Human World." It is presented in an imaginary conversation between Confucius and his beloved disciple Yen Hui. Yen Hui was contemplating on making a missionary trip to the state of Wei to convert its unruly prince and to save his people writhing under his tyranny. On taking leave of Confucius, Yen Hui explained why he must go, saying, "I have heard you, Master, say, 'Leave alone the well-governed states, but go to those where disorder prevails. The place of a physician is with the sick.' My present move is motivated by your teaching. I will go in the hope of curing the ills of that state." Confucius poured cold water on the ardors of his disciple's generous soul, saying, "Alas! Your going will only land you in trouble! The practice of Tao does not admit of complexity. Complexity is the source of multiplicity; multiplicity causes confusion; confusion breeds worry and anxiety. A man weighed down by worry and anxiety can be of no help to others. The ancient men of Tao had it first in themselves before they came to find it in others. If you have no firm grasp of it in yourself, how can you bring it to bear upon the conduct of the reckless ones? Besides, do you know what dissipates virtue and what gives rise to cleverness? Virtue is dissipated by the love of name; and cleverness is born of contention. Both of them are instruments of evil; and certainly they are incapable of furnishing the ultimate norms of conduct. Granting that you have attained substantial virtue and genuine sincerity, and granting further that you do not strive for name and reputation, yet, so long as these qualities of yours have not effectively communicated themselves to the spirit and mind of men, if you force your norms of humanity and justice upon men of confirmed wickedness, this would be tantamount to exposing their evils by the display of your own righteousness. This is to call calamity upon others. He who calls calamity upon others only provokes others to call calamity on him. I am afraid that this is what is awaiting you!"

Not to be daunted, Yen Hui said, "If I try to act rightly and remain humble inside, to use all my resources and still maintain the unity of my purpose, will this do?" This again failed to satisfy Confucius, who took exception to the glaring disparity between the inner and the outer.

Yen Hui then offered his pièce de résistance. "Let me then be upright within but bending without, and support my own convictions by quoting appropriate words from the ancients. Now, to be upright within is to be a friend of Heaven. A friend of Heaven knows in his heart that he is as truly a child of God as the 'son of Heaven' (the king). How can a child of God be affected by the approval or disapproval of men? Such a man is truly to be called an innocent child, a friend of Heaven. To be bending without is to be a friend of men. To bow, to kneel, and to bend the body belong properly to the manners of the ministers. I will do as others do. He who acts as others do will incur no criticism. This is what I call being a friend of men. Again, to support my own convictions by quoting appropriate words from the ancients is to be a friend of the ancients. Even though their words are condemnatory of the conduct of the prince, they represent in reality time-honored truths, not my private views. This being the case, I can get away with my straightforwardness. This is what I call being a friend of the ancients. Would that do?" "Pooh!" replied Confucius, "How can it? You have too many ways and means, and too little peace of mind. You may indeed get away with it, but that's about all. As for transforming another, it is far from adequate. The trouble is that you are still taking your guidance from your own mind."

Yen Hui said, "I can proceed no farther. Can you tell me the way?" "Fast," Confucius replied, "and I will tell you the way. But even if you have the way, will it be easy to act on it? Anyone who deems it easy will incur the disapproval of the Bright Heaven." Yen Hui said, "My family being poor, I have not tasted wine or meat for several months. Is this not enough of a fast?" "It is merely liturgical fast," said Confucius, "but not the fast of mind." "What is the fast of mind?" asked Yen Hui, and Confucius answered, "Maintain the unity of your will. Cease to listen with the ear, but listen with the mind. Cease to listen with the mind, but listen with the spirit. The function of the ear is limited to hearing; the function of the mind is limited to forming images and ideas. As to the spirit, it is an emptiness responsive to all things. Tao abides in emptiness; and emptiness is the fast of mind."

At this, Yen Hui was enlightened, as we may infer from what he remarked: "The only obstacle which keeps me from practicing the fast of mind lies in my self. As soon as I come to practice it, I realize that there has never been my self at all. Is this what you mean by emptiness?" "Exactly," said Confucius, "that is all there is to it! I can tell you that you are now prepared to enter into any circle without being infected by its name. Where you find a receptive ear, sing your song. Otherwise, keep your mouth shut. Let there be one single dwelling place for your spirit, and that is wherever the necessity of circumstances leads you. In this way, you will not be far from your goal. It is easy to walk without leaving a trace; the hard thing is to walk without touching the ground at all. A missionary of man can easily resort to human devices and tricks; but a missionary of heaven can have no use for such artificial means. You have heard of flying with wings; but you have not heard of flying without wings. You have heard of knowing through knowledge; but you have not heard of knowing through unknowing. Ponder the effect of emptiness. An empty room invites brightness and attracts all kinds of felicitous influences to dwell therein. Nay more, it will radiate its light and happiness all around. Thus, while remaining still, it moves like a galloping horse. Indeed, if you can turn your ear and eye inwards and cast out all discriminating knowledge of the mind, even spiritual beings will make their home in you, not to mention men. All things thus undergo a transforming influence."

*Confirmed in forgetting.* The original phrase *tso-wang* has been translated by Legge as "I sit and forget everything," by Giles and Lin Yutang as "I can forget myself while sitting," by Fung Yu-lan as "I forget everything," and by Suzuki as "mind-forgetting." I feel sure that the word *tso* in this context must not be taken literally, but rather figuratively. It means, to my mind, "being seated or steeped in forgetting." The forgetting is universal in scope. You forget yourself and you forget everything. But it is not only while you are sitting that you forget yourself and everything, but at all times and under all circumstances.

As usual, Chuang-tzu presented his teaching in the form of a story. Once Yen Hui said to Confucius, "I am making progress." "In what way?" "I have forgotten humanity and justice," said Yen Hui. "Very well," said Confucius, "but that is not enough." Another day, Yen Hui reported that he had forgotten the rites and music. This again failed to impress Confucius. A third day, he reported that he "was steeped in forgetting." This time, Confucius was excited and asked him what he meant. Yen Hui replied, "I have dropped the body and the limbs and discarded intelligence and consciousness. Freed from the body and knowledge, I have become one with the Infinite. This is what I mean by being *steeped in forgetting*." Confucius said, "To be one with the Infinite is to have no more preferences. To be thoroughly transformed is to have no more fixations. In this you have gone ahead of me. Let me follow in your steps."

*Clear as the Morning.* This phrase is found in a remarkable story that Chuang-tzu told about the method of a Taoist master training his chosen pupil. Somebody once said to the Taoist master Nü Yü, "You, sir, are advanced in years, and yet you still have the complexion of a child. What can be the secret?" "Well," said Nü Yü, "I have been instructed in Tao." "Can I learn to attain Tao?" asked the other. "Oh no," said the master, "you are not the man for it. In the case of Pu-liang I, he had the potentiality of Sagehood, but was not acquainted with the Way of Sagehood. In my own case, I know the Way of Sagehood, but I do not have the potentiality of Sagehood. So I was desirous of teaching him the Way in the hope that his potentiality might develop into actuality. But do not imagine that the task of imparting the Way even to a potential sage was an easy one. Even in his case, I had to wait and watch for the proper time to start the instruction. After three days of training, he became detached from the world. This accomplished, I watched and guided him for seven days before he was detached from things sensual and material. Then again I had to watch and guide him for nine more days before he was detached from the clinging to life. Only when one has been detached from the clinging to life can one be as clear as the morning. When one is as clear as the morning, one is capable of seeing the Unique One. Seeing the Unique One, one transcends the past and present. To transcend the past and present is to enter the realm of no-death and no-birth, of the one who dispenses death and life to all things while He himself does not die nor is ever born. When a man is in this state, he becomes infinitely adaptable to external things, accepting all and welcoming all, equal to all tasks, whether in tearing down or in building up. This is what is called 'Peace in the midst of trials and sufferings.' How can one maintain peace in the midst of trials and sufferings? Because it is precisely through these that peace is perfected."

I have reproduced these three passages in detail because they contain so many seed-thoughts of Zen. This is not to deny that the Zen masters were Buddhists; but the point is that their predilection for the insights of Lao-tzu and Chuang-tzu conditioned their choice of similar Buddhist ideas for their special attention and development.

Besides, Chuang-tzu's ideas of the "true man" and Self-discovery have exerted a profound influence on all the Zen masters. This influence is particularly evident in the doctrines of Lin-chi and his house.

One of the profoundest insights of Chuang-tzu is that "only the true man can have true knowledge." The emphasis is on being rather than knowing. It will be seen that this is one of the distinctive features of Zen. Be and you will know. Instead of "Cogito, ergo sum," Zen says, "Sum, ergo cogito."

## II. THE VITAL RELEVANCE OF ZEN TO THE MODERN AGE

In his remarkable article, "It's What's Bugging Them," William C. McFadden reports a recent three-day conference on student stress in college experience. I am especially struck by this:

When the causes of stress had been exhaustively set down, one student could still remark: "It's all those things—and none of those things. It's something else." A second readily agreed, "All I know is that something is bugging me." A third demanded to know what this something was. It sounded like a void, or a nothing; but then how do you talk about it?

Someone identified the missing factor as truth, and another, as beauty, but both suggestions were quickly rejected. The "something" was much more vague and undefined. A fellow named Mike expressed it best at the end of a stirring speech: "The heart needs more room to breathe!"

The writer's comments on this are no less striking:

The restless heart has been with man for a long time. The philosopher seeks some absolute; mortal man yearns for immortality; temporal man seeks to be grounded in the eternal; finite man longs for the infinite.

But precisely because this absolute is infinite, it must be vague and ill-defined, a "something" that seems a void, a nothing. The infinite that is clearly defined ceases thereby to be infinite.

The writer was not thinking of Taoism and Zen. But he has brought up a vital point in the spiritual situation of the contemporary age, which makes me understand why Taoism and Zen exercise such an irresistible attraction upon the minds of the young generation in the West. It is in the Taoist paradoxes and enigmas of Zen that they hope to find that "something" which is bugging them. Their spirit feels ill at ease with the neatly defined concepts and dogmas of their traditional religion. The traditional theology appears too much to them like a book on geometry. It has laid too much emphasis upon the communicable aspect of things spiritual, while neglecting, almost completely, that which is incommunicable. This is where Taoism and Zen come in. They do not try to communicate the incommunicable, but they have a way of evoking it, thereby broadening your mental horizons and creating more room for the heart to breathe.

One of the most characteristic traits of the Chinese spirit is its predilection for the suggestive and evocative as against a well-rounded and systematic exposition of ideas. The most charming poems in Chinese are those quatrains, of which it may be said that "the words have stopped, but the sense goes on without end." Realizing that what is expressible in words, colors, and sounds must always fall short of reality, the Chinese spirit finds its home in what is beyond words, colors, and sounds. It uses words to evoke the indefinable, sounds to evoke silence, and colors to evoke the formless Void. It uses all the material things to evoke the Spirit.

In a review of Herbert Giles's translation of Chinese poems, Lytton

Strachey has brought out the differences between Greek and Chinese art and poetry.

> Greek art is, in every sense of the word, the most finished in the world; it is for ever seeking to express completely and finally. Thus the most exquisite of the lyrics in the Greek Anthology are, fundamentally, epigrams. . . . Different, indeed, is the effect of the Chinese lyric. It is the very converse of the epigram; it aims at producing an impression which, so far from being final, must be merely the prelude to a long series of visions and of feelings. It hints at wonders; and the revelation it at last gives us is never a complete one, it is clothed in the indefinability of our subtlest thoughts.

Take, for instance, a lovely quatrain of twenty words by Li P'o:

> A fair girl draws the blind aside
> And sadly sits with drooping head;
> I see the burning tears glide,
> But know not why those tears are shed.

Commenting on this poem, Strachey wrote: "The blind is drawn aside for a moment and we catch a glimpse of a vision which starts us off on a mysterious voyage down the widening river of imagination. Many of these poems partake of the nature of the *chose vue;* but they are not photographic records of the isolated facts; they are delicate pastel drawings of some intimately seized experience."

This is the style of Chinese poetry, painting, and art of living. And this is also the style of Zen. It is in this sense that Zen is truly one of the most typical flowers of the Chinese spirit.

Western civilization, on the other hand, is predominantly a product of the Greek spirit. By this time, it has been developed to a saturating point, so that the profounder spirits in the West have begun to feel what it lacks, just at a time when the more progressive elements in the East have begun to sense its strength. Hence the paradox that Zen seems to be of a greater impact on the western than on the oriental intellectuals, whose greatest ambition is to catch up with the West in its scientific civilization. However, the fact that the spirit of Zen has begun to permeate the vanguards of western thinkers is bound to affect the East in the long run. Humanity is one, and it is moving beyond East and West. It is only by moving

beyond that the East and the West will be vitally synthesized. If I may
venture on a prediction in such unpredictable matters, this vital synthesis
will probably be attained first in the West. But once attained, it will spread
to the whole world.

It is well for the East to remember that even on the natural plane, the
philosophy of Chuang-tzu, a main source of Zen, has, as Alan Watts so
keenly perceives, an "astonishing relevance to modern man's predicament." Watts sees much in common between Chuang-tzu and Teilhard de
Chardin in their vision of the universe as an organic whole. This vision is
"far more consistent with twentieth-century science than Newton's essentially mechanical model of the universe as an interaction of atomic 'bil-
liard balls.' "

On the other hand, the West should remember that Zen is not something entirely without reason or rhyme, for certainly there is method in its
madness. No one has put it better than Thomas Merton:

> The fashion of Zen in certain western circles fits into the rather con-
> fused pattern of spiritual revolution and renewal. It represents a certain
> understandable dissatisfaction with conventional spiritual patterns and
> with ethical and religious formalism. It is a symptom of western man's
> desperate need to recover spontaneity and depth in a world which his
> technological skill has made rigid, artificial, and spiritually void. But in
> its association with the need to recover authentic sense experience,
> western Zen has become identified with a spirit of improvisation and
> experimentation, with a sort of moral anarchy that forgets how much
> tough discipline and what severe traditional mores are presupposed by
> the Zen of China and Japan. So also with Chuang-tzu. He might easily
> be read today as one preaching a gospel of license and uncontrol.
> Chuang himself would be the first to say that you cannot tell people to
> do whatever they want when they don't even know what they want in
> the first place! Then also, we must realize that while there is a certain
> skeptical and down-to-earth quality in Chuang-tzu's critique of Con-
> fucianism, Chuang-tzu's philosophy is essentially religious and mysti-
> cal. It belongs in the context of a society in which every aspect of life
> was seen in relation to the sacred.

It is with the hope of showing the true face of Zen that the present
book has been written. I have confined myself to the treatment of the

giants of Zen in the T'ang period, because it was they who created the school of Zen by dint of their original insights and powerful personalities.

It was in the hands of the Sixth Patriarch Hui-neng that the school of Zen took form. A succession of men of spiritual genius like Huai-jang, Ch'ing-yüan, Ma-tsu, Shih-t'ou, Pai-chang, Nan-ch'üan, Chao-chou, Yüeh-shan, and Huang-po, developed it into full maturity, and prepared it for the rich and refreshing ramification into the Five Houses of Zen. Actually the five branches are homogeneous in their origin and in their aim. They were all derived from Hui-neng, and rooted in the Taoism of Lao-tzu and Chuang-tzu, although each in its own way and measure. The House of Kuei-yang laid stress upon the distinction between the potential and the actual, between the conceptual and experiential ("faith stage" and "personality stage"), and between letter and spirit. Kuei-shan saw eye-to-eye with Chuang-tzu that when Truth is attained words should be thrown overboard.

The House of Ts'ao-tung depicted the process of self-realization in terms of progressive self-loss. The House of Lin-chi focused its attention on the "true man of no title" who is none other than everybody's true self. The House of Yün-men soared directly to the indefinable ne plus ultra, and then showed the way of returning to the world of things, the realm of relativity. Finally, the House of Fa-yen started from the fundamental insight of Chuang-tzu that "heaven and earth and I spring from the same root, and all things are one with me."

Zen may therefore be regarded as the fullest development of Taoism by wedding it to the congenial Buddhist insights and the powerful Buddhist impulse of apostolic zeal. If Buddhism is the father, Taoism is the mother of this prodigious child. But there can be no denying that the child looks more like the mother than the father.

CHAPTER II

# Bodhidharma, the "Wall-Gazing Brahman," and His Immediate Successors

The school of Zen as we know it was actually founded by Hui-neng the Sixth Patriarch. But it must be remembered that by his time there was already a legend about Bodhidharma and his immediate successors, of whom Hui-neng was the heir. The Chinese records about Bodhidharma are hopelessly in conflict with one another, so that it is not possible in the present state of scholarship to say definitely who he was and when he came to China. According to one account, he was a Persian monk, who arrived in China probably around 480. Another account has it that he came from a Brahman family in southern India, and that he arrived in China in 527 and died in 536. For the purposes of this book, it is not necessary to pass upon the relative merits of the two accounts. What is important is that the second account was already the accepted one by the time of Hui-neng, who referred to Bodhidharma's encounter with Emperor Wu of Liang as an established fact. Whether this and other stories about Bodhidharma possessed historical truth is far from certain. What is certain is that the Bodhidharma legend was believed in as a fact by the actual founders of the school of Zen in the T'ang dynasty, when it had already become a living tradition.

According to this tradition, Bodhidharma arrived in southern China in 527 and was immediately invited by Emperor Wu of Liang to his capital, Nanking. In his audience with the emperor, a devout Buddhist, the latter is said to have asked, "Since I came to the throne, I have built countless temples, copied countless *sūtras*, and given supplies to countless monks. Is there any merit in all this?" "There is no merit at all!" was the unexpected reply of the Indian guest. "Why is there no merit?" the emperor asked. "All these," said Bodhidharma, "are only the little deeds of men and gods, a leaking source of rewards, which follow them as the shadow follows the body. Although the shadow may appear to exist, it is not real." "What then is true merit?" "True merit consists in the subtle comprehension of pure wisdom, whose substance is silent and void. But this kind of merit cannot be pursued according to the ways of the world." The emperor further asked, "What is the first principle of the sacred doctrine?" "Vast emptiness with nothing sacred in it!" was the answer. Finally the emperor asked, "Who is it that stands before me?" "I don't know!" said Bodhidharma, and took his leave.

Finding that the emperor was not someone who could see eye-to-eye with him, he crossed the Yangtze river and went to Mount Sung in Ho-nan, where he resided in the Shao-lin Temple. It is said that he took to sitting-in-meditation before a wall, keeping silence throughout the day. This mystified all who saw him, and they called him "the wall-gazing Brahman."

With regard to the term *wall-gazing* (*pi-kuan* in Chinese), many have taken it in the literal sense. But some have given it a spiritual interpretation by saying that the word *wall* has the connotation of shutting out external dust or distractions. Following this line, Suzuki observes that "the underlying meaning of 'wall-contemplation' must be found in the subjective condition of a Zen master, which is highly concentrated and rigidly exclusive of all ideas and sensuous images." Suzuki identifies pi-kuan with the *chüeh-kuan* of the *Vajrasamādhi Sūtra* that is, "enlightened or awakened contemplation." To my mind, the word *wall* evokes still other images or ideas, such as abruptness and precipitousness, something rising overtoppingly before you, which cannot be scaled or surmounted by ordinary means. It reminds me of what the sage disciple of Confucius, Yen Hui, referred to when he related how, after he had been led step by step by his master and after he had exhausted all his natural talents, there suddenly appeared something like an insurmountable wall right before him, which prevented him from following him further. In the spiritual doctrine of the Christian fathers, this crucial juncture in the life of the spirit represents a transition from the natural to the supernatural state or from active contemplation to passive contemplation.

Be that as it may, it is not necessary to confine ourselves to either the literal sense or the spiritual interpretation of the term *wall-gazing*. It may well have included both of the senses.

It is interesting to note that Bodhidharma was not averse at all to the study of scriptures. In fact he earnestly recommended the study of the *Laṅkāvatāra Sūtra*, a highly metaphysical and somewhat discursive piece of work. He remained at heart an Indian, a Buddhist who was at the same time well steeped in the best of Hinduism. It was certainly not for nothing that he was called a "Brahman."

The only piece of writing that has been attributed to him is an essay on the twofold entrance to Tao and Truth. This little discourse is important, even though its mode and style are quite different from that of the later Zen masters who imprinted upon Zen the distinctive characteristics with which it has since been identified. At least the fundamental thoughts embodied in it may serve as a background to the later development of Zen. Therefore I have thought it worthwhile to give a translation of the whole discourse here.

## A DISCOURSE ON THE TWOFOLD ENTRANCE TO THE TAO

There are many roads leading to the Tao, but essentially they can be subsumed under two categories. The one is "entrance by way of reason" and the other "entrance by way of conduct."

By "entrance by way of reason" we mean the understanding of the fundamental doctrines through the study of the scriptures, the realization, upon the basis of a deep-rooted faith that all sentient beings have in common the one True Nature, which does not manifest itself clearly in all cases only because it is overwrapped by external objects and false thoughts. If a man abandons the false and returns to the true, resting single-heartedly and undistractedly in pure contemplation (pi-kuan), he will realize that there is neither self nor other, that the holy and profane are of one essence. If he holds on firmly to this belief and never swerves from it, he will never again be a slave to the letter of the scriptures, being in secret communion with reason itself and altogether emancipated from conceptual discrimination. In this way, he will enjoy perfect serenity and spontaneity. This is called "entrance by way of reason."

"Entrance by way of conduct" refers to the four rules of conduct under which all other rules can be subsumed. They are (1) the rule of requital of hatred, (2) the rule of adaptation to variable conditions and circumstances of life, (3) the rule of non-attachment, and (4) the rule of acting in accord with the Dharma.

1. *The Requital of Hatred.* When a pursuer of the Tao falls into any kind of suffering and trials, he should think and say to himself thus: "During the innumerable past *kalpas* I have abandoned the essential and followed after the accidentals, carried along on the restless waves of the sea of existences, and thereby creating endless occasions for hate, ill will, and wrongdoing. Although my present suffering is not caused by any offenses committed in this life, yet it is a fruit of my sins in my past existences, which happens to ripen at this moment. It is not something which any men or gods could have given to me. Let me therefore take, patiently and sweetly, this bitter fruit of my own making without resentment or complaint against anyone." The scripture teaches us not to be disturbed by painful experiences. Why? Because of a penetrating insight into the real cause of all our sufferings. When this mind is awakened in a man, it responds spontaneously to the dictates of reason, so that it can even help him to make the best use of other people's hatred and turn it into an occasion to advance toward the Tao. This is called "the rule of requital of hatred."

2. *The Rule of Adaptation.* We should know that all sentient beings are produced by the interplay of karmic conditions, and as such there can be no real self in them. The mingled yarns of pleasure and pain are all woven of the threads of conditioning causes. If therefore I should be rewarded with fortune, honor, and other pleasant things, I must realize that they are the effects of my previous deeds destined to be reaped in this life. But as soon as their conditioning causes are exhausted, they will vanish. Then why should I be elated over them? Therefore, let gains and losses run their natural courses according to the ever-changing conditions and circumstances of life, for the mind itself does not increase with the gains nor decrease with the losses. In this way, no

gales of self-complacency will arise, and your mind will remain in hidden harmony with the Tao. It is in this sense that we must understand "the rule of adaptation to the variable conditions and circumstances of life."

3. *The Rule of Non-Attachment.* Men of the world remain unawakened for life; everywhere we find them bound by their craving and clinging. This is called "attachment." The wise however understand the truth, and their reason tells them to turn from the worldly ways. They enjoy peace of mind and perfect detachment. They adjust their bodily movements to the vicissitudes of fortune, always aware of the emptiness of the phenomenal world, in which they find nothing to covet, nothing to delight in. Merit and demerit are ever interpenetrated like light and darkness. To stay too long in the triple world is to live in a house on fire. Everyone who has a body is an heir to suffering and a stranger to peace. Having comprehended this point, the wise are detached from all things of the phenomenal world, with their minds free of desires and craving. As the scripture has it, "All sufferings spring from attachment; true joy arises from detachment." To know clearly the bliss of detachment is truly to walk on the path of the Tao. This is "the rule of non-attachment."

4. *The Rule of acting in accord with the Dharma.* The Dharma is nothing else than reason which is pure in its essence. This pure reason is the Formless Form of all Forms; it is free of all defilements and attachments, and it knows of neither "self" nor "other." As the scripture says, "In the Dharma there are no sentient beings, that is, it is free from the stain of sentient beings. In the Dharma there is no self, that is, it is free from the stain of the self." When the wise are convinced of this truth, they should live in harmony with the Dharma.

As there is no shadow of pusillanimity in the whole body of the Dharma, so the wise are ever ready to put their body, life, and property at the service of charity, never ceasing to be generous and gracious. Having thoroughly pierced through the threefold nature of emptiness, they are no longer dependent upon or attached to anything. Even in their work of converting all living beings, their sole motive is to cleanse them of their stains; and while they are among them as of them, they would take care not to be contaminated by a possessive love. In this way, they manage to keep themselves perfect and at the

same time to benefit others. Besides, they glorify the true Tao of Enlightenment. As with the virtue of charity, so with the other five of the
*prajñāpāramitā*. The wise practice the six virtues of perfection in order to
sweep away all confused thoughts, but they feel as though they were
doing nothing to speak of. This is indeed acting "in accord with the
Dharma."

This discourse is a gem of spiritual literature. It shows that the author
was in the grand tradition of Buddhist and Hindu writers. His two entrances are on a par with what the Christian writers have called the "active
way" and the "contemplative way." The ideas of *samsāra* and *karma* belong
to the domain of faith held by Buddhists and Hindus alike. But assuming
them as the premises, there is nothing in the essay which goes beyond the
realm of rational thinking. Bodhidharma's treatment of the "entrance by
way of conduct" is particularly noteworthy, not only because it is so
practical and down-to-earth, but also because his frequent reference to
reason and Dharma tend, implicitly, to show that reason and conduct are
really but one way. This blending of the abstract and the concrete was
due probably to the subtle influence of the Chinese spirit upon the mind
of Bodhidharma.

But, profound as it is as a piece of spiritual literature, it is certainly not
Zen at its most characteristic. We have here nothing of the breathtaking
abruptness, the blinding flashes, the deafening shouts, the shocking out-
bursts, the mystifying kōans, the rocket-like soarings beyond the sphere
of reason, the tantalizing humor and whimsicality, the unaccountable
beatings, which were to fill the pages of Zen literature as such.

If there is any connecting link between Bodhidharma and the later
masters, it is to be found in the via negativa which he employed in
leading his disciples to enlightenment. For instance, Hui-k'o said to him,
"My mind has not found peace. I beg you, Master, to pacify it for me." He
said, "Bring forth your mind to me and I will pacify it for you." After a
long silence, Hui-k'o told his master that he had searched for the mind
but could not find it. Thereupon the master said, "Behold, I have already
pacified the mind for you!"

This marked the beginning of the transmission of the lamp, and
Bodhidharma became the First Patriarch of the Chinese school of Zen.
The method he employed is a typical instance of the via negativa, so

characteristic of the whole tradition of Zen. Bodhidharma did not deny, anymore than the later masters, the existence of the mind. But the "mind" which Hui-k'o was trying so desperately to find and to pacify was not the true mind, but merely a faint reflection of it. The true mind is always peaceful; there can be no restlessness about it. Besides, the true mind is the *subject* that thinks. As soon as we begin to think about it or try to do something about it, it is no longer the subject, but an object, which cannot be the true mind. By saying that he had already pacified it, the master was pointing at the true mind, which, being always in peace, really has no need of pacification. By asking the disciple to bring forth the mind, he made him discover for himself that the falsely objectified mind was but an illusion. This prepared him for the discovery of the true mind through a direct intuitive perception called into action by the unexpected words of the master.

In 536, when he felt that the day of his departure was drawing near, he called his four disciples to come and ordered them to state their original insights. Tao-fu was the first to respond: "According to my view, we should neither cling to words and letters nor dispense with them altogether, but only use them as an instrument of Tao." "You have got my skin," said the master. Then the nun, Tsung-chih, came forward, saying, "In the light of my present comprehension, it is like Ānanda's viewing the Buddha land of Akṣobhya, seeing it once and never again." "You have got my flesh," said the master. Tao-yü said, "The four elements are all empty; the five skandhas are all unreal. Looking from where I stand, there is not a thing that can be grasped." "You have got my bone," the master commented. Finally, it was Hui-k'o's turn to show his insight. But he did not open his mouth. Bowing reverently to the master, he kept standing in his place. The master remarked, "You have got my marrow;" and Hui-k'o came to be recognized as the Second Patriarch.

The whole scene can be looked at as a graphic footnote to Lao-tzu's

> *He who speaks does not know:*
> *He who knows does not speak.*

It is impossible to tell how much of the legend about Bodhidharma was invented by Chinese ingenuity and how much of it he had brought with him from India. The only thing that one can confidently aver is that it is a blend of the two. India furnished the impulse, and China gave it a unique style. No one can deny that the later masters of Zen were inspired by the personality and thought of Bodhidharma. On the other hand, it is equally clear that Bodhidharma himself had become sinicized during his stay in China. The very analogies he employed in describing the relative degrees of attainment on the part of his disciples is typically Chinese, recalling to mind a well-known passage in the *Book of Mencius,* where it is stated that most disciples of Confucius had only got one limb or organ of the master, while Yen Hui and two others had got his whole body, though in miniature.

After Hui-k'o had succeeded to the patriarchate, there came to him a Buddhist layman of over forty years of age with a strange request; he begged the master to purify him of his sins. Hui-k'o told him to bring forth his sins that he might expiate them for him. The layman, after a long silence, said, "I have searched for the sins, but I have not been able to find them." Thereupon, Hui-k'o remarked, "Behold, I have expiated them for you!" The layman became a monk under the name of Seng-ts'an, destined to be the Third Patriarch.

Seng-ts'an carried on the tradition and proved to be a chip off the same block. One day, a young monk came to pay his homage, saying, "I beg you, Master, to show your compassion and lead me to the Dharma Gate of liberation." "Who has bound you?" asked Seng-ts'an. "Nobody has bound me," answered the monk. "That being the case," said the master, "Why should you continue to seek for liberation?" The monk was thoroughly enlightened. This was Tao-hsin, who was destined to be the Fourth Patriarch. Seng-ts'an is well known to the modern world by his essay, "On Believing in Mind." This may be called a Buddhist interpretation and restatement of the Taoist doctrine of the all-embracing reality. Especially noteworthy are the following passages:

> *There is no difficulty about the Perfect Way:*
> *Only we must avoid the making of discriminations.*
> *When we are freed from hate and love,*
> *It will reveal itself as clearly as broad daylight.*
>
> *Do not pursue the outer entanglements,*
> *Nor dwell in the inner void.*
> *Rest in peace in the oneness of things,*
> *And all barriers will vanish without a trace.*

*The more you strive to stop motion in order to attain rest,*
*The more your rest becomes restlessness.*
*As long as you are stuck in dualism,*
*How can you realize oneness?*

*The object is an object for the subject,*
*The subject is the subject for the object:*
*Know that the relativity of the two*
*Rests ultimately on one emptiness.*

# CHAPTER III

# Hui-neng
# the Sixth Patriarch

Like the wind that blows where it wills, genius often appears where it is least expected. Hui-neng (638–713) is one of such cases. He is assuredly one of the superlative geniuses that China has ever produced. He belongs to the company of Lao-tzu, Confucius, Mencius, and Chuang-tzu. His sermons and conversations, as recorded, collected, and printed by his disciples under the title of *Fa-p'ao T'an-ching*, or *The Altar Sūtra of the Dharma Treasure*, constitute the greatest masterpiece of Buddhist literature of Chinese authorship. It is by no accident that in the whole Tripiṭaka this little volume is the only Chinese work which bears the title of a "sūtra." Even among the sūtras, it seems to have found its level with some of the greatest, such as the *Diamond*, the *Lotus*, and the *Vimalakīrti*.

The *Altar Sūtra* is not the work of a scholar, smelling of the lamp. It is the work of a true sage who speaks from the fullness of his heart and mind. His words are like the spontaneous spurts of water from a living fountain. Anyone who has tasted this water will discern at once its soul-refreshing quality and know in his heart that it comes from the same fountain as Buddha carried within him. It takes a Buddha to recognize a Buddha; and only a Buddha could have discovered the Buddha nature in himself and in all sentient beings.

Like Confucius and Mencius, Hui-neng lost his father in his childhood, and was brought up by his mother in poverty and distress. He was born into a Lu family in 638 in Ling-nan of Kwangtung. Soon afterwards his family moved to Canton. In his youth, he supported his mother and himself by selling firewood in the marketplace. He did not have any chance of learning to read and write.

One day a customer bought some firewood from him and ordered him to carry it to his shop. After he had delivered his wood, received his money, and was leaving the shop, he chanced upon a man reciting a sūtra at the door. As soon as he heard the words, his mind was immediately awakened to their meaning. He asked the reciter for the name of the sūtra and was told that it was the *Diamond Sūtra*. It was from the same person that he learned for the first time the name of the master Hung-jen, the Fifth Patriarch of Ch'an, who was teaching in Huang-mei Mountain in Hupeh, far away from Canton. By a queer coincidence, which Hui-neng himself believed to be due to a cooperating cause in former life, another stranger urged him to go to Huang-mei to call on the Fifth Patriarch, and, to make the trip possible, he generously gave him ten silver taels for his old mother's upkeep during his absence. Taking leave of his mother, Hui-neng traveled for more than thirty days before he reached Huang-mei. When he saw Hung-jen, the latter asked, "Where do you come from and what do you want?" He replied, "I, your humble disciple, am a commoner from Hsin-chou in Ling-nan, and I have come a long way to pay my obeisance to Your Reverence, with no other aim than to become a Buddha." Hung-jen must have been impressed by the guileless straightforwardness of the uncouth visitor, but, being a very tactful teacher, he tested him by uttering an insulting remark, "So you are from Ling-nan and, besides, a barbarian! How can you ever become a Buddha?" This drew from the newcomer a sharp retort: "Although men can be classified into southerners and northerners, the Buddha nature knows of no south and north. The body of a barbarian may be different from the body of a monk; but what difference can there be from the standpoint of the Buddha nature?" Convinced that this barbarian had the real stuff in him, Hung-jen was inclined to converse more with him but he hesitated for fear of scandalizing the crowd of his disciples around him, who understandably were not prepared to appreciate the quality of the uncultivated stranger. So he ordered him to do some manual labor. But Hui-neng, unaware of the delicate tact of the master, continued to say, "I confess to Your Reverence that I feel wisdom constantly springing from my own heart and mind. So long as I do not stray from my nature, I carry within me the field of bliss. I wonder what kind of labor Your Reverence wants me to do." The master had to cut him short by saying, "This barbarian is too sharp in his nature and character. Don't speak any more!" Thereby he ordered him away to work in the backyard as a rice pounder.

More than eight months later, the master dropped in to see Hui-neng, saying, "In my heart I approved your views, but for fear lest certain wicked elements might entertain jealousy against you and attempt to harm you, I have refrained from speaking further with you. Are you aware of this?" Hui-neng replied, "I, your humble disciple, have also come to realize my Master's mind. This is why I have not ventured to come to the hall, in order that the others might not entertain any suspicions about what had happened between us."

One day, the patriarch, knowing that the time for transmitting the patriarchate was ripe, summoned all his disciples before him and said to them, "I have something to tell you. The question of life and death is the most important concern for everyone in the world. All day long, you look only for blessings, but you do not seek to get out of the bitter sea of birth and death. But as long as you remain deluded about your self-nature, no amount of blessings can save you. Now I want each of you to retire and look into his own inner wisdom. In other words, let each of you draw upon the prajñā-wisdom of his own mind and compose a *gāthā* [verse] for me to see. He who understands the essential truth will inherit the robe and the Dharma as the Sixth Patriarch. Go away quickly and do not linger over the gāthā, for by thinking and reasoning you will surely miss the point. The man who perceives his self-nature perceives it at a word. He will perceive it even in the heat of a battle."

In obedience to the order, all the disciples retired to their own quarters. They said to one another, "There is no need for all of us to cudgel our brains over the composition of a gāthā. The head monk Shen-hsiu, who is our present instructor, is sure to get the patriarchate. It would be presumptuous and most silly for us to waste our mental energy in producing a shabby gāthā or hymn to enter into a hopeless competition." In fact, all of them would be contented to follow their present instructor Shen-hsiu as their new patriarch.

Now, Shen-hsiu was a deeply spiritual man, a man of true piety and modesty. Knowing that none of his present pupils would present a gāthā before the patriarch, he composed one, more in the spirit of obedience than with a craving for the patriarchate. As he candidly said, "If I do not submit a gāthā, how can the master know the degree of my attainment? In submitting it, my motive is good since I seek only the Dharma, while it would be base should I seek the patriarchate, as it would amount to snatching a holy office with an unholy ambition. Anyway, if I do not submit a gāthā, I may never attain the right Dharma. Oh, what a dilemma, what a predicament!"

These words have an unmistakable ring of candor and sincerity about them. And when we remember that it was none other than Hui-neng himself who reported these words, we are warranted in concluding that neither of the two great masters was responsible for the later bickerings between the Northern School and the Southern School.

Let us then see what gāthā Shen-hsiu composed and wrote on the wall of the corridor for the patriarch to see and judge. It read:

> The body is the tree of enlightenment.
> The mind is the stand of a bright mirror.
> Wipe it constantly and with ever-watchful diligence,
> To keep it uncontaminated by the worldly dust.

When the patriarch came to see it, he knew that it was from the hands of Shen-hsiu and was sorely disappointed. However, in the presence of Shen-hsiu's pupils he uttered some guarded compliment, saying that this gāthā was worthy of being committed to memory and reverently observed, and that the cultivation of one's conduct in conformity with the gāthā would keep the devotee from falling into evil ways. Late in the evening, the patriarch secretly called Shen-hsiu to him and told him, "This gāthā which you have composed reveals that you have not yet seen the self-nature. You have only arrived at the threshold, but have not entered the door. Ordinary people, by conducting themselves according to your gāthā, will be prevented from falling into a worse state. But it is impossible to attain the highest wisdom on the basis of such a view. To aspire to the highest wisdom, one must be able to recognize by direct intuition one's own mind, and to perceive one's self-nature as beyond birth and death. This self-perception is perpetual and pervades every thought, so that nothing in the world can ever obstruct it. The realization of a single truth is the realization of all truths. Then you will see that all the infinitely variable and shifting scenes of the world remain really in the state of suchness. Reality is nothing other than the Bhutatathatā mind.

This insight is one with the self-nature of supreme wisdom." He then bade him submit another gāthā. But in the next few days, Shen-hsiu's mind knew no peace, and he was not able to write another gāthā.

In the meantime, a young novice passed by the rice-pounding area, chanting aloud Shen-hsiu's gāthā. When Hui-neng heard it, he knew right away that its author had not perceived the self-nature. So he asked the boy whose gāthā it was that he had just chanted. The boy said, "True barbarian, you! You even do not know what has happened recently?" Then he told him everything. Hui-neng said, "Sir, you see I have been pounding rice here for over eight months, and I have never come near the hall. Will you, Sir, lead me to where the gāthā is that I too may pay my respect to it." When they arrived at the place, Hui-neng said to the boy, "Your servant is illiterate, will you, Sir, read it to me?" It happened that a governmental clerk was also there visiting, and he chanted the gāthā aloud. Having heard it, Hui-neng said to the reciter that he too had got a gāthā and asked him if he would graciously write it out for him. "What!" replied the clerk, "even *you* can compose a gāthā? How extraordinary!" Hui-neng fired back, "Anyone who wishes to attain the highest wisdom must not despise a beginner. For even the lowest kind of people may have the highest kind of wisdom, while the highest kind of people may have the most senseless kind of wisdom. To despise any man is to be guilty of immeasurable sin." This rebuke humbled the clerk, who finally consented to write out the gāthā for him, which read:

> *Enlightenment is no tree,*
> *Nor is the bright mirror a stand.*
> *Since it is not a thing at all,*
> *Where could it be contaminated by dust?*

When the monks saw the gāthā, they were all struck with a sense of wonder. Sighing and exclaiming, they said to one another, "How marvellous! We must not judge any man by appearance. Here we have a bodhisattva in the flesh! How could we have treated him like a menial servant for so long?"

Seeing the general commotion and excitement, the patriarch was afraid that some people might do harm to Hui-neng, so he rubbed off the gāthā with his shoe, saying, "This also has not seen the self-nature." The commotion was thereby quieted down.

The next day, the patriarch went secretly to the rice-pounding area. He saw Hui-neng working intently away with a stone tied around his waist. He called out to him, saying, "Should a seeker of Truth forget his body for the Dharma in such a manner?" He then proceeded to ask Hui-neng, "Is the rice ripe?" "The rice has been ripe for a long time," said Hui-neng; "only it still waits to be sifted in a sieve." The patriarch struck the pestle with his staff three times, to indicate that he wanted Hui-neng to come to his chamber at the third watch in the evening, which Hui-neng understood and acted upon accordingly. When the two were face to face in the stillness of the night, the patriarch expounded the *Diamond Sūtra* to his disciple. When he came to the sentence: "Keep your mind alive and free without abiding in anything or anywhere," Hui-neng was suddenly and thoroughly enlightened, realizing that all dharmas are inseparable from the self-nature. Ecstatically he said to the patriarch, "How could I expect that the self-nature is in and of itself so pure and quiet! How could I expect that the self-nature is in and of itself unborn and undying! How could I expect that the self-nature is in and of itself self-sufficient, with nothing lacking in it! How could I expect that the self-nature is in and of itself immutable and imperturbable! How could I expect that the self-nature is capable of giving birth to all dharmas!"

Knowing that Hui-neng had truly comprehended the self-nature, the patriarch commented, "He who does not know his fundamental mind can derive no benefit from the study of the Dharma. He who knows his fundamental mind and perceives his self-nature is called a man who has realized his manhood, a teacher of *devas* and men, a Buddha." It was in the depth of the night that he transmitted to Hui-neng the robe and the bowl together with the doctrine of instantaneous enlightenment, saying, "You are now the Sixth Patriarch. Take good care of yourself, liberate as many living beings as possible, and transmit the teaching to the future generations in uninterrupted continuation. Now listen to my gāthā:

> Sow the seed widely among the sentient beings,
> And it will come to fruition on fertile ground.
> Without sentience no seed can grow;
> Nor can there be life without nature.

All this happened in 661, when Hui-neng was barely twenty-three years old and still a lay brother. It took extraordinary courage on the part of Hung-jen to have picked out for his successor a man from the extreme south who was not only illiterate but to all appearances untrained in Ch'an and Buddhism in general. But he was as tactful as he was courageous. He knew that Hui-neng was thoroughly enlightened, but he also knew that it would be too much to expect his disciples to see eye-to-eye with him concerning his handpicked successor. He therefore sent the new patriarch off to his native place with the utmost secrecy, bidding him to live a hidden life for a period before entering upon his public life as a patriarch. In view of the fact that the transmission of the robe might easily become an occasion of contention, he told Hui-neng that there was to be no more transmission of the robe after him, and that thereafter it was to be a purely spiritual transmission of truth from mind to mind. They then ferried over to the southern shore of the Yangtze river. At first, the old patriarch took the oar and rowed the boat, bidding Hui-neng to sit in it as his passenger. This was too much for Hui-neng, who insisted that he should do the labor and the master should be seated. But the master said, "It is for me to ferry you over." Hui-neng replied, "When a disciple is still under delusion, it is for the master to ferry him over. When he is already enlightened, it is for him to ferry himself over." The old patriarch was greatly delighted with these words. "In the future, the Buddha dharma will greatly prevail through you," he predicted. Then they parted, never to see each other again in this life. The old patriarch returned to his monastery, where he died three years later; and the new patriarch went deep into the south. How he spent the next fifteen years nobody knows exactly. It is likely that he was nourishing his insight by meditation and preparing himself for his future work by learning to read so that he could have more knowledge of the scriptures. He himself has told us that for a period he mixed with a band of hunters in Szu-hui. Without revealing his identity, he often tried to infiltrate into the minds of the hunters some essential principles of the Dharma, whenever he saw an opportunity to do so. On some occasions when the hunters charged him with the task of watching the traps, he made it a point to free the animals caught therein. At meals, he would put his own vegetables into the pots in which they were cooking meat, declaring that he liked to eat vegetables by the side of meat.

He managed to keep his anonymity until 676, when he was approaching forty. On a certain day of that year, he felt strongly that the time was ripe for him to come out from his hiding to spread the Dharma. He went to the Fa-hsin monastery in Canton, where the Dharma master Yin-tsung was lecturing on the *Mahāparinirvāna Sūtra*. One day, two monks, watching a banner streaming in the wind, entered into a heated debate. One of them maintained that it was the wind that was moving, the other that it was the banner that was moving. Hui-neng intervened, saying, "That which is moving is neither the wind nor the banner, but your mind." All those who were present were amazed by the remark, and it attracted the attention of Yin-tsung himself, who discussed with him the spiritual sense of scriptural teachings. Deeply impressed by the simplicity of the newcomer's words and the directness of his insight, which could not have come from mere book learning, Yin-tsung remarked, "Lay Brother, you are an extraordinary man. I heard long ago that the successor to the robe and Dharma of Huang-mei had come to the south. I wonder if you are not the one." Hui-neng was too modest to say "Yes," but he was too honest to say "No." So he answered, "Oh, I am not worthy!" which in Chinese polite conversation amounts to an affirmative answer. Yin-tsung then paid him homage with due rites and requested him to bring out the transmitted robe and bowl that the whole community might have the pleasure of seeing them.

When Yin-tsung asked him whether the Fifth Patriarch had transmitted to him any particular methods, he answered, "He had no particular methods, but only stressed the necessity of seeing one's self-nature. He did not even speak of deliverance through dhyāna." He went on to explain that to speak of deliverance through the practice of dhyāna is to introduce a dual Dharma, which is not the true Dharma, because the Buddha dharma is the Dharma of nonduality. He pointed out that the *Nirvāna Sūtra* speaks of "comprehending the Buddha nature," and that this alone is the non-dual Buddha dharma. Then he cited from the same sūtra that Śākyamuni had said in answer to the Bodhisattva Kao-kuei Teh-wang: "The good roots are of two classes: the permanent and the impermanent. But the Buddha nature is neither permanent nor impermanent, therefore it never ceases to be." According to Hui-neng, the Buddha nature is beyond permanent and impermanent, beyond good and evil, beyond content and form. This is what he meant by the "essential nonduality of the Buddha nature." Yin-tsung was so delighted with his teaching that he brought together his palms in reverence and said, "My discourses on the scriptures are like bricks and tiles, while your interpretation of their meaning is like pure gold." Thereupon he shaved Hui-neng's head, and wished to become his disciple.

In the following year (677), Hui-neng went to Ts'ao-ch'i, and established himself in the Pao-lin monastery, which he built with the generous contributions of his lay devotees, notably Chen Ya-hsien. There he stayed and taught for thirty-six years till his death in 713. The magistrate of the Shao-chou district, to which Ts'ao-ch'i belonged, was Wei Ch'ü, who became a lay disciple of the patriarch. It was at his request that the patriarch delivered the sermons which form the main bulk of the *Platform Sūtra* as we find it today. The rest of the sūtra consists in his dialogues with the new-coming disciples and visitors to his monastery, whom he led to enlightenment. The sermons constitute, as it were, the *Ch'an Dharma*, and the dialogues the *Ch'an Yoga* of the Sixth Patriarch. But the Dharma and the Yoga are essentially one, as the body and its function are one.

In 705, Dowager Empress Wu Tse-t'ien and Emperor Chung-tsung sent a special envoy with a mandate to invite the patriarch to come to the capital. Hui-neng declined on ground of illness and old age. But it is interesting to note that in the mandate it was stated that the two great masters, Hui-an and Shen-hsiu had recommended Hui-neng as the one who "had truly inherited the robe and the Dharma from the great master Hung-jen." This shows how highly he was regarded by Shen-hsiu, and at the same time it reveals what a great-souled man Shen-hsiu was. Hui-neng too was fair in his judgment of Shen-hsiu's teachings. The only difference between the two great masters is that while Shen-hsiu taught gradual enlightenment, Hui-neng taught instantaneous enlightenment. Shen-hsiu's doctrine of *śīla*, *prajñā*, and *dhyāna* (moral discipline, wisdom, and recollection and peace) was based upon the famous precept from the *Dharmapada*: "Not to commit any sin, to do good, and to purify one's mind, that is the teaching of all the Awakened." To Shen-hsiu, this sums up the whole spiritual doctrine of Buddhism. For what is śīla but abstention from all evil? What is prajñā but the pursuing of all good? And what is dhyāna but the purification of one's mind? These are the three stages in Shen-hsiu's program of gradual enlightenment. Hui-neng did not deny the value of this teaching. As he told one of Shen-hsiu's disciples, "Your master's expounding of śīla-dhyāna-prajñā is ineffably profound." Only it was meant to guide "men of Mahāyāna," while his own teaching of instantaneous enlightenment was meant for "men of the highest Vehicle." To Hui-neng, the all-important thing is to recognize the self-nature, of which all dharmas such as śīla, dhyāna, and prajñā are but functions. In this view, they are not so much stages of spiritual life as streams flowing from the self-nature as the sole fountain of wisdom. Everything depends upon awakening. The self-awakened will spontaneously avoid all evil and pursue all good. He enjoys an ineffable freedom and peace and carries within him a living fountain of wisdom.

The way of Hui-neng was, then, professedly opened for men of the highest spiritual gifts. But taking mankind as it is, one cannot but admit that even "men of Mahāyāna" are rare enough, to say nothing of "men of the highest Vehicle." One wonders how many monks and lay devotees who have claimed themselves to be members of the southern school of instantaneous enlightenment have in truth been men of the supreme vehicle as envisaged by Hui-neng.

Even among the immediate disciples of Hui-neng, there were, traditionally, only five outstanding men. Let us take a brief look at each of them.

The first was Nan-yüeh Huai-jang (677–744), a native of Chin-chou in Shensi, from a Tu family. He began as a novice in the Vinaya order, and was professed in 697. For a time he steeped himself in the *Vinaya-piṭaka*. Later, feeling an impulse to transcend the realm of learning, he went to Sung-shan Mountain to visit the Ch'an master Hui-an, who, after giving him some initial instructions so as to open his mental horizons, recommended that he go down south to Ts'ao-ch'i to visit Hui-neng. When he arrived, Hui-neng asked him where he came from, and he replied that he had come from Sung-shan. Thereupon, the patriarch asked, "What thing is it that thus comes?" Huai-jang said, "To say that it is like a thing is to miss the point altogether!" The patriarch asked again, "Can it still be cultivated and verified?" Huai-jang replied, "I would not say that there is no more cultivation and verification; only it can never be contaminated." The patriarch was so delighted with the answer that he exclaimed, "Just this noncontamination is what all the Buddhas have been careful to preserve. As it is so for you, so it is for me." Huai-jang stayed with the master and served him for fifteen years, during which period he grew steadily in the penetration of the mystical and profound. Later he went to the Nan-yüeh Mountain, greatly spreading the Ch'an teaching. Among his disciples was Ma-tsu Tao-i, with whom we shall deal at length in a later chapter.

Of equal importance with Huai-jang was Ch'ing-yüan Hsing-ssu (d. 740), a native of Chi-chou in Kiangsi, from a Liu family. Very little is known about his life except that he joined a monastery in childhood, and that he was taciturn by nature. On his first visit to the patriarch, he asked, "What should one do in order not to fall into the sphere of relative degrees?" The patriarch asked back, "What have you been doing of late?" Hsing-ssu replied, "I have not even practiced the fourfold Noble Truth." "What degree have you arrived at?" asked the patriarch. Hsing-ssu said, "Since I have not even practiced the Noble Truth, how can I speak of any degrees?" The patriarch was deeply impressed by the depth of his insight, and made him the leader of the community. Later, he was sent to the Ch'ing-yüan Mountain in Chi-chou, where he spread the Dharma and continued the tradition of Hui-neng. So far as the records go, he had only one disciple, Shih-t'ou Hsi-chien (700–790). But as Ch'ing-yüan himself put it, "Although there are innumerable horned animals, a single unicorn suffices."

Another outstanding disciple of Hui-neng was Yung-chia Hsüan-chüeh (665–713), who is famous for his *Song of the Realization of Tao*. He was born in Yung-chia, Chekiang, into a Tai family. He began as a member of the T'ien-t'ai school, and he was well steeped in its contemplative lore. Quite independently of the Sixth Patriarch or any other Ch'an masters, Hsüan-chüeh had arrived at certain mystical insights along the lines of Ch'an. But at the advice of some of his Ch'an friends, he went to visit Hui-neng for the "verification" of his insights. On arrival, he circumambulated the patriarch thrice, and then, holding his staff straight, he stood still before him. In order to test him, Hui-neng said, "A monk is supposed to embody three thousand rites and eighty thousand minor rules of conduct. Where does the Virtuous One come from, and what makes him appear so haughty and proud?" Ignoring the question, Hsüan-chüeh remarked, "The question of birth and death is of capital importance. Everything is impermanent and fleeting." "Why not embody that which is unborn and realize that which is not fleeting?" asked the patriarch. Hsüan-chüeh replied, "The very act of embodying is itself unborn, and the very realization is itself unfleeting." The identification of the subject and the object won a hearty approval from the patriarch, who exclaimed, "Exactly so, exactly so!" Thereupon

Hsüan-chüeh made obeisance to the patriarch with due rites, after which he wished to take leave. "Why are you going back in such a hurry?" asked the patriarch. He replied, "Fundamentally, I have not moved at all; how can there be hurry?" The patriarch again asked, "Who is it that knows there is no motion?" Hsüan-chüeh replied, "Your Reverence is creating vain distinctions!" The patriarch remarked, "You have firmly grasped the meaning of the 'unborn.' " Hsüan-chüeh said, "How can the 'unborn' have any meaning?" "If there is no meaning, how can anyone discern it?" asked the patriarch. "Discernment itself is no meaning," Hsüan-chüeh retorted. The patriarch exclaimed, "Good, good!" He urged him to stay overnight. This was why he was called by his contemporaries "the Overnight Enlightened."

Nan-yang Hui-chung (677–775) is everywhere listed as one of the "Big Five" among the disciples of Hui-neng, although there is no record to show when he visited the master and how he came to his enlightenment. All that we know is that after he had received the seal of the Buddha mind from Hui-neng, he retired to Pai-yai Mountain in Nan-yang, where he stayed over forty years without once descending from the mountain. In 761, he was invited by Emperor Su-tsung to the capital and honored as "National Teacher." Once in an audience, the emperor asked him many questions, but he did not even look at the emperor. The latter became annoyed, saying, "I am the Emperor of the great T'ang! How is it that my Master does not even deign to look at me?" Hui-chung asked him in turn, "Does Your Majesty see the empty space?" "Yes," replied the emperor. Then Hui-chung asked again, "Does the empty space wink at Your Majesty?" This concluded the conversation.

What a severe master Hui-chung was can be seen from his treatment of his disciple and attendant Tan-yüan. One day, one of Hui-chung's younger friends, Tan-hsia came to call on him. Hui-chung happened to be taking a nap. When Tan-hsia asked Tan-yüan whether the master was at home, Tan-yüan, who had just been initiated into Ch'an, replied, "At home he is, only he is not to be interviewed by any guest." Tan-hsia remarked, "You are being too profound and remote." "Not even the Buddha eye can see him," Tan-yüan added. Thereupon Tan-hsia remarked sarcastically, "Indeed, it takes a dragon to beget a little dragon, and a phoenix to bear a baby phoenix!" and went away. When the master got up, Tan-yüan reported Tan-hsia's visit and the interesting conversation that had taken place. To the great surprise of Tan-yüan, the master gave him twenty blows with his cane, and drove him away from his door. When Tan-hsia heard of this, he said, "It is not for nothing that Hui-chung has been honored as National Teacher!" This anecdote is important as a warning to all students of Ch'an. A Ch'an insight is valuable in itself, but when a neophyte uses it the first opportunity that comes his way, he is apt to be like a child of three playing with a razor, cutting everything that he could reach and ending up by cutting his own fingers. Tan-yüan must have become wiser after this painful experience, for eventually he became Hui-chung's successor.

The last of the "Big Five" was Ho-tse Shen-hui (670–758). Although he seems to have had little significance in the inner tradition of Ch'an, yet as a popularizer and defender of Hui-neng's position in the world his merit was second to none. It was through his vigorous efforts and struggles that the Southern School of Sudden Enlightenment achieved its great triumph over the Northern School of Gradual Attainment. But here we are more interested in his encounters with his master Hui-neng.

Shen-hui was born in 670 in Hsiang-yang, Hupeh, into a Kao family. It was in 682 that he first came to visit Hui-neng. He was then barely twelve years of age, a novice from another monastery. The master said, "Learned friend, you have come from a long distance and must have had an arduous journey, but have you brought the *fundamental* along with you? If you have the *fundamental*, then you should know the *host* or *subject* to whom it belongs. Can you tell me something about it?" Shen-hui replied, "The fundamental is nothing else than the non-abiding; the subject is nothing else than the seeing." The master remarked, "Oh, this little monk, how glibly he talks!" Shen-hui then asked, "When Your Reverence sits in meditation, is there seeing or no seeing?" The master struck him thrice, saying, "When I strike you do you feel pain or no pain?" Shen-hui answered, "I feel both pain and no pain." The master said, "I see and yet I do not see." Shen-hui asked, "What do you mean by seeing and yet not seeing?" The master said, "Seeing, I see constantly the errors and faults of my own mind; not seeing, I do not see other people's rights and wrongs, goodness and evil. This is what I mean by saying that I see and yet I don't see. But what do you mean by feeling pain and yet not feeling pain? If you do not feel pain, then you are as insensible as wood and stone. If you feel pain, then you are no more than an ordinary man, who will immediately feel anger and resentment. Come nearer (and I will tell you). Seeing and not seeing are but two aspects, while feeling pain and not feeling pain belong to the two different planes of existence and extinction. You do not even see your self-nature. How dare you mock others?" Shen-hui made obeisance and apologized. He became a faithful attendant. One day at a regular assembly, the master said, "I have here something, which has no head and no tail, no name and no attribute, no front and no back. Does any of you recognize it?" Shen-hui stood forth, saying, "It is the original source of all the Buddhas, the Buddha nature of Shen-hui!" The master remarked, "I said explicitly to you that it has no name and no attribute; yet you still call it the 'original source' and 'Buddha nature!' Hereafter, even if you should spend your life in a thatched hut, you will at most become a speculative and intellectual propagator of the Way." And this was exactly what he turned out to be, no more but no less!

Early in the autumn of 713, the master announced that he was to depart from the world in the next month. Fa-hai and other devoted disciples were with him. Of the "Big Five," only Shen-hui was present. At the hearing of this news from the mouth of their master, all the disciples burst out crying. Shen-hui alone remained calm, nor did he weep. The master said, "The little master Shen-hui alone has risen above what is good and what is not good. He has attained the state in which honor and dishonor can no longer move him, and there is no more sorrow and joy for him. The rest of you have not attained it. What kind of Tao have you been cultivating these many years on the mountain? For whom are you worrying that you should cry so piteously today? Are you worrying that I do not know where I am going? But I know very well where I am going. If I don't know where I am going, why should I announce it beforehand to you? You are lamenting perhaps, because you do not know where I am going. If you knew, you would not have lamented. The Dharma nature is not subject to birth and death."

CHAPTER IV

# Hui-neng's Fundamental Insights

Bodhidharma's mission has been summarized by later Zennists in a formula, which may be called a "four-point program":

> *Special transmission outside the scriptures.*
> *No setting up of words and letters.*
> *Point directly at man's mind.*
> *See self-nature and attain Buddhahood.*

It is to be noted that this formula did not make its appearance until some time after Hui-neng's death. At any rate, it expresses more characteristically the spirit of Hui-neng than that of Bodhidharma, whose predilection for the *Laṅkāvatāra Sūtra* was so explicit that his school was at first known as the school of Laṅkāvatāra. But even as applied to Hui-neng, the formula must not be taken literally. In fact Hui-neng's mind works intuitively, and his perceptions and insights are too much like a rapidly flowing stream to be dammed up within the four corners of a formula.

If, therefore, we use the four-point program in treating of Hui-neng's teaching, we are only employing an expedient means in order to recall what he actually taught. In proceeding from point to point, we must at the same time remember that the four points are interdependent and interpenetrated with each other, so that a certain amount of anticipation and overlapping is unavoidable.

1. By a "special transmission outside the scriptures," is meant that the Dharma or reality and truth can only be "transmitted" from mind to mind,

that the scriptures are only a means of evoking or rousing our true insights, that besides the scriptures there are other means which may serve as an occasion to awake us to reality, that this waking is a strictly personal experience, as personal as eating and drinking. All external things are but a reflection of our "original face," and all external teachings are but an echo of the true music of our self-nature. Let no one identify himself with his mere reflection or echo; it is only by seeing one's self-nature that he becomes actually what he is in essence.

A Zen master, however enlightened he might be, cannot infuse or instil his own insights into the mind of another. He is at most a midwife who helps a pregnant woman whose hour has come to give birth to her own child. There is no better illustration of this point than the very first experience that Hui-neng had in converting another person, after his accession to the patriarchate. As he was escaping from the Mount Huang-mei, he was overtaken by a monk named Ch'en Hui-ming, who, whatever may have been his real motive, declared that he had come, not for the robe, but for the Dharma, imploring Hui-neng to expound the Truth to enlighten him. "Since you have come for the Dharma," said Hui-neng, "I will explain it to you, if you would banish all distracting tangles and thoughts." After waiting a long while, Hui-neng resumed, "When you are not thinking of the good and evil, what is your original face?" At those words, Hui-ming was instantaneously enlightened. Then he inquired whether there was any ultrasecret teaching over and above the esoteric expression and teaching handed down by the patriarchs. To this Hui-neng replied, "What has been communicated to you is really no secret at all. But if you turn your light inward, the secret is within you." "Although I have been in Huang-mei for some time, I never have recognized my own original face. But now, thanks to your pointing out, I feel like a drinker of water who alone knows its coldness and hotness."

Unlike technical knowledge, which can be communicated through the intellect alone, spiritual wisdom must be experienced and realized by your whole being—head and heart, body and spirit. When David sang, "Taste and see that the Lord is good," he was uttering a Zen experience.

Hui-neng's attitude toward the study of scriptures is not inhibitory. In fact, it was through the hearing of the *Diamond Sūtra* that he was first awakened to reality; and although he might have been illiterate then, he certainly picked up enough knowledge of the written characters to read the scriptures. Otherwise, how could he have quoted appropriate passages in his sermons from such sūtras as *Nirvāṇa, Vimalakīrti, Laṅkāvatāra, Amitābha,* and *Bodhisattva-śīla,* to mention nothing of the *Diamond* and the *Lotus.* What is true is that he did not approach the scriptures as a scholar or erudite annotator, but as a sage who understands their spiritual sense. In his hands the scriptures became alive and subservient to the great purpose of spiritual liberation. This is what he meant when he said:

> *The mind that is deluded is spun around by the* Lotus:
> *The mind that is enlightened spins the* Lotus *around.*

To Hui-neng, all books, to the extent they are true, are but streamlets flowing from the living fountain within you. When the great Neo-Confucian philosopher, Lu Hsiang-shan, said, "In learning, if we know the fundamentals, all the 'six classics' are but so many footnotes to the truths we carry within us," he was apparently under the liberating influence of Zen.

2. *No setting up of words and letters.* This phrase has often been rendered as "no dependence on words and letters" *(pu li wen tze).* The word *li* means to set up as the pattern. The idea is that, just as we must not cling to the letter of the scriptures, so we should not expect others to be enslaved by our own words. A typical instance of this is where after he had spoken of the "true void of the self-nature," Hui-neng immediately warned his audience against clinging to the word *void.* "Learned friends," he said, "when you hear me speaking of the void, please do not cling to the void. It is of first importance not to cling to the void. If you sit in meditation with a vacant mind, you will fall into a spiritless apathy." In fact, the true void is the same as infinite reality. "The self-nature of man is so great that all things and laws are contained in it."

In his last instruction, he said, "Those who cling to the void vilify the scriptures by saying they have no use for words and letters. But anyone who says that he has no use for words and letters contradicts himself by his very speech, because this too is a form of words and letters." Against those who cling literally to "No setting up of words and letters," Hui-neng said, "Even this phrase 'No setting up' belongs to words and letters. As soon as they see someone expounding the Dharma, they would immediately jump upon him as one attached to the use of words and letters! You should know that such people are not only deluded in themselves, but are actually disparaging the scriptures."

By "No setting up of words and letters" is meant merely that there should be no attachment to the letter. It does not mean that they cannot be used as an expedient means of pointing to the truth. The one thing necessary is to realize one's self-nature. "The one who has realized his self-nature may do as he sees fit, whether to set up or not to set up the dharmas; for he comes and goes freely without any inhibition or impediment. He will act whenever called upon to exercise his function and respond readily to questions asked of him. He plays all roles in all situations without departing for a single moment from his self-nature. In this way he attains the ineffable state of sovereign liberty and enjoys the perennial delights of playful *samādhi*. This is what I mean by 'seeing one's self-nature.' "

3. *Pointing directly at the mind of man.* "Mind" is a weasel word. My mind always feels confused when I have to speak about the mind. But the mind is the very hinge of Zen, and there can be no comprehension of Zen without a clear understanding of what the Zennists mean by the mind. For, although the ultimate aim of Zen is to see one's self-nature and attain Buddhahood, it takes the mind to see it, and therefore we must first point at the mind.

"The *bodhi* or wisdom, which constitutes our self-nature, is pure from the beginning. We need only use our mind to perceive it directly to attain Buddhahood." These are the words with which Hui-neng opened his sermon at the T'a-fan Temple in Canton; they present in a nutshell his fundamental insight which underlies all his teachings. The insight was genuine, but he did not claim any originality for himself, for he supported it with a quotation from the *Bodhisattva-śīla Sūtra*: "Our self-nature is pure in and of itself. If only we are aware of our mind and see our self-nature, we should all attain Buddhahood."

Hui-neng regards the self-nature as the king, with the mind as his land and minister. In other words, the self-nature is the substance or essence of the mind, while the mind is the function of the self-nature. In this interior kingdom of ours, the king is absolutely perfect, only the minister is not always loyal. If he functions as he ought to, the whole kingdom will enjoy peace and the blessings of peace. But if he functions ill, if he turns away from the king, the whole kingdom may be wrecked. The power of the mind is infinitely great. It is through the mind that we achieve self realization, becoming what we are. It is through the same mind that we may land ourselves in hell. Without the mind there can be neither virtues nor sins, neither detachment nor attachment, neither enlightenment nor delusion, neither *bodhi* nor *kleśa*. Hui-neng speaks of pure mind, good mind, impartial mind, straightforward mind, wise or Tao-mind. But he also speaks of the evil mind, impure mind, warped mind, distracted mind, the deluded mind. This does not mean that there are two different kinds of minds. There is only one mind, and it is not a static entity but a dynamic process like an ever-flowing stream, sometimes pure and sometimes muddy, sometimes flowing smoothly and sometimes impeded. The insight that the mind must flow on and never stop is the key to the whole philosophy of Hui-neng. As we have seen, he himself was awakened to this truth at the hearing of the words of the *Diamond Sūtra*: "Let your mind function freely without abiding anywhere or in anything." As we shall see, his whole philosophy of the mind springs from this basic insight.

It must be pointed out, however, that the mind we are thinking of here is not the real mind, for the simple reason that the real mind is that which is thinking, not that which is thought about. The mind is the subject, which cannot be objectified without losing its intrinsic nature. As soon as it becomes a *Gegenstand* (an object of study or philosophy), it is no longer the real mind but only a concept or an abstraction of it. In speaking of the mind, therefore, we are not really pointing directly at the mind, but at best pointing to the pointing. So long as we are aware of this, we are in no danger of clinging to the static, conceptualized entities as if they were realities. But if we should identify the concept of the mind with the real mind, we would become attached to the letter that kills and confined in a cocoon woven of our thoughts. This is the reason why Hui-neng and his followers have never wearied of stressing the vital importance of "no-thought" or "mindlessness."

For Hui-neng, "no-thought" simply means "the seeing of all things with your mind without being tainted or attached to them." Let your mind function actively and freely in all things without being stuck in anything. The doctrine of no-thought must never be understood as demanding that we must think of nothing or cut off all thoughts. This would be turning a liberating doctrine into a cage. Truth should make us free; but the literal minded have the knack of turning everything into a chain.

…view must have been to the contemporaries of Hui-neng
…ed from the fact that a Zen master called Wo-lun could have
…sed a gāthā like the following:

> Wo-lun possesses a special aptitude:
> He can cut off all thoughts.
> No situation can stir his mind.
> The Bodhi tree grows daily in him.

One day a monk was chanting the gāthā, apparently with approval.
When Hui-neng heard it, he commented that its composer had not realized his mind and that to act upon it would only create more shackles for
oneself. He therefore answered it with a gāthā of his own:

> Hui-neng has no special aptitude:
> He does not cut off any thoughts.
> His mind responds to all situations.
> In what way can the Bodhi tree grow?

Hui-neng's doctrine of "no-thought" is on a par with Lao-tzu's doctrine
of "non-ado." Lao-tzu had said, "Non-ado, yet nothing is left undone."
Similarly, Hui-neng maintained that so long as our mind remains unattached to any particular thought, it is capable of thinking all thoughts
suitable to all situations. The pure or unattached mind "comes and goes
freely and functions fluently without any hindrance."

Hui-neng's attitude toward sitting-in-meditation is inspired by the
same solicitude to keep the mind perfectly free. When he learned how
Shen-hsiu taught his disciples to "keep the mind still to contemplate
silence and quiet and to keep up the sitting posture without lying down,"
he remarked that "to keep the mind still to contemplate silence and quiet
is a disease rather than Zen" and that "to keep sitting for a long time
only shackles the body with no profit to the mind." He composed a
gāthā:

> When alive, one keeps sitting without lying down:
> When dead, one lies down without sitting up.
> In both cases, a set of stinking bones!
> What has it to do with the great lesson of life?

Not that he rejected categorically the practice of zazen any more than
he rejected the use of words and letters. But he was careful to remind his

disciples of the one thing necessary: to realize the ever-abiding mind and to see one's self-nature to attain Buddhahood. All other things must be subordinated to the supreme end of *satori* (enlightenment). There is only one tragedy in life and that is to forget the end as a consequence of our attachment to the means.

Hui-neng was one of the most thoroughgoing teachers of nonattachment. To him it makes no difference whether you are a monk or a layman; but it makes a world of difference whether you are attached or non-attached in spirit to the externals. "Attachment to externals gives rise to birth and extinction like the waves in the sea; this is to remain on 'this shore.' Detachment from the externals brings about freedom from birth and extinction, like a river flowing freely and calmly; this is called 'reaching the other shore.' "

It goes without saying that our mind must not cling to our sins. Hui-neng, like many other Buddhist philosophers, insists that we must be detached even from our virtues. Perhaps their doctrine of going beyond good and evil can best be understood in the light of Lao-tzu's aphorism: "High virtue is not self-virtuous; hence it has virtue. Low virtue never frees itself from virtuousness; hence it has no virtue." But the question is, when we are detached from all things, including our good deeds, are we to be attached to detachment, or must we be detached even from detachment? Hui-neng's answer to this crucial question is to be found in a splendid passage which represents one of the highest peaks in the whole landscape of Buddhist literature: "When your mind is free from all clinging and thinks of neither good nor evil, you should be careful not to sink into a sheer emptiness and stick to a deathlike stillness; you should rather try to broaden your learning and increase your knowledge, that you may become aware of your own mind and thoroughly comprehend the essential teaching of all the Enlightened Ones; you should cultivate a spirit of congenial harmony in your fellowship with others and free yourself of the cramping idea of the 'self' and 'other,' until you attain complete enlightenment and realize your true nature which is immutable."

4. *To see the self-nature and attain Buddhahood.* To Hui-neng, to perceive the self-nature *is* to attain Buddhahood. In fact, as he says, "Our original nature is Buddha, and apart from this nature there is no other Buddha." He conceives of the self-nature of man as "so great that it can contain all things." "All the Buddhas of the past, present, and future ages and all the

twelve parts of the scriptures are immanent in the nature of man as its original endowment."

In the history of Chinese thought, Hui-neng's vision of the nature of man finds its prototype in Mencius, who had said: "All things are complete within us, and there is no greater joy than to turn our look inwards and to find ourselves true to our nature." For Hui-neng as for Mencius, our nature is one with reality. In the words of Hui-neng, "One reality is all reality."

Hui-neng uses the term *Buddhahood* as equivalent to "enlightenment." And when he speaks of the "Buddhas" he means simply the "enlightened ones." With this in mind, we can understand him perfectly when he says, "Our self-mind has its own Buddha and the self-Buddha is the true Buddha." In his hands everything is interiorized and spiritualized. Nothing can be more interesting than his theory of the "Triple Gem of our self-nature." The traditional Buddhist teaching is that the believers should surrender themselves to and rely on the Buddha, the Dharma, and the *sangha* or *ecclesia* of monks. Hui-neng, on the other hand, preaches that they should surrender themselves to and rely on enlightenment, rightness, and purity. This is really a tremendous revolution, quietly effected through a subtle interpretation. He sums up his doctrine of Triple Gem of the self-nature in these words: "Within, keep the mind in perfect harmony with the self-nature; without, respect all other men. This is surrender to and reliance on one's self."

When he speaks in terms of "within" and "without," he is referring only to the effects of the self-nature's functioning. In itself, the self-nature is identical with the nondual real, which is beyond space and time and above all attributes that human language can offer. Human language is at home dealing with the things of the phenomenal world, the field of relativity where all things seem to go in endless pairs of opposites. For Hui-neng as for Shankara, the nondual is that "before whom all words recoil." Whenever a mystic tries to express himself, his words are like so many thirsty blinded lions running in all directions in search of a hidden spring of water. In this sense alone can we see eye-to-eye with Hui-neng when he asserts that there is no difference between the enlightened and the unenlightened, or between bodhi and kleśa, and that the self-nature is neither good nor evil. In his answer to the special envoy of the emperor, he expounds the nonduality of the real nature in these terms: "Light and darkness are two different things in the eyes of ordinary people. But the wise and understanding ones possess a penetrating insight that there can be no duality in the self-nature. The nondual nature is the real nature. Real nature does not decrease in the fool nor increase in the sage; it is unperturbed in the midst of trials, nor does it stay still in the depth of meditation and samādhi; it is neither impermanent nor permanent; it neither comes nor goes; it is neither in the middle, nor in the interior, nor in the exterior; it is not born and does not die; both its essence and its manifestations are in the absolute state of suchness. Eternal and unchanging, we call it the Tao." If I say that whole passage shows that Hui-neng saw eye-to-eye with Chuang-tzu, it is not because he happens to use the word *Tao*. Or perhaps it would be more accurate to say that Hui-neng's vision transmutes the insights of Mencius and Chuang-tzu into a living whole.

Hui-neng's philosophy is as transcendental as that of Lao-tzu and Chuang-tzu; but at the same time it is as man-centered as that of Confucius and Mencius. He holds that all scriptures are devised for man and built upon the inherent prajñā-mind of his self-nature. "If there were no human beings, there would have been no dharmas whatever from the beginning." This is why he interprets all doctrines and dogmas in the light of the mind and nature of man. His theory of the Trikāya is as revolutionary as his theory of the Triple Gem. He preaches the threefold body of the Buddha of your self-nature. Your own body contains the Trikāya Tathāgata. In the sense that your self-nature is fundamentally pure and clean and that all the dharmas have their source in it, it is truly the *dharmakāya* Buddha. When all illusions and passions have been swept sway by the piercing light of the prajñā mind, which is the self-nature's own mind, your self-nature appears in its full splendor like the sun in a cloudless sky, this is called the *sambhogakāya* Buddha. But nowhere is his faith in the creative power of the mind more clearly shown than in his treatment of the *nirmāṇakāyas* (transformation bodies). It is our thought that makes us what we are. "If our mind dwells upon evil things, they will be transformed into a hell for us. If our mind dwells upon good things, they will be transformed into heaven for us." If we harbor malice and venomous hatred, we are transformed into dragons and snakes. If we are full of mercy and compassion, we are transformed into bodhisattvas. People under delusion do not understand this and persist in evildoing, while at the same time seeking external blessings, which are of no avail for bringing about their enlightenment. If, however, they should turn their mind to the good even for a single moment, prajñā would instantly arise, and their self-nature becomes the true *nirmāṇakāya* of Buddha.

In Hui-neng's hands, Buddhist doctrines are deepened and universal-ized, and the barriers between monks and laymen, between saints and sinners, between Buddhism and other schools of thought, are broken down. For instance, no Confucian scholar can have any objection to the following gāthā which he composed specially for lay people:

> *If your mind is right and without bias,*
> *What is the need of observing the śīla?*
> *If your conduct is upright,*
> *What is the use of practicing dhyāna?*
> *To cultivate the virtue of gratitude,*
> *Nothing is better than to love and serve your parents.*
> *To practice good faith and justice,*
> *Let superiors and inferiors be considerate to each other.*
> *The virtue of courtesy and deference is shown*
> *In the harmony between master and servant.*
> *The effect of patience and long-suffering is shown*
> *In the quieting down of all evils.*
> *If you know how to bore into wood*
> *In order to get a spark of fire,*
> *Your life will be like a red lotus flower*
> *Growing unsullied from mire and mud.*
> *Know that all effective medicines*
> *Taste bitter in the mouth.*
> *Remember that what is unpleasant to your ear*
> *Must come from the mouth of a loyal friend.*
> *Repentance and amendment are sure*
> *To give birth to knowledge and wisdom,*
> *While the defense of your shortcomings*
> *Reveals only the lack of goodness in your heart.*
> *In your daily life, make it a point*
> *To do always what is beneficial to others.*
> *The attainment of the Tao does not depend*

*Upon the mere giving of money.*
*Bodhi is to be found only in your mind;*
*Why waste your effort in seeking inner truth outside?*
*If you conduct yourself according to this gāthā,*
*You will see "Paradise of the West" right before your eyes.*

From the above, we can easily discern the element of Confucian ethics in the system of Hui-neng. On the other hand, he is so dialectically minded that one cannot help noting the profound affinity between him and Lao-tzu. The second chapter of the *Tao-te ching* gives us the classic statement of the Taoistic dialectics:

*When all the world recognizes beauty as beautiful, there emerges ugliness.*
*When all the world recognizes good as good, there emerges evil.*
*Likewise, the hidden and the manifest give birth to each other,*
*Difficult and easy complement each other,*
*Long and short set measure to each other,*
*High and low have reference to each other,*
*Tones and voice harmonize each other,*
*Back and front follow each other.*

All these pairs of opposites belong to the realm of relativity; and the sage, according to Lao-tzu, does not dwell on them but rises above them.

Similarly Hui-neng, in his last instruction to his disciples, enumerated no less than thirty-six pairs of opposites, such as light and darkness, yin and yang, form and the formless, the phenomenal and the void, activity and tranquility, the pure and the muddy, the worldly and the saintly, the monk and the layman, the great and the small, long and short, perversion and rectitude, delusion and wisdom, klésa and bodhi, kindness and cruelty, permanent and impermanent, real and unreal, joy and anger, advance and retreat, birth and death, spiritual body and physical body, etc. "If you know the proper way of using these pairs of opposites, you will be able to go freely in and out through the scriptural dharmas, steering clear of the two extremes by letting the self-nature stir and function spontaneously. In conversation with others, externally be detached from phenomena in the midst of phenomena; internally be detached from the void in the midst of the void. If you are entirely attached to the phenomenal, you would fall into perverted views. On the other hand, if you are entirely attached to the void, you would only sink deeper into your ignorance." "If someone asks you about the meaning of existence, answer him in terms of nonexistence. If he asks about the worldly, speak of the saintly. If he asks of the saintly, speak of the worldly. In this way, the interdependence and mutual involvement of the two extremes will bring to light the significance of the Mean." "Suppose someone asks you: What is darkness? Answer him thus: 'Light is the primary cause of darkness and darkness is the secondary cause of light. It is the disappearance of light that causes darkness. Light and darkness exhibit each other, and their interdependence points inevitably to the significance of the Mean.'"

It should be noted that the "mean" spoken of here is found invariably in a principle which is beyond the realm of relativity. Ultimately it is none other than the self-nature, which in the system of Hui-neng is one with the nondual reality, which transcends all the pairs of opposites while at the same time embracing them all. It was Justice Holmes who said it takes a man of profound and sustained insight to distrust the dilemma as an instrument of logic and to discern "that a thing may be neither A nor not A, but the perpendicular, or, more plainly, that the truth may escape from the limitations of a given plane of thought to a higher one." Herein lies the greatness of Hui-neng as a thinker. What is more, he had the knack of using the dilemma to point at the perpendicular, and to goad the spirit of man to rise to the Absolute.

# CHAPTER V

# Ma-tsu Tao-i

Ma-tsu Tao-i (709–788) was the most important figure in the history of Ch'an after the Sixth Patriarch, Hui-neng. The fact that he has been called since his death "Ma-tsu," literally "Patriarch Ma," is an eloquent testimony to the veneration that all students of Ch'an have held for him. It is well known that the transmission of the patriarchal robe had ceased once and for all after Hui-neng, and that there were to be no more patriarchs in the school of Ch'an. The name "Ma-tsu" must therefore have originated by a sort of popular acclaim. But what makes the name doubly exceptional is that "Ma" was the name of his family. Ma-tsu is a rare instance where a Buddhist monk has been called by his family name.

Probably a legend contributed in no small degree toward the retaining of the family name. It is said that after the enlightenment of Huai-jang, who was to become the master of Ma-tsu, the Sixth Patriarch had confided a secret to him: "In India, Prajñātāra (the twenty-seventh Indian patriarch) had predicted that under your feet will come forth a spirited young horse who will trample the whole world." As the Chinese word for "horse" is *ma*, which happened to be the family name of Ma-tsu, and since Ma-tsu was the only outstanding disciple of Huai-jang, it is only natural that later writers should have interpreted the prophecy as referring to Ma-tsu. And if we are to judge a tree by its fruits, we cannot but admit that Ma-tsu must have been a man of destiny.

A native of Hangchow in what is now Ch'eng-tu, Szechwan, he joined

a local monastery in his childhood. Before he was twenty, he was already
a professed monk. After his profession, he went to Nan-yüeh Mountain,
where he practiced by himself sitting-in-meditation. At that time Huai-
jang was the abbot of the Prajñā temple on Nan-yüeh Mountain. Seeing
Ma-tsu, he recognized him by intuition as a vessel of the Dharma. So he
visited him in his cell, asking, "In practicing sitting-in-meditation, what
does Your Reverence aspire to attain?" "To attain Buddhahood!" was the
answer. Huai-jang then took up a piece of brick and began to grind it
against a rock in front of Ma-tsu's cell. After some moments Ma-tsu became curious and asked, "What are you grinding it for?" "I want to grind it
into a mirror," Huai-jang replied. Greatly amused, Ma-tsu said, "How can
you hope to grind a piece of brick into a mirror?" Huai-jang fired back,
"Since a piece of brick cannot be ground into a mirror, how then can you
sit yourself into a Buddha?" "What must I do then?" Ma-tsu inquired.
Huai-jang replied, "Take the case of an ox cart. If the cart does not move,
do you whip the cart, or do you whip the ox?" Ma-tsu remained silent. "In
learning sitting-in-meditation," Huai-jang resumed, "do you aspire to learn
the sitting Ch'an, or do you aspire to imitate the sitting Buddha? If the
former, Ch'an does not consist in sitting or in lying down. If the latter, the
Buddha has no fixed postures. The Dharma goes on forever and never
abides in anything. You must not therefore be attached to nor abandon
any particular phase of it. To sit yourself into Buddha is to kill the Buddha.
To be attached to the sitting posture is to fail to comprehend the essential
principle." When Ma-tsu heard these instructions, he felt as though he
were drinking the most exquisite nectar. After doing obeisance to the
master according to the rites, he further asked, "How must one apply
one's mind to be attuned to the formless samādhi?" The master said,
"When you cultivate the way of interior wisdom, it is like sowing seed.
When I expound to you the essentials of the Dharma, it is like the showers from heaven. As you are happily conditioned to receive the teaching,
you are destined to see the Tao." Ma-tsu again asked, "Since the Tao is
beyond color and form, how can it be seen?" The master said, "The
Dharma Eye of your interior spirit is capable of perceiving the Tao. So it
is with the formless samādhi." "Is there still making and unmaking?" Ma-tsu
asked. To this the master replied, "If one sees the Tao from the standpoint
of making and unmaking or gathering and scattering, one does not really
see the Tao. Listen to my gāthā:

*The ground of the mind contains many seeds.*
*Which will all sprout when heavenly showers come.*
*The flower of samādhi is beyond color and form:*
*How can there be any more mutability?*

At this point Ma-tsu was truly enlightened, his mind being transcended from the world of phenomena. He attended upon his master for a full ten years. During this period, he delved deeper and deeper into the inner treasury of mystical truth. It is said that of six outstanding disciples of Huai-jang, Ma-tsu alone got the mind of the master.

After leaving his master, Ma-tsu went to Chiang-hsi, and became abbot in the 670s. In his sermons, he followed closely the basic insights of the Sixth Patriarch, such as that there is no Buddha outside one's mind. According to him, "The phenomenal is identical with the transcendent, and the born is none other than the unborn. If you have a thorough realization of this idea, you can live your daily life, wear your clothes, eat your meals, rear and nourish your inner 'womb of holiness' and pass your time as befitting your conditions and the tides of human affairs." This passage is important for several reasons. To begin, it is to be noted that the phrase "womb of holiness" is borrowed from the current Taoist lore, although given a new connotation. In the Taoist lore, the "womb of holiness" is the germ of the immortal man in the physical sense. In the hand of Ma-tsu, it is transmuted into the seed of eternal life. It is the prototype of Lin-chi's "true man of no title." In the second place, the emphasis on living the ordinary life, which is in accord with the spirit of the teachings of Lao-tzu and Chuang-tzu, constitutes one of the recurrent themes in the sayings of later Ch'an masters. When Nan-ch'üan, Ma-tsu's favorite disciple, said that "Tao is nothing but the ordinary mind," he was evidently echoing the voice of his master. Likewise the same philosophy is clearly embodied in the following gāthā by Ma-tsu's outstanding lay disciple, P'ang Yün:

*In my daily life there are no other chores than*
*Those that happen to fall into my hands.*
*Nothing I choose, nothing reject.*
*Nowhere is there ado, nowhere a slip.*
*I have no other emblems of my glory than*
*The mountains and hills without a speck of dust.*

*My magical power and spiritual exercise consist in*
*Carrying water and gathering firewood.*

Ma-tsu's greatness lies not so much in his sermons as in his marvellous skill and resourcefulness as a teacher. Once a disciple asked him, "Why does Your Reverence say that this very mind is Buddha?" "In order to stop the crying of little children," Ma-tsu replied. The disciple asked further, "When the crying has stopped, what then?" Ma-tsu said, "Then I would say that this very mind which is Buddha is in reality neither mind nor Buddha." "What would you say to people outside of these two classes?" "I would tell them that it is not a thing either." "If you unexpectedly meet someone from the inner circle, what would you say?" "I would simply tell him to embody the great Tao."

This dialogue reveals an important secret about Ma-tsu's art of teaching. Sometimes he used a positive formula, sometimes he used a negative formula. On the surface, they are contradictory to each other. But when we remember that he was using them in answering persons of different grades of attainments and intelligence, the contradiction disappears at once in the light of a higher unity of purpose, which was in all cases to lead the questioner to transcend his present state. Of course, this does not apply to a person who "comes from the inner circle," which is another way of saying that he is an enlightened one. All that Ma-tsu could say to such a one was that he should continue in his present state.

This leads us to an interesting story about one of Ma-tsu's disciples, Ta-mei Fa-ch'ang. On his very first visit to Ma-tsu, he asked, "What is Buddha?" "This very mind itself is Buddha" was Ma-tsu's answer. At this word Ta-mei was enlightened. Later, he settled on a mountain. Ma-tsu sent a monk to test him. The monk asked Ta-mei, "When you were with the great Master Ma, what did you learn from him?" Ta-mei replied, "The great Master told me that this very mind itself is Buddha." The monk said, "The great Master has lately changed his way of teaching the Buddha dharma." Ta-mei asked how he had changed. The monk said, "He is now saying that this very mind which is Buddha is neither mind nor Buddha." Ta-mei said, "That old fellow, when will he cease to confuse the minds of men? Let him go on with his 'neither mind nor Buddha.' I will stick to 'this very mind itself is Buddha.'" When the monk returned to report the conversation, Ma-tsu remarked, "The plum is ripe!"

In saying, "The plum is ripe," Ma-tsu was making a pun of Ta-mei's name, "Ta-mei" in Chinese being "big plum." Obviously, Ta-mei was an enlightened person; and in sticking to the master's positive formula, he knew what he was doing. Perhaps, his own disciples were still little children whose crying had yet to be stopped. Moreover, Ta-mei showed his spirit of independence, which pleased the master. If he had been shaken by the new teaching and adopted it blindly simply because the master had changed his teaching, Ma-tsu would have said that the plum was far from ripe.

Ma-tsu's way of teaching is most varied. He is said to have been instrumental to the enlightenment of one hundred thirty disciples, "each of whom became the master of a particular locality." This does not mean that all of them were of the same stature. Even enlightenment has different grades and modes. For instance, Ma-tsu had three outstanding disciples who enjoyed a special intimacy with him. They were Nan-ch'üan P'u-yüan, Hsi-t'ang Chih-ts'ang, and Pai-chang Huai-hai. One evening, as the three disciples were attending on their master enjoying the moon together, he asked them what they thought would be the best way of spending such a night. Hsi-t'ang was the first to answer, "A good time to make offerings." Pai-chang said, "A good time to cultivate one's spiritual life." Nan-ch'üan made no answer but shook his sleeves and went away. Ma-tsu said, "The sūtras will join the *pitaka (ts'ang)*; dhyāna will return to the sea *(hai)*; P'u-yüan alone transcends the realm of things all by himself."

In the school of Ma-tsu, Nan-ch'üan had a special place in the master's heart, just as Yen Hui had a special place in the heart of Confucius. Yet, in the line of transmission Pai-chang became the successor of Ma-tsu, just as Tseng-shen was the successor of Confucius. Perhaps it takes a man of tough fiber and administrative ability like Pai-chang to lay the foundations of a properly organized monastic community. Although the *Holy Rule of Pai-chang* has undergone successive revisions through the centuries and the original text has long been lost, no one can deny the lasting contribution of Pai-chang in transmuting what used to be a floating population of monks into a real community.

Here, however, we are more interested in the training Pai-chang received at the hands of Ma-tsu. Once, as the master and disciple were promenading together, they saw a flock of wild geese flying over. Ma-tsu asked, "What is it?" Pai-chang said, "Wild geese." "Where have they gone?" "They have flown away." At this point Ma-tsu caught hold of his disciple's nose and twisted it with all his force. This made Pai-chang scream with pain. But Ma-tsu merely remarked, "So you thought that they had flown away, eh?" At this word, Pai-chang had a flash of apprehension. Yet when he returned to the attendants' quarters, he began to cry most piteously. His colleagues asked him whether he was crying because he was homesick or because somebody had scolded him. To all such questions he answered "No." "Then why are you crying?" they pursued. Pai-chang said, "Because the great Master twisted my nose so hard that I am still feeling pain." "What was the conflict that led to this?" they asked. "Go ask the abbot himself?" said Pai-chang. When they went to ask Ma-tsu, the latter said, "He himself understands it perfectly well. Go ask him. He has the answer." Then they returned to Pai-chang, saying, "The abbot says that you understand it and refers us back to you for the true answer." Upon this Pai-chang laughed aloud. His colleagues, amused as well as amazed, queried, "A moment ago you were crying. What makes you laugh now?" Pai-chang said, "I cried then and I laugh now." They were mystified.

The next day, at a regular assembly, Ma-tsu had hardly sat down when Pai-chang came up to roll up his mat, which made the master descend from the platform. Pai-chang followed him into his room. Ma-tsu said, "Just now, before I had begun my sermon, what made you roll up my mat?" Pai-chang said, "Yesterday Your Reverence twisted my nose and I felt acute pain." "Where did you apply your mind yesterday?" asked the master. All that the disciple said was, "I feel no more pain in the nose today." Thereupon the master commented, "You have profoundly understood yesterday's episode."

Frankly, I do not know what to make of this dialogue. Pai-chang's "answers" sound more like a lunatic's talking to himself than sensible replies to the questions. And what is stranger still, the master was impressed! It takes a lunatic to understand and appreciate a lunatic! But since it can be reasonably assumed that neither of them was a lunatic, there must be some meaning behind it all, although the meaning cannot be found by logical reasoning, but can only be hit upon by intuition.

I feel that the clue to the whole thing lies in Pai-chang's cryptic remark to his colleagues: "I cried a moment ago, but I am laughing now." Although the scenes and actions had changed, the subject remained the same. All the tactics of Ma-tsu were meant only to lead his disciple to discover the "I." So, when Pai-chang said, "Yesterday I felt acute pain. . . . I feel no pain today," Ma-tsu was satisfied that his disciple had discovered his self, and this was all the more certain as his statement had no logical relevance whatever to the questions.

Self-discovery, then, is the real meaning of Ma-tsu's teachings, as indeed it is the real meaning of all Ch'an. This will be plainly seen from what Ma-tsu said to Ta-chu Hui-hai, another of his outstanding disciples. When Ta-chu visited Ma-tsu for the first time, the master asked him where he had come from. Ta-chu replied that he had come from the Ta-yün Temple in Yüeh-chou. Then Ma-tsu asked, "What do you come here for?" "I have come to seek the Buddha dharma," said Ta-chu. "I have here not a thing to give you," said Ma-tsu. "What Buddha dharma can you expect to learn from me? Why do you ignore the treasure of your own house and wander so far away from home?" Greatly mystified, Ta-chu asked, "What is your humble servant's treasure?" "None other than the one who is questioning me now is your treasure?" replied the master. "All things are complete in it, with nothing lacking. You can use it freely and its resources are inexhaustible. What is the use of seeking in the exterior?" At these words Ta-chu had a sudden recognition of his own mind, by direct intuition and not through reasoning or the senses. This is how Ma-tsu pointed directly at the mind so as to make it perceive the self-nature.

Another disciple Wu-yeh of Fen-chou was enlightened in a similar way. Wu-yeh originally belonged to the Vinaya order and was versed in scriptural learning. On his first visit, Ma-tsu, impressed by his towering physical stature and sonorous voice, remarked, "What a magnificent temple of Buddha! Only there is no Buddha in it!" Wu-yeh thereupon knelt down gracefully and said, "The literature of the Three Vehicles I have roughly studied and understood. However, I have often heard about the doctrine taught by the school of Ch'an that this very mind itself is Buddha. This truly is beyond my comprehension." Ma-tsu said, "Just this mind that does not comprehend is the very mind that is Buddha, and there is nothing else." Still unenlightened, he proceeded to ask, "What is the mind-seal transmitted secretly by the patriarch coming from the West?" So Ma-tsu said, "Your Reverence is still busied about nothing. Suppose you retire for the moment and come back some other time." Wu-yeh had just started to leave when the master called after him, "Your Reverence!"

As Wu-yeh turned his head, Ma-tsu asked, "What is it?" At this question, Wu-yeh was instantaneously enlightened.

Sometimes Ma-tsu resorted to rough tactics to expedite the process of self-discovery, as when the monk Shui-liao called on him asking, "What was the purpose of Bodhidharma's coming from the West?" (In the jargon of Ch'an, this question is equivalent to: What is the essential principle of Buddhism?) Instead of answering, Ma-tsu bade him to bow down in reverence. No sooner had Shui-liao bowed down than Ma-tsu stamped him to the ground. Curiously enough, Shui-liao was enlightened right on the spot. Rising up, he clapped his hands and laughed aloud, saying, "How marvelous! How marvelous! Hundreds and thousands of samādhis and innumerable spiritual insights have their root and source in the tip of a feather!" After bowing once more in reverence, he retired. When Shui-liao became an abbot, he often told his assembly, "Ever since I received Ma-tsu's stamping, I have never ceased to laugh."

From what we read in the records, Ma-tsu must have been of strong physical build and a man of extraordinary vigor. It is said that he walked like an ox and gazed like a tiger. His tongue was so long that it could touch the tip of his nose. Although the books do not tell us that he could roar like a lion, it is certain that he had a tremendous voice, as is clear from the story of Pai-chang's final enlightenment. As Pai-chang was attending upon the master, the latter looked at the duster hanging at a corner of his couch. Pai-chang remarked, "In the very act of using it, you are detached from its use," and then took up the duster and held it straight. Ma-tsu said, "In the very act of using it, you are detached from its use." Pai-chang then placed the duster in the original place. Thereupon Ma-tsu uttered such a terrific shout that the disciple's ears were deafened for three days. It was that shout that wrought a complete enlightenment in Pai-chang.

But it must not be imagined that Ma-tsu was always shouting or stamping. In most cases he was much more gentle and subtle, although the element of shock was seldom absent. For instance, when a high official asked him whether it was right to eat meat and drink wine, Ma-tsu replied, "Eating and drinking are Your Excellency's due. Refraining from eating and drinking is Your Excellency's bliss."

How resourceful he was in the use of *upāya* (expedient means) finds an illustration in his conversion of Shih-kung Hui-ts'ang, who was originally a hunter loathing the very sight of Buddhist monks. On a certain day, as he was chasing after a deer, he passed by Ma-tsu's monastery. Ma-tsu came forward to meet him. Shih-kung asked him whether he had seen the deer pass by. Ma-tsu asked, "Who are you?" "A hunter," he replied. "Do you know how to shoot?" "Of course I do." "How many can you hit with one arrow?" "One arrow can only shoot down one deer." "In that case, you really don't know how to shoot." "Does Your Reverence know how to shoot?" "Of course I do." "How many can you kill with one arrow?" "I can kill a whole flock with a single arrow." At this, Shih-kung spoke up, "After all, the beasts have life as you do, why should you shoot down a whole flock?" Ma-tsu said, "Since you know this so well, why don't you shoot yourself?" Shih-kung answered, "Even if I wanted to shoot myself, I would not know how to manage it." At this point, Ma-tsu remarked, "This fellow has accumulated klésa from ignorance for numberless aeons. Today the whole process has come to a sudden stop." Tossing his arrows and bow to the ground, Shih-kung became a monk and a disciple of Ma-tsu. Once as Shih-kung was working in the kitchen, Ma-tsu asked him what he was doing. "I am tending an ox," the disciple answered, meaning that he was trying to tame himself. "How do you tend it?" asked Ma-tsu. Shih-kung replied, "As soon as it goes back to the grass, I ruthlessly pull it back by its nostrils." This won a hearty approval from the master, who remarked, "You certainly know the true way of tending an ox!" With all their jolly actions and humorous speeches, one can hardly guess with what ruthlessness and fierce energy the holy monks have controlled and disciplined their unruly natures.

Ma-tsu lost no opportunity for encouraging in his disciple the spirit of violence and fearlessness. It happened once that his disciple Yin-feng of Wu-t'ai was pushing along a cart, while Ma-tsu was sitting on the road with his feet stretched out. Yin-feng requested him to draw back his feet; but Ma-tsu said, "What is stretched is not to be drawn back again!" Yin-feng retorted, "Once advanced, there is no turning backward!" Disregarding the master, he kept pushing the cart till it ran over and injured his feet. Ma-tsu returned to the hall with an axe in his hand, saying, "Let the one who a few moments ago injured my feet with his cart come forward!" Yin-feng, not to be daunted, came forward stretching his neck in front of the master. The master put down his axe.

Sometimes Ma-tsu took delight in leading his novices on a wild goose

chase. Once a monk asked him, "Without resorting to the 'four affirmations and hundred negations,' will you please point out directly the reason
why Bodhidharma came from the West?" Ma-tsu said, "I am too tired
today to speak with you. Go ask Chih-ts'ang about it." The monk went to
ask Chih-ts'ang, who said, "Why don't you ask the abbot about it?" "The
abbot it was who referred me to you," the monk replied. Chih-ts'ang
evaded the question by saying, "I have a headache today and am not in a
position to speak with you. Go ask my elder brother Huai-hai about it."
So the monk went to Huai-hai with the same question. Huai-hai said,
"Arrived at this point, I really do not know what to say." The monk then
went back to Ma-tsu, reporting what the two had said. Ma-tsu remarked,
"Chih-ts'ang wears a white cap, while Huai-hai wears a black cap."

The "white cap" and the "black cap" refer to an old story of two robbers. One of the robbers wore a white cap, while the other wore a black
cap. As the story goes, the black-capped one, by a clever ruse, despoiled
the white-capped one of all things that he had robbed from others. That
is to say, the former was more ruthless and radical than the latter. Likewise, Pai-chang Huai-hai was more ruthless and radical than Hsi-t'ang
Chih-ts'ang. When Chih-ts'ang evaded the answer by pleading a headache, he thereby implied that if he was not ill, he could still formulate the
right answer. On the other hand, Huai-hai's declination was final and
honest. According to him, since the question has to do with something
transcending all affirmations and negations, what words can he possibly
find in answer to it? As Lao-tzu had said, "If Tao could be expressed in
words, it would not be Tao as it is in itself."

We have already mentioned P'ang Yün and quoted his gāthā in the
preceding pages. It would be interesting to know how his enlightenment
came about. At first he visited Shih-t'ou Hsi-ch'ien, whose importance was
only second to that of Ma-tsu. When he asked "Who is the one that finds
no mate in the universe of things?" Shih-t'ou immediately covered his
mouth with his hand. This initiated P'ang Yün into Ch'an. Later he visited
Ma-tsu and asked the same question, to which Ma-tsu replied, "I will tell
you about him when you have drunk up the waters of the West River at a
single quaff." At this word P'ang Yün was thoroughly enlightened.

In reality, the two great masters were of the same mind. In covering up
his own mouth with his hand, Shih-t'ou meant that it is impossible to
speak about it. Similarly, what Ma-tsu meant to say was that just as it is

impossible to drink up the waters of the West River, so it is impossible to speak about the Transcendent One. The fact is that both Shih-t'ou and Ma-tsu were steeped in the philosophy of Lao-tzu and Chuang-tzu. And so was P'ang Yün. Although P'ang Yün is usually placed in the lineage of Ma-tsu, he can be with equal appropriateness called a disciple of Shih-t'ou.

Although Ma-tsu and Shih-t'ou were said to "divide the world between them," they were entirely free of any sense of rivalry. It is a delight to see how they cooperated with each other in bringing others to enlightenment. Yüeh-shan Wei-yen (751–834) is a case in point. Yüeh-shan began in the school of Vinaya, well versed in scriptural studies and ascetic discipline. However, he came to feel that this was not yet the ultimate goal of the life of the spirit. He aspired to attain true freedom and purity beyond the formulas of the Law. So he called on Shih-t'ou, seeking guidance. He said to the master, "I have only a rough knowledge of the Three Vehicles and the twelve branches of the scriptural teaching. But I hear that in the South there is a teaching about 'pointing directly at the mind of man and attaining Buddhahood through the perception of the self-nature.' Now this is beyond my comprehension. I humbly beseech you to graciously enlighten me on this." Shih-t'ou replied, "It is to be found neither in affirmation nor in negation nor in affirming and negating at the same time. So what can you do?" Yüeh-shan was altogether mystified by these words. Hence, Shih-t'ou told him frankly, "The cause and occasion of your enlightenment are not present here in this place. You should rather go to visit the great Master Ma-tsu." Following the suggestion, he went to pay his respects to Ma-tsu, presenting before him the same request as he had addressed to Shih-t'ou. Ma-tsu replied, "I sometimes make *him* raise his eyebrows and turn his eyes; at other times I do not let him raise his eyebrows and turn his eyes. Sometimes it is really *he* who is raising his eyebrows and turning his eyes; at other times it is really *not he* who is raising his eyebrows and turning his eyes. How do you understand it?" At this Yüeh-shan saw completely eye-to-eye with Ma-tsu and was enlightened. He bowed reverently to the master who asked him, "What truth do you perceive that you should perform these ceremonies?" Yüeh-shan said, "When I was with Shih-t'ou, I was like a mosquito crawling on a bronze ox." That is to say, he found no entrance. Ma-tsu, discerning that the enlightenment was genuine, asked him to take good care of the insight.

He attended upon Ma-tsu for three years. One day, Ma-tsu asked again, "What do you see recently?" Yüeh-shan replied, "The skin has entirely moulted off; there remains only the one true reality." Ma-tsu said, "What you have attained is perfectly in tune with the innermost core of your mind, and from thence it has spread into your four limbs. This being the case, it is time to gird your waist with three bamboo splints and go forth to make your abode on any mountain you may like." Yüeh-shan replied, "Who am I to set up any abode on any mountain?" Ma-tsu said, "Not so! One cannot always be traveling without abiding, nor always be abiding without traveling. To advance from where you can no longer advance and to do what can no longer be done, you must make yourself into a raft or ferryboat for others. It is not for you to abide here forever." Only then did he go back to Shih-t'ou. Although Yüeh-shan is usually placed in the lineage of Shih-t'ou, he is really the bridge between Shih-t'ou and Ma-tsu. When Yüeh-shan became an abbot he had Tao-wu and Yün-yen for his disciples. One day, as these two were attending upon him, he pointed at two trees on the mountain, one flourishing and the other withering, and asked Tao-wu, "Which of these is: the flourishing or the withering?" Tao-wu said, "The flourishing one is." Yüeh-shan said, "Splendid! Let all things shine with glorious light everywhere!" Then he put the same question to Yün-yen, who replied, "The withering one is." Yüeh-shan said, "Splendid! Let all things fade away into colorless purity!" Just at that moment there arrived unexpectedly the Śramaṇera Kao, to whom the master put the same question. The Śramaṇera answered, "Let the flourishing flourish, and the withering wither!" Then Yüeh-shan turned to Tao-wu and Yün-yen, saying, "It is not! It is not." Is this not in the style and spirit of Ma-tsu, who had taught Yüeh-shan that one cannot always abide without travel-ing nor always travel without abiding? In fact, Ma-tsu, Shih-t'ou, and Yüeh-shan seem to have seen eye-to-eye with Lao-tzu who had said:

> For all things there is a time for going ahead, and a time for following
>       behind:
> A time for slow breathing and a time for fast breathing;
> A time to grow in strength and a time to decay;
> A time to be up and a time to be down.

Like the Sixth Patriarch, Ma-tsu was adept in the use of polarities to lift the mind of his disciples from the physical world to the metaphysical, from the realm of relativity to the Absolute, from the world of things to the Infinite Void. Whether he used the via positiva or the via negativa, it was in all cases according to the needs of the individual inquirer. But his sayings were never clear-cut, but always enigmatic so as to tease the mind of the listener. Even during his last illness he did not cease to utter enigmas. When someone came to ask about his health, all that he said was, "Sun-faced Buddhas, Moon-faced Buddhas." Now, in the Buddhist lore, the Sun-faced Buddhas lived a long life on earth, while the Moon-faced Buddhas lived only a day and a night. What Ma-tsu probably meant to say was that it makes not the slightest difference whether one lives long or short, so long as one has found one's Self.

Chuang-tzu used to say that no one was more short-lived than Peng-tsu, the Chinese counterpart of the Sun-faced Buddha. On the other hand, no one was more long-lived than the Shang-tsu, the Chinese counterpart of the Moon-faced Buddha. Perhaps, Chuang-tzu would have smiled at the words of Ma-tsu.

But I cannot dismiss Ma-tsu without introducing a touching episode, which goes to show that, with all his detachment from the world, there still remained something human deep down in him. We are told that when he returned to his native place for a temporary visit, he was warmly welcomed by his countrymen. But an old woman, who used to be his next-door neighbor, said, "I thought that all the commotion was caused by the visit of some extraordinary personage. In fact, it's none other than the little chap of the family of Ma the garbage cleaner!" This made Ma-tsu improvise a half-humorous and half-pathetic poem:

> I advise you not to return to your native place:
> For no one can be a sage in his own home.
> The old woman by the side of the old brook
> Still calls me the garbage man's son!

Anyway, he came back to Chiang-hsi, where he spent fifty years of his life, dying at the age of eighty.

# CHAPTER VI

# Pai-chang
# and Huang-po

We have already referred to the *Holy Rule of Pai-chang*. Although the original text of the rule laid down by Pai-chang Huai-hai (720–814) has not been preserved, the *Holy Rule of Pai-chang*, as we have it in the Chinese Tripiṭaka, which was the work of Pai-chang Te-hui of the Yüan dynasty, published in 1282, was explicitly modeled upon Pai-chang Huai-hai's original rule. It was this rule that instituted for the first time the Zen monastic system. In its emphasis on moral discipline and in its matter-of-factness, it is comparable to the Holy Rule of St. Benedict. The duties of the abbot and various functionaries under him are meticulously defined. The daily life of the monks is regulated in detail. Of particular interest are the rites of taking vows and the universal duty of working in the fields. To become a *śrāmana*, the postulant must take the first vow, which consists in pledging oneself to the observance of the five moral precepts:

> *Not to kill.*
> *Not to sin sexually.*
> *Not to steal and rob.*
> *Not to lie or speak wildly.*
> *Not to drink wine.*

This fivefold vow is said to be the "first condition for entering into the Tao or Right Path." But to be a professed śrāmana, one must take a second vow which imposes five "pure rules" in addition to the above five moral precepts. The five pure rules are:

*Not to sit or sleep in a high and wide bed.*

*Not to wear any flower or gem on the head, or to apply perfume on the body.*

*Not to sing and dance like a professional actor, or to go deliberately to see a play.*

*Not to lay hold of gold and silver or any treasure.*

*Not to eat outside of the regular meals.*

It is only after taking this second vow, which together with the first is called the "tenfold vow of purity," that the shaving of the head is administered to. This makes the śrāmana a full *bhiksu*.

But the most original feature of Pai-chang's monastic system lies in his introduction of the duty of working in the fields, a duty which is required of all, including the abbot himself. Before Pai-chang's time, monks were not supposed to be engaged in productive labor. They depended for their livelihood entirely on alms begging. Buddhists in India were originally forbidden to till the ground, lest in hoeing and ploughing they might perhaps injure and kill the worms and insects. This system might have been workable in a tropical zone like India, where one could possibly avert starvation by feeding on fruits and dates. The practical sense of Pai-chang revolted against the idea of exclusive dependence on alms. Why should able-bodied monks live like parasites on the sweat and labor of lay people? So he required all his monks to spend part of the day in reclaiming wastelands and in tilling the fields, so that they could live primarily on their own labor, and only secondarily on alms begging. Furthermore, Pai-chang insisted that the crops yielded should be subject to the assessment of taxes on an equal basis with those of lay people. This was so revolutionary a step that at first Pai-chang became the target of criticisms by all the conservative Buddhist monks. But like all great reformers, he had the courage of his convictions; and he as the abbot of a large community worked hardest of all. His favorite motto: "One day without working, one day without eating" has become a well-known proverb among monks of all sects.

Pai-chang lived to be ninety-four. There is a touching story about his last days. It is said that his disciples, out of respect for his age, tried to dissuade him from continuing to work on the farms; but the old man would not hear of it. Then they hid away his tools. As the old man sought for them everywhere and could not find them, he stayed away from meals until the tools were returned to him.

Historically, Pai-chang's healthy innovation had a vital importance which he probably could not have foreseen. Pai-chang died in 814. In the 840s, Buddhism was to suffer the worst blow in its history in China, from which it has never fully recovered. Emperor Wu, who reigned from 814 to 847, was bent upon wiping out this "foreign religion." The main reason for this terrible persecution was economical, as may be gathered from the following passage in the edict of 845:

> Now, when one man does not farm, others suffer hunger, and when one woman does not weave, others suffer from the cold. At present the monks and nuns of the empire are numberless, and they all depend on agriculture for their food and on sericulture for their clothing. The monasteries and temples are beyond count, but they all are lofty and beautifully decorated, daring to rival palaces in grandeur. None other than this was the reason for the decline in material strength and the weakening of the morals of the Chin, Sung, Ch'i, and Liang [dynasties].

More than 4,600 monasteries, and more than 40,000 temples and shrines throughout the empire were destroyed. More than 260,500 monks and nuns were returned to lay life; and 150,000 slaves were taken over by the government.

But the wonder of it is that of all the sects of Buddhism, the school of Zen alone managed to survive the holocaust and to continue to flourish in the succeeding dynasties as a vigorous movement. As Kenneth Ch'en so keenly observes, this survival of Zen might be attributed to two of its features.

> In the first place, its lack of dependence on the external paraphernalia of the religion, such as the scriptures, images, and so forth, enabled it to function and carry on even after the destruction of such externals. In the second place, it escaped the charge of being a parasite on society, for one of the cardinal rules of the school was that every monk must perform some productive labor every day. The Ch'an master responsible for the rule was Huai-hai (720–814), who even in his old age insisted on working in the fields.

But it would be superficial to regard Pai-chang as merely a far-sighted sociological reformer of the monastic system. His insistence on manual labor had a deep spiritual significance and carried with it an intimate sense of involvement with the common lot of mankind. As the disciple of Ma-tsu, he had taken to heart the utter nonduality of the transcendent and the immanent. To him, a one-sided attention to the transcendent would tend to cut reality into two. His vision of reality includes the phenomenal world of causal relations, as well as the world beyond. In this light we can fully understand the story—mythical though it is—of how he helped an old fox to his enlightenment. We are told that everytime Pai-chang ascended the platform to preach, an unknown old man followed the monks into the hall to listen. One day, after the whole community had retired, the old man lingered on. Pai-chang asked him who he was. He replied, "I am actually not a human being. Long, long ago, in the time of Kāśyapa Buddha, I used to be an abbot on this mountain. When a student asked if a man of high spirituality was still subject to the law of causality, I answered, 'He is not subject to the law of causality.' This answer caused me to fall into the body of a wild fox for five hundred births. Now I beseech Your Reverence to utter for me the right word that I may be rid of the body of the wild fox." Pai-chang said, "Suppose you ask me." The old man repeated the question of his student. Pai-chang replied, "He does not ignore the law of causality." The old man was thoroughly enlightened at this word. Doing obeisance, he told the master, "I am already rid of the body of the wild fox. I dwell on the other side of the mountain. I beg you to bury me according to the rites as a deceased monk." Pai-chang ordered the superintendent of his monastery to announce to the whole community to be ready after the meal to attend the funeral of a deceased monk. All the monks were surprised, because they knew of no one being sick. After the meal, the abbot led them to a cave at the back of the mountain. There they found the corpse of a wild fox. The abbot ordered it to be cremated according to the rites.

At the evening assembly on the same day, Pai-chang related to the monks the whole story. Huang-po asked, "In the case of this ancient abbot, a single erroneous answer caused his fall into the body of a wild fox for five hundred lives. What will happen to an abbot who gives the right answer to every question?" Pai-chang said, "Come near me, and I will tell you." Huang-po approached right away and gave the master a slap on the face. The master clapped his hands and laughed, saying, "I thought you were the red beard of a Tartar; in fact, you are a Tartar with a red beard."

The story of the wild fox can hardly be taken literally, but the meaning is clear. A truly enlightened man does not ignore the phenomenal world, which is governed by the law of causality. He sees the immutability of the transcendent, and he sees also the changes of the phenomenal world. Tao is beyond these two spheres and therefore comprehends both. In the words of Chuang-tzu, "The truly wise man, considering both sides of the question without partiality, sees them both in the light of Tao. This is called following two courses at once." To follow two courses at once is the only way to rise above monism and dualism. As Chuang-tzu puts it else-where,

> Can a man cling only to heaven
> And know nothing of earth?
> They are correlative: to know one
> Is to know the other.
> To refuse one
> Is to refuse both.
> Can a man cling to the positive
> Without any negative
> In contrast to which it is seen
> To be positive?
> If he claims to do so
> He is a rogue or a madman.

The error of the wild fox is easy to detect. But if Pai-chang should cling to his answer as the only right and sufficient explanation of the whole ineffable reality, his error would be just as serious if not worse. Herein is to be found the piercing point hidden in the question of Huang-po: "What would happen to an abbot who gives the right answer to every question?" In calling him to come near, Pai-chang probably intended to give him a slap, pointing to the Ultimate Reality, the "true self," beyond all attributes, positive as well as negative. But instead of waiting for the master's slapping, Huang-po was quick enough to slap the master, point-ing exactly to the same Absolute. How could Pai-chang help laughing? He had thought that his disciple might still be moving in the sphere of attributes; but he found to his greatest delight that he had moved beyond it. The "red beard of a Tartar" is but an attribute. After all, the important thing is not the red beard, but the Tartar!

Once a monk asked Pai-chang, "Who is the Buddha?" The master asked him in turn, "Who are *you*?" It is only by being yourself that you can move freely in and out of the world without contradictions and obstacles. Once you have found your true self, you are emancipated from your little ego with all its selfish interests, because the true self is one with reality and embraces all beings. In this state you can live and work in the world without being a worldling, and you can be a contemplative and a hermit without being a self-enclosed and egocentric seeker of happiness.

This leads us to an interesting anecdote about Huang-po Hsi-yün (d. 850). A native of Fukien, he became a monk early in his life. When he was traveling in T'ien-t'ai Mountain, he encountered a strange monk, who conversed and joked with him as though he were an old friend of his. One day as they were walking together, they found the streams flooded, and the monk suggested to Huang-po that they should cross over together. Huang-po did not feel like crossing and said, "Brother, if you want to cross over, go ahead by yourself." The monk walked on water as though he was walking on solid ground, and, turning his head, he said to Huang-po, "Come along, come along!" Huang-po said, "Fie upon this self-server! Had I known it, I should have cut off your shins!" The monk appeared to be deeply impressed by this response and remarked, "You are truly a vessel of the Mahāyāna! I am no match for you!" Thereupon he vanished.

To Huang-po, as to all Zen masters, the "self-server" does not really attain selfhood. He is a self-enclosed and egocentric seeker of happiness. But he will not attain true happiness because, instead of *being* the "true man" that he is, who is happiness itself, he places happiness outside himself, as something to be strained after. In fact, he is pursuing an illusory object.

Huang-po envisaged the Ultimate Reality as mind, the One Mind. This mind is the creator of all things, visible and invisible. It is the fountain of true wisdom. We have this living fountain within us, but our hearts run after external things and our minds are busy weaving hair-splitting distinctions and rigid concepts to serve as a cocoon for our little ego. Consequently, our inner fountain of wisdom is stopped up. As Huang-po puts it, "If the pursuers of Tao do not awake to this fundamental mind, they are apt to create a mind over and above the mind, seek Buddha outside of themselves, and remain attached to forms and practices in the cultivation of their spiritual life. All these are erroneous ways which do not lead to supreme enlightenment. Adoration of and devotion to all the Buddhas in the universe are nothing in comparison with the following of a single *mindless* man of Tao." In other words, if we want to get at the fundamental mind within us, we must first rid ourselves of the clever conceits of our petty minds or at least set no store by them, for they only distract us from the living source of true wisdom. Thus, Huang-po's doctrine of universal mind is at the same time a doctrine of mindlessness. It is through mindlessness that we can return to the mind.

As Huang-po sees it, this universal mind is no mind in the ordinary sense of the word, and it is completely detached from form. Therefore, it is beyond "good" and "evil." For as he says, "To engage in good actions and bad actions equally implies attachment to form." The one thing necessary is to realize this universal mind in us, which is nothing else than our original Buddha nature. "It is void, omnipresent, silent, pure; it is glorious and mysterious peace and that is all that can be said about it. You yourself must awake to it, fathoming its depths." "This spiritually enlightened nature is without beginning or end, as old as space, neither subject to birth nor to death, neither existing nor non-existing, neither defiled nor pure, neither clamorous nor silent, neither old nor young, occupying no space, having no inside, outside, size, form, color, or sound." In short, it is beyond all attributes. It cannot be communicated in words but can only be apprehended by direct intuition. Words and actions on the part of the master serve only to evoke your direct intuition, when the time is ripe. When this happens, there is a tacit understanding between you and your master. This is what is called "transmission from mind to mind."

With Huang-po, as with Chuang-tzu, the aspiration to move beyond good and evil does not entail an encouragement of license and moral anarchy. The man of Tao does not seek the good as an object. He views it as a streamlet flowing spontaneously from the fountain of wisdom within him. He will perform acts of charity when there is occasion for them; and when the occasion has passed, he remains quiescent. In doing good, he has not the slightest intention of seeking merits for himself, because he knows that his self-nature is complete in itself, with nothing lacking.

Huang-po's position towards the accumulation of merits, which come from performing the six pāramitās and innumerable similar practices, is on a par with Chuang-tzu's position towards the cultivation of moral life as stressed by the Confucian scholars. He vigorously advocated sudden enlightenment as against gradual advancement. "To practice the six pāramitās and a myriad of similar methods with the intention of attaining Buddhahood thereby is to try to advance by stages, but the Buddha who has always existed is not a Buddha of stages. Only awake to the universal mind and realize that there is nothing whatever to be attained. This is the real Buddha. For the Buddha and all sentient beings are nothing but the universal mind." This revolt against traditional Buddhism is as apt to be misunderstood as Chuang-tzu's strictures against traditional Confucianism. In an illuminating study of Chuang-tzu, Thomas Merton has written:

> If Chuang-tzu reacted against the Ju doctrine, it was not in the name of something lower—the animal spontaneity of the individual who does not want to be bothered with a lot of tiresome duties—but in the name of something altogether higher. This is the most important fact to remember when we westerners confront the seeming antinomianism of Chuang-tzu and the Zen masters. Chuang-tzu was not demanding less than Jen and Yi, but more. His chief complaint of Ju was that it did not go far enough. It produced well-behaved and virtuous officials, indeed cultured men. But it nevertheless limited and imprisoned them within fixed external norms and consequently made it impossible for them to act freely and creatively in response to the ever new demands of unforeseen situations.

No one has, to my knowledge, made a fairer and more penetrating observation on this point. It is as true of the Zen tradition as it is of Lao-tzu and Chuang-tzu. I only wish to add that what Father Merton says of the Confucian scholars is not meant to apply to Confucius himself, who in his later years attained remarkable spontaneity and flexibility in his outlook and conduct.

To say that Huang-po's Dharma agrees closely with the philosophy of

Chuang-tzu is not to deny his originality. Both of them were discoursing on the Absolute, although Huang-po called it the universal mind while Chuang-tzu called it Tao. Since both of them were profound thinkers and great mystics, it would be strange if they did not arrive at somewhat the same insights about the Absolute. In fact, Western mystics like Ruys-broeck, John of the Cross, and Meister Eckhart have uttered insights surprisingly similar to those of the great Zennists and Taoists.

Huang-po's importance in the history of Zen lies not only in the fact that he was one of the most explicit in his views, but also in the fact that his strong personality and drastic methods have impressed themselves on his disciple Lin-chi and the whole House of Lin-chi. There was such fierceness, if not ferocity, about him that even his master Pai-chang compared him to the tiger. One day, as he returned from work, Pai-chang asked him where he had been; and he answered that he had been gathering mushrooms at the foot of the Ta-hsiung Mountain. Pai-chang further asked, "Did you see the tiger there?" Huang-po roared like a tiger. His master took up an axe as if to kill the tiger. Thereupon, Huang-po gave the master a slap. Smiling affably, Pai-chang retired to his room. At the regular assembly, Pai-chang announced to his community, "At the foot of the Ta-hsiung Mountain there is a tiger. All of you must watch out for your safety. I have already been bitten today." This was but a symbolic way of saying that he had found his successor in the person of Huang-po.

Once Huang-po was visiting the master Hsien-kuan, and as he was doing obeisance to the statue of Buddha, a novice took him to task, saying, "In our pursuit of Tao, we must not be attached to the Buddha, nor to the Dharma, nor to the *sanga*. What does Your Reverence seek after in performing these rites of obeisance?" Huang-po replied, "I am attached neither to the Buddha, nor to the Dharma, nor to sanga. I am only performing the usual rites." The novice asked, "What is the use of rites?" Huang-po thereupon gave him a slap. "You are being too rough," said the novice. Huang-po fired back, "What kind of thing do you find here in this place that you should speak of 'rough' and 'refined'?" And he gave him another slap. The reader will be interested to know that the novice was none other than the future Emperor Suan-tsung, destined to succeed Wu-tsung, the terrible persecutor of Buddhism, in 847.

Huang-po found a great lay disciple in the person of P'ei Hsiu, a scholar-statesman, who held the premiership for several years during the reign of Suan-tsung. P'ei Hsiu was a devout Buddhist. Once he brought a statuette of Buddha; and kneeling before Huang-po he besought him to give it a name. Huang-po called out, "P'ei Hsiu!" "Yes, Your Reverence!" he responded. "I have already done the naming for you!" said Huang-po.

Once P'ei Hsiu submitted to Huang-po a manuscript of his reflections on Buddhism. The master laid it aside without even looking at it. He remained silent for a long time and then asked P'ei Hsiu, "Do you understand?" The latter replied, "It is beyond my comprehension." The master said, "If only you could understand it in this manner, it would be of some account. As to expressing it by means of paper and ink, what has that to do with the teaching of our school?"

Yet it was due to the diligence of P'ei Hsiu that we are able to read the two works of Huang-po in the Chinese Tripiṭaka, the *Ch'uan-hsin Fa-yao* and the *Wan-ling lu*. The first has been rendered into English in two versions. The second is a record of Huang-po's dialogues with P'ei Hsiu and other disciples. It ends, significantly, with a special stress on *kung-an* (Japanese, *kōan*) as a way to enlightenment, showing that this particular method, which was to become one of the characteristic features of Zen, had begun to emerge with Huang-po. He was telling his community that Zen was a life-and-death struggle, and therefore it must not be taken lightly.

If you are a full-grown man of heroic determination, you should resort to pondering on kung-an. Take, for instance, Chao-chou's answering "No!" to the question whether there is Buddha nature in a dog. You should meditate on this word *wu* day and night without cease. Keep at it while you are walking, resting, sitting, and sleeping, while you are putting on clothes, taking meals, sitting on the stool, making water. Let every thought of your mind be focused on it, fiercely stir up your spirits, and never lose hold of the word *wu*. After holding on for days and months, your whole being becomes one continuous attention. Suddenly the flower of your mind will burst in no moment; and you will apprehend the initial insight of all the Buddhas and patriarchs. You will have such a firm grasp on it that you can no longer be deceived by the tongues of all the old monks of the world; and great truths will flow from your wide-open mouth. You will realize that the coming of Bodhidharma is like the rising of a wave without wind and that the

Buddha's holding of the flower is but a fiasco. Once arrived at this state, all the holy ones can do nothing to you, to say nothing of the old fellow Yama. Who can ever believe in the possibility of such inconceivable wonders? Yet nothing is impossible to him who has set his heart and his mind to it.

He concluded the talk with a great gāthā:

> To detach oneself from the dust of the world,
> This is no ordinary task.
> Hold firmly to the end of the rope and go at it
> With all your might.
> Without undergoing a whole spell of cold
> That bites into your bones,
> How can you have the plum blossoms regale you
> With their piercing fragrance?

My impression is that for all the great Zen masters, our whole life is one big kōan, which we must break through before we begin to be really alive. To one who is really alive, the most ordinary things become a wonder of wonders. When a monk asked Pai-chang what was the most wonderful thing in the world, the master answered, "That I am sitting all alone on the peak of Ta-hsiung Mountain!" The realization of this state admits of infinite levels of depth. To understand it speculatively or even intuitively is one thing. To realize it with every fiber of our being is quite another. Unless we are thoroughly dead, we cannot be thoroughly alive. This is certainly easier said than done, for we are all hemmed in by contradictions, and we are all diehards. In the meantime let us take to heart what Chuang-tzu said:

> Where the fountains of passion
> Lie deep
> The heavenly springs
> Are soon dry.

In the writings of Chuang-tzu we often come across unmistakable prototypes of the kōan. Let one instance suffice. Once an earnest beginner in the pursuit of Tao came to visit Lao-tzu. As soon as Lao-tzu saw him, he asked, "Who are all those people whom you have brought with you?" The disciple whirled around to look. Nothing there. Panic! Lao-tzu said,

"Don't you understand?" This only added confusion to his panic. Lao-tzu then pressed him to tell him what was ailing him. The disciple said (to use the version of Thomas Merton),

> *"When I don't know, people treat me like a fool.*
> *When I do know, the knowledge gets me into trouble.*
> *When I fail to do good, I hurt others.*
> *When I do good, I hurt myself.*
> *If I avoid my duty, I am remiss,*
> *But if I do it I am ruined.*
> *How can I get out of these contradictions?*
> *That is what I came to ask you."*

Lao-tzu replied:

> *"A moment ago*
> *I looked into your eyes.*
> *I saw you were hemmed in*
> *By contradictions. Your words*
> *Confirm this.*
> *You are scared to death,*
> *Like a child who has lost*
> *Father and mother.*
> *You are trying to sound*
> *The middle of the ocean*
> *With a six-foot pole.*
> *You have got lost and are trying*
> *To find your way back*
> *To your own true self.*
> *You find nothing*
> *But illegible signposts*
> *Pointing in all directions.*
> *I pity you."*

> *The disciple asked for admittance,*
> *Took a cell, and there*
> *Meditated,*
> *Trying to cultivate qualities*
> *He thought desirable*

*And get rid of others*
*Which he disliked.*
*Ten days of that!*
*Despair!*

*"Miserable!" said Lao.*
*"All blocked up!*
*Tied in knots! Try*
*To get untied!*
*If your obstructions*
*Are on the outside,*
*Do not attempt*
*To grasp them one by one*
*And thrust them away.*
*Impossible! Learn*
*To ignore them.*
*If they are within yourself,*
*You cannot destroy them piecemeal,*
*But you can refuse*
*To let them take effect.*
*If they are both inside and outside,*
*Do not try*
*To hold on to Tao—*
*Just hope that Tao*
*Will keep hold of you!"*

There are present here all the elements of a kōan. Here we find a man trying desperately to get out of a self-created dilemma. The master just bypassed his questions and pointed him directly to Tao, that he might lift himself to a higher standpoint from which the dilemma is seen to be an illusion. The questions of the student are not solved, but dissolved. The experience is like waking suddenly from a nightmare.

# CHAPTER VII

# Ts'ung-shen
# of Chao-chou
# (778–897?)

Master Ts'ung-shen is commonly known as "the ancient Buddha of Chao-chou," or simply as "Chao-chou," in Ch'an circles, because he was for a long period the Abbot of the Kuan-yin Monastery in the district of Chao-chou, in what is today the province of Hopeh. In these pages, we shall call him Chao-chou in conformity to the general custom.

Chao-chou came from a Ho family of Ts'ao-chou in Shantung. Born in 778, he is said to have lived to his one hundred and twentieth year, according to the *Record of Transmission of the Lamp*. But another source tells us that Chao-chou died in 863. In that case, he would have lived no more than ninety-one years. It is hard to tell which statement is correct, although the former view represents the prevailing tradition.

He began early in life as a novice in a local monastery. Before his profession he travelled southward to visit Master Nan-ch'üan in Chi-chou, Anhwei. It happened that at the time of his arrival Nan-ch'üan was resting, stretched out on his back on his couch. On seeing the young visitor, the master asked, "Where do you come from?" "I come from the Jui-hsiang (holy image) monastery," Chao-chou replied. "Do you still see the holy image?" the master asked. "No," answered the visitor, "I do not see the holy image, I only see the sleeping Tathāgatha!" Struck by the strange answer, the master sat up and asked him, "Are you a free śrāmana (monk), or one belonging to a master?" "One belonging to a master," declared Chao-chou. Upon being asked who his master was, Chao-chou made no answer but simply paid his obeisance, saying, "In this wintry season the weather is so very cold. I wish Your Reverence good health." This was how Chao-chou chose his predestined master. As for Nan-ch'üan, he must have welcomed his predestined disciple as a windfall. At any rate, he had the highest esteem for the newcomer and admitted him immediately into his inner chamber.

When Chao-chou asked his master, "What is the Tao?" the latter replied, "Tao is nothing else than the ordinary mind." "Is there any way to approach it?" pursued Chao-chou further. "Once you intend to approach it," said Nan-ch'üan, "you are on the wrong track." "Barring conscious intention," the disciple continued to inquire, "how can we attain to a knowledge of the Tao?" To this, the master replied, "Tao belongs neither to knowledge nor to no-knowledge. For knowledge is but illusive perception, while no-knowledge is mere confusion. If you really attain true comprehension of the Tao, unshadowed by the slightest doubt, your vision will be like the infinite space, free of all limits and obstacles. Its truth or falsehood cannot be established artificially by external proofs." At these words Chao-chou came to an enlightenment. Only after this did he take his vows and become a professed monk.

On another day, Chao-chou asked his master, "When one realizes that 'there is,' where should he go from there?" "He should go down the hill," came the surprising answer, "to become a buffalo in the village below!" But even more surprising was Chao-chou's reaction. Far from being mystified, he thanked his master for having led him to a thorough enlightenment. Thereupon, Nan-ch'üan remarked, "Last night at the third watch, the moon shone through the window."

The above two conversations are of capital importance. They establish the foundation of Chao-chou's inner vision and spiritual realization. They furnish the key to the understanding of all his sayings and actions in his long pilgrimage of life. Let us, therefore, look at them more closely before we proceed to the rest.

In the first dialogue, Nan-ch'üan began by uttering one of the central insights of Ch'an: "Tao is nothing else than the ordinary mind." Then he proceeded to point out that Tao is beyond knowledge and no-knowledge, that it cannot be attained by deliberate seeking, nor proved or disproved by discursive arguments. Nan-ch'üan does not tell us how to attain a true comprehension of Tao; but he has stated very clearly the effect of such comprehension: "Your vision will be like the infinite space, free of all limits and obstacles." This, I believe, points up the transcendence of Tao. If Tao is nothing else than the ordinary mind, then the ordinary mind must be very extraordinary indeed.

In the second dialogue, we first encounter a typical Ch'an idiom: To realize that "there is." In ordinary language, it signifies "To comprehend reality or pure being," which is none other than Tao. By direct comprehension one becomes one with the Tao. Chao-chou was asking where a man could go when he has become one with Tao, since Tao, as Chuang-tzu had truly said, is nowhere and everywhere. Meaning to bring out graphically the immanence of Tao, Nan-ch'üan declared that such a man should go down the hill to become a buffalo in the village below. The buffalo was, of course, only a random instance employed by the master to clinch the attention of the disciple. This was on a par with Chuang-tzu's pointing to a particular pile of excrement saying that Tao was *there*. But Nan-ch'üan was more fortunate than Chuang-tzu; for while Chuang-tzu's words only resulted in driving away his listener, Nan-ch'üan's words occasioned a complete enlightenment in his disciple. To be one with Tao is to be one with the whole universe and each and everything in it! Chao-chou was inundated with this wonderful insight, until his whole being was filled with it. As Nan-ch'üan put it, the bright moonlight had penetrated the windows of his soul.

Now, to be enlightened is to be emancipated from illusions and inhibitions. This explains certain actions, especially in the case of newly enlightened persons, which might easily shock the usual conventionally minded gentlemen. In the exercise of their newly won freedom, their master has often been the first person to receive their rough handling. Curiously enough, many a master seems to have enjoyed the apparent indignities received from his disciple. When Lin-chi slapped Huang-po, the latter burst out laughing. Nan-ch'üan fared no better with Chao-chou. Once Nan-ch'üan said to Chao-chou, "Nowadays it is best to live and work among members of a different species from us." (This statement may be unintelligible to those who are unfamiliar with the Buddhist proverb: "It is easier to save the beasts than to save mankind." Chao-chou, however, thought otherwise. He said, "Leaving alone the question of 'different,' let me ask you what is 'species' anyway?" Nan-ch'üan put both of his hands on the ground to indicate the species of the quadrupeds. Chao-chou, approaching him from behind, trampled him to the ground and then ran into Nirvana Hall crying, "I repent, I repent!" Nan-ch'üan, who appreciated his act of trampling, did not understand the reason of his repentance. So he sent his attendant to ask the disciple what he was repenting for. Chao-chou replied, "I repent that I did not trample him twice over!" Thereafter the master esteemed and loved him more than ever.

What a topsy-turveydom is the world of Ch'an! Yet, if we remember that Nan-ch'üan made that statement with no other purpose than to test the authenticity and depth of his disciple's enlightenment, and if we understand that Chao-chou's act of trampling was meant only to wipe out the very notion of "species," we could easily realize that there is method in all their madness.

Although Nan-ch'üan was the abbot of a large community of monks and novices, Chao-chou was the only man after his heart. In fact the master and the disciple seem to have cooperated closely in the work of initiating the others. At first Chao-chou was made to serve in the kitchen as the stoker. One day he closed all the doors and piled wood on the fire until the whole kitchen was filled with smoke. Then he shouted, "Fire! Fire! Come to my rescue!" When the whole community had flocked to the door, he said, "I will not open the door unless you can say the right word." No answer came from the crowd. But the abbot silently passed the key through a window hole. This was the right word that Chao-chou had in mind, and he opened the door immediately.

No one knows exactly what was behind it all. But if we take the whole episode as a pointer to the process of enlightenment, it may reveal to us a part of its hidden significance. For, is not enlightenment after all the opening of the mind's door at the occasion of the "right word?" It is also interesting to note that the "right word" is not necessarily something oral, but may consist in silence or in a simple action like the passing of the key in this case. Another lesson is that the door, if it is to be opened at all, must be opened from the inside. Finally, as the story shows, the stoker could have opened the door even without the key. The master, in passing the key through the window hole, actually did not contribute anything substantial to the opening of the door. His action was no more than an echo to the voice inside. That's why no Ch'an master has ever boasted of his power even though he should have been instrumental to the enlightenment of a great number of his disciples. This is what Thomas Merton calls "ontological" or "cosmic" humility, which he has so aptly attributed to Lao-tzu and Chuang-tzu. It can with equal appropriateness be attributed to the great masters of Ch'an, who, as Merton observes, are the "true inheritors of the thought and spirit of Chuang-tzu."

How completely Chao-chou saw eye-to-eye with his master can be inferred from another episode. It happened that the monks of the eastern and western halls of the monastery were quarreling over the possession of a cat. Nan-ch'üan seized the cat, saying to the monks, "If any of you can say the right word, the cat will be spared." As no one answered, he ruthlessly cut the cat in half. When Chao-chou returned in the evening, the master told him about the whole incident. Chao-chou did not say anything, but, removing his sandals from his feet and putting them on his head, he walked out. The master said, "If you had been here, you would have saved the cat!"

This is one of the most frequently discussed cases in the literature of Ch'an. Why did Nan-ch'üan take such a drastic and merciless action upon the innocent cat? What did he wish to teach by cutting it into two pieces by a single stroke of his knife? What did Chao-chou mean by putting his sandals on his head and walking out? Why did Nan-ch'üan say that this eccentric action would have constituted the right word he had expected from the community, which would have saved the life of the poor cat? The simplest way of disposing of all these questions would be to say that Ch'an is something beyond sense and therefore cannot be explained at all. No doubt Ch'an is beyond sense; but it must be remembered that it is also beyond nonsense. Although there can be no logical answer to any of these questions, nothing prevents us from perceiving some of the psychological and spiritual motives impelling the two masters of Ch'an to act the way they did. If Nan-ch'üan's action was shocking, it was intended to shock his monks out of their attachment to the cat. Nan-ch'üan himself must have been shocked to find the "home-leavers"—as monks were called—still tied to a cat. All ties must be cut once and for all if one is to be a true monk. It is only through ruthless violence that one can be started on the road to freedom and spontaneity. I am not sure whether the means Nan-ch'üan employed were the best under the circumstances; but there can be no question that the end-in-view was to teach his monks an unforgettable lesson in spiritual liberation. Likewise Chao-chou's action of putting his sandals on his head and walking out may appear completely arbitrary; but it was certainly meant to remind his fellow monks of the realm of reality in which the values of this world are turned upside down, and in which the legal rights and wrongs, over which the worldlings fight so seriously, exist no more. Incidentally his funny behavior must have served to soothe the nerves of his excited master—for even enlightened ones have their emotional life—as if he were saying, "Good night, Master! Take it easy and have a good rest."

After his enlightenment, Chao-chou spent many years in traveling and visiting contemporary Ch'an masters, not so much in order to receive further instruction from them as to exchange notes with them. He was fond of mountains and rivers and was very much at home roaming from one place to another. Several of his friends advised him to settle down with a community of his own, but he had no such desire. Once, as he was visiting Chu-yu, the latter said, "A man of your age should try to find a place to settle down and teach." "Where is my abiding place?" Chao-chou asked back. "What?" said his host. "With so many years on your head, you have not even come to know where your permanent home is!" Chu-yu was, of course, referring here to the obvious truth that the true man is his own abiding place. It is so obvious a truth as to make its articulation quite silly. So Chao-chou said, "For thirty years I have roamed freely on horseback. Today, for the first time I am kicked by an ass!"

When he was on the point of starting for the Ch'ing-liang temple on Five-Story Mountain in Shansi, a learned monk wrote a gāthā to tease him:

> What green mountain is not a center of Tao?
> Must you, cane in hand, make a pilgrimage to Ch'ing-liang?
> Even if the golden-haired lion should appear in the clouds,
> It would not be an auspicious sight to the Dharma Eye!

(Note: The temple on Five-Story Mountain was built in honor of National Teacher Ch'ing-liang, the Fourth Patriarch of the Hua-yen sect. It is said that when he preached on the mountain, a golden-haired lion appeared in the clouds.)

But Chao-chou was not to be dissuaded from his trip. He answered the gāthā by asking back, "What is the Dharma Eye?" The monk could find no answer. He should have known that together with the cane Chao-chou brought the Dharma Eye wherever he went.

It was not until he was around eighty that he settled at the Kuan-yin Monastery in the eastern suburb of Chao-chou. It is said that he was extremely ascetic in his habits. During the forty years of his abbotship, he did not install a single piece of new furniture, nor did he write a single letter to any patron to ask for alms. (He would be considered a very inefficient abbot according to the standards of the modern West.)

But Chao-chou was too well known to be left alone by the world. Once a very powerful prince came to visit him. Chao-chou kept seated and asked the visitor, "Does Your Highness understand?" The prince said, "I do not understand." The master said, "Since my childhood I have been keeping fasts. Now that I am old, I do not possess enough energy to rise from my Ch'an couch to receive my guests." Far from being offended, the prince respected him all the more. The next day he dispatched a general to convey his appreciation. The master came down immediately to receive him. After the general was gone, an attending monk asked the master, "When the great prince came, you did not come down from the couch to welcome him. But today, as soon as you saw his general, you came down immediately to greet him. What kind of protocol is that?" The master replied, "This is something you do not understand. When a first-rate man comes, I receive him while remaining seated. When a second-rate man comes, I come down from my seat to receive him. When a man of the lowest class comes, I would go out of the front gate to receive him." Evidently he was no longer speaking of the protocol of social intercourse, but expounding the degrees of accommodation in dealing with different grades of spiritual potentiality.

We have already mentioned that Chao-chou was called "the ancient Buddha of Chao-chou." This title was given him by Hsüeh-feng, a prominent Ch'an master in southern China. It is not known whether they ever met in person. But on a certain day, a monk, who came from the south to visit Chao-chou, related to him the following dialogue between Hsüeh-feng and a disciple of his:

> Disciple: *Can you tell me something about the "cold spring of the ancient brook?"*
> Hsüeh-feng: *However hard you gaze into it, you cannot see its bottom.*
> Disciple: *What happens to the drinker?*
> Hsüeh-feng: *He does not drink it with his mouth.*

At this point, Chao-chou remarked humorously, "Since he does not drink it with his mouth, I suppose he does it with his nose." The visitor said, "What would *you* say about the 'cold spring of the ancient brook?'" "It tastes bitter," he replied. "What happens to the drinker?" the visitor further asked. "He dies!" said Chao-chou.

When Hsüeh-feng heard of this dialogue, he burst into praise, saying, "The ancient Buddha! The ancient Buddha!" This was how the title originated.

The "cold spring of the ancient brook" signifies nothing else than the Tao. That "it tastes bitter" means that you have to go through the strictest self-discipline and deprivation in the pursuit of Tao, till you are thoroughly dead to the world and to yourself. Without bitterness there can be no true joy. Without death there can be no real life. This dialogue reveals the hidden spring of Chao-chou's gaiety and vitality, his profound wisdom and light-hearted humor.

Once a Confucian scholar came to visit him. Greatly impressed by his wisdom, the guest exclaimed, "Your Reverence is indeed the ancient Buddha!" He immediately returned the compliment by saying, "But you are the new Tathāgata!" This was, in fact, more than a mere exchange of compliments. The repartee of Chao-chou was meant, I think, to be a subtle rectification of the term *ancient Buddha*. The true self is ever new. An ancient Buddha would be a dead Buddha.

It is the common aim of all Ch'an masters to lead their novices to the true self. This is also the end of Chao-chou's teachings. But his way of accomplishing it was altogether original and funny.

One morning, as he was receiving new arrivals, he asked one of them, "Have you been here before?" "Yes," the latter replied. "Help yourself to a cup of tea," he said. Then he asked another, "Have you been here before." "No, Your Reverence, this is my first visit here." Chao-chou again said, "Help yourself to a cup of tea." The prior of the monastery took the abbot to task, saying, "The one had been here before, and you gave him a cup of tea. The other had not been here, and you gave him likewise a cup of tea. What is the meaning of all this?" The abbot called out, "Prior!" "Yes," responded the prior, "what's your bidding?" "Help yourself to a cup of tea!" said the abbot.

The act of drinking tea is but the functioning of someone, and in each case it should evoke the question, who is drinking the tea? Besides, if Tao is nothing else than the ordinary mind, every ordinary action is an expression of Tao. A novice once said to the master, "I am only newly admitted into this monastery, and I beseech Your Reverence to teach and guide me." The master asked, "Have you taken your breakfast?" "Yes, Master, I have." "Go wash your bowl," said the master. At these words, the novice experienced an instantaneous enlightenment.

Like Chuang-tzu, Chao-chou may be called a "cosmic democrat." In his weltanschauung, all things are equal, because Tao is present even in what the world looks upon as the lowest things.

On a leisurely summer day, Chao-chou was sitting idly in his room, with his faithful disciple Wen-yüan attending on him. By a fluke a bright idea came into the head of the jolly old man. "Wen-yüan," he said, "let us enter into a contest as to which of us can identify himself with the lowest thing in the scale of human values." It was agreed that the winner was to pay the loser a cake. Wen-yüan gladly accepted the challenge but deferred to the master to start. Chao-chou began: "I am an ass." Wen-yüan: "I am the ass's buttock." Chao-chou: "I am the ass's feces." Wen-yüan: "I am a worm in the feces." At this point, Chao-chou could not go further, so he asked, "What are you doing there?" Wen-yüan replied, "I am spending my summer vacation there." Thereupon, Chao-chou said, "You win!" and demanded the cake.

This was the only recorded case where the resourceful abbot admitted his defeat. But I suspect that the old man was hungry, and he was only too eager to lose the contest in order to win the cake.

I have often wondered why certain sages seem to have taken a delight in mentioning things which are offensive to delicate ears. Chuang-tzu used to say that Tao is in the excrement. Justice Holmes used to doubt if cerebration had a greater cosmic validity than the movement of bowels. But to Chuang-tzu and the Ch'an masters, there can be no doubt that the movement of bowels possesses cosmic validity, though the same cannot be said of mere cerebration.

To the pure all things are pure. But to the impure, even the purest things can be impure. One morning a nun besought Chao-chou to tell her "the secret of all secrets," which in Buddhist parlance means the most fundamental principle. The ancient Buddha just patted her on the shoulder. Evidently he wished thereby to indicate that the most fundamental principle was within her. But the nun was taken aback by the ancient

Buddha's unexpected action. "I am shocked," she exclaimed, "to see that Your Reverence has still got *that* in him!" "Rather it is you, Sister," Chao-chou retorted, "who have still got *that* in you!" The very quickness of his repartees reveals that they flowed from an unencumbered heart.

To Chao-chou, reality is not to be found in formulated principles and mottoes. Once a monk asked him, "What is the one motto of this monastery of Chao-chou?" The master replied, "There is not even a half motto here." "Don't we have Your Reverence here as the abbot?" the monk queried. "But this old monk is not a motto!" said Chao-chou.

A true descendant of Hui-neng, Chao-chou's eyes were steadfastly focused on the self-nature, which was for him but another name for Tao or reality. In a remarkable sermon, he declared, "Thousands upon thousands of people are only seekers after Buddha, but not a single one is a true man of Tao. Before the existence of the world, the self-nature is. After the destruction of the world, the self-nature remains intact. Now that you have seen this old monk, you are no longer someone else, but a master of yourself. What's the use of seeking another in the exterior?" On another occasion he said, "The one word which I dislike to hear is 'Buddha.' "

For Chao-chou, as for Ma-tsu and Nan-ch'üan, Tao or reality is neither mind, nor Buddha, nor a thing. It transcends the universe of time and space, yet it pervades all things. It is only against this metaphysical background that we can understand some of his enigmatic sayings. For instance, when a monk asked him, "What is the real significance of Bodhidharma's coming from the West?" (By a consensus of opinion among Ch'an masters, this question meant nothing else than: "What is the essential principle of Buddhism?" or, to put it more simply, "What is Tao?") His answer was, "The cypress tree in the courtyard." When the monk protested that the abbot was only referring him to a mere object, the abbot said, "No, I am not referring you to an object." The monk then repeated again the question. "The cypress tree in the courtyard!" said the abbot once more.

Stripped of the jargon of Ch'an, all that Chao-chou was saying was that Tao is in the cypress tree in the courtyard. In fact, it is in all things. The cypress tree was mentioned simply because it happened to be the first thing that he saw. If he had seen an eagle flying over, he would have said, "The eagle in yonder sky!" True, he mentioned an object; but he was using it to point to Tao. He was not referring the monk to a mere object;

it was the monk whose vision was glued to the object so that it could not pass beyond it.

Chao-chou's view of Tao is on all fours with that of Lao-tzu and Chuang-tzu. This is not because he followed them deliberately, but because his insights happened to coincide with theirs. On the other hand, he did not agree entirely with the view of Seng-ts'an, the Third Patriarch of Ch'an, as presented in the following stanza:

> There is no difficulty about the pursuit of Tao,
> Except that we must refrain from making discriminations.
> If a man can only free himself of likes and dislikes,
> He will see clearly as in broad daylight.

Chao-chou took exception to it in a conference. "The moment you utter a single word, you have already made a choice, while imagining yourself to be in the light. As for me, I am not in the light about it. I only want to know whether you still cherish it and preserve it intact in your heart." At this point, a monk asked him, "Since you are not in the light about it, what is it, then, that you wish us to cherish and preserve intact?" "I don't know any more than you do," the abbot replied. The monk further asked, "Since you are so clear about your not knowing, how can you say that you are not in the light?" Instead of giving the final answer, the master evaded the question by saying, "Please confine your questions to the realm of things." After performing the rites of worship, the assembly was dismissed.

The monk in this case was probably not a neophyte in Ch'an learning. He was perhaps trying to press the master to articulate his philosophic creed somewhat in the way Lao-tzu had done when he said:

> To realize that our knowledge is ignorance,
>     This is a noble insight.
> To regard our ignorance as knowledge,
>     This is mental disease.

But Chao-chou had the knack of glancing off the target instead of sticking in the bull's-eye. Like all the great masters of Ch'an, Chao-chou kept the feet of his disciples on a slippery ground in order to prevent them from slipping into the snug den of a clean-cut formula. When Ma-tsu said,

"Slippery is the road of Shih-t'ou!" it was meant as a compliment to his great contemporary in the world of Ch'an.

But no one can be more slippery than Chao-chou. Once a monk asked him, "It is said that all things return to the One. Where does the One return to?" The master said, "When I was in Ch'ing-chou, I made a robe of cotton cloth, weighing seven catties." What an irrelevant answer! This dialogue has been used in succeeding generations as a typical *kung-an* to tease the minds of neophytes. But we must remember that to Chao-chou the One and many are relative and interpenetrated. If the many return to the One, the One returns to the many, so that any particular event, however trivial it may appear, in whatever place and time it may happen, is inseparably connected with the One and may therefore serve as a pointer to it. Now, nothing could be more particular than the fact that when he was in Ch'ing-chou he had a robe of cotton cloth made for him, which weighed seven catties. On the other hand, nothing could be more universal than the One. Yet, in none of the infinite number of particulars is the One ever absent!

But did Chao-chou equate the One with Tao? By no means! If he did, Tao itself would have been conceived as relative. The truth is that in his view, Tao is absolutely beyond one and many. This seems to be the pivotal point in his philosophy. Even in his early days, when he was with Nan-ch'üan, he already had a clear grasp of the utter transcendence of Tao. After quoting to his master a popular saying: "Tao is not outside of the realm of things; outside of the realm of things there is no Tao"; he asked, "What about the transcendent Tao?" Nan-ch'üan struck him. Catching hold of the cane, Chao-chou said, "Hereafter, take care not to hit the wrong person!" That won from Nan-ch'üan a wholehearted commendation: "It is easy to distinguish the dragon from the snake, but it is next to impossible to deceive a true monk."

Tao is not only beyond the one and many, but also beyond *yu* and *wu* (the phenomenal and the noumenal). Chao-chou's extreme flexibility in handling all relative terms springs directly from his constant awareness of the utter transcendence of Tao. Once he was asked if the dog possessed the Buddha nature. He answered, "No!" This flatly contradicts an essential tenet of Buddhism. So the questioner further asked, "There is Buddha nature in all beings, from the Buddhas to the ants. How can you say that the dog has no Buddha nature?" The master replied, "Because of its habit of discrimination." On another occasion when exactly the same question was put to him, he answered, "Yes." But the questioner said, "Since the dog has Buddha nature, how did he come to assume the body of a dog?" "He acted against his better knowledge," the master replied.

If the same question were put to Chao-chou for the third time, he might well have answered, "Yes and no!" Yes, that is, in one sense, and no, in another sense.

Chao-chou seldom if ever repeated his answers to any question, however frequently it might be put to him. Not that he hankered after novelty, but that his single-hearted fidelity to the end—to pave the way to enlightenment for others—compelled him to use different answers in response to the exigencies of each case. Only such answers as these are living answers, flowing spontaneously from the heart. On the other hand, if you repeat the same answer to the same question, it becomes a dead formula, mechanically remembered and perfunctorily delivered. Even if the answer was original with you and had a wiggle of life in the beginning, your systematic repetition of it is liable to take all life out of it until it becomes as dead and dry as a sucked lemon. In this way, you easily degenerate from a speaker into a parrot.

It was by this test, I suppose, that Chao-chou is said to have exposed certain fakers. He had a keen nose for the counterfeits. Often clever neophytes came from famous centers of Ch'an south of the Yangtze river, after they had learned many a stock phrase and slogan from the lips of their masters. In their conversation with Chao-chou, they talked glibly of profound subjects and made frequent use of their masters' words. Chao-chou called them "traveling peddlers." When he was on the way to Five-Story Mountain, he encountered a strange old woman. His fellow travelers had told him how she waited at the roadside and greeted every monk, and whenever a monk asked her to point the way to the monastery on the mountain, she would say, "Just go straight ahead!" And as the monk went his way, she would say, "So he passes on like this!" Many people suspected that she must be deeply versed in Ch'an. But Chao-chou said to them, "Let me try her out." When he approached her, she greeted him as usual. When he asked her to point the way to the monastery, she answered, "Just go straight ahead!" As he was going his way, she said, "So he passes on like this!" Next day, he announced to his fellow travelers, "I have found her out!" The spirit of Ch'an refuses to be stereotyped.

It was Chuang-tzu who said, "Only the true man can have true knowledge." Chao-chou was very much of the same mind, for he maintained that in the practice of Ch'an, everything depends upon the person. He went to the extent of saying, "When the right person expounds a wrong doctrine, even the wrong doctrine becomes right. When the wrong person expounds a right doctrine, even the right doctrine becomes wrong."

The wonderful thing about Chao-chou is that his advancing age did not tarnish the freshness of his mind. He was immune to senility. Few of his younger contemporaries could measure up to him in mental vigor. In his last years he already discerned certain signs of degeneration in the Ch'an tradition. "Ninety years ago," he said, "I saw more than eighty enlightened masters in the lineage of Ma-tsu; all of them were creative spirits. Of late years, the pursuit of Ch'an has become more and more trivialized and ramified. Removed ever farther from the original spirit of men of supreme wisdom, the process of degeneration will go on from generation to generation."

Assuming that these words were uttered in the last decade of the ninth century, when Chao-chou was in his 110s, we cannot but admit the accuracy of his observation. By that time the golden age of Ch'an was over. He had lived to be the last spiritual giant of the period of T'ang—the last, but not the least.


## MORE ABOUT CHAO-CHOU

Chao-chou did not found a house of his own. He was too much of a free-lancer to be interested in being an "ancestor" of brilliant descendents bearing his image and continuing his lineage. But all the Five Houses have drawn upon the "ancient Buddha of Chao-chou" as their common source of inspiration and wisdom. Therefore, I have collected some more anecdotes about him and some more wise saws from him, which appeal to me as typical expressions of the spirit of Ch'an.


### 1. CHAO-CHOU AND HIS IMAGE

A monk had drawn a portrait of the master. When it was presented to him, he said, "If it is really a true image of me, then you can kill me. But if it is not, then you should burn it."

## 2. "LAY IT DOWN!"

A new arrival said apologetically to the master, "I have come here empty-handed!" "Lay it down then!" said the master. "Since I have brought nothing with me, what can I lay down?" asked the visitor. "Then go on carrying it!" said the master.

To be initiated into Ch'an, it is not enough to be empty-handed. What is more important, you must be empty-hearted. To feel ashamed of your ignorance shows that your heart is still full of yourself.

## 3. CHAO-CHOU'S FAMILY TRADITION

When a monk asked, "What is the abbot's family tradition?" the abbot replied, "I have nothing inside, and I seek for nothing outside."

## 4. THE BEGGAR LACKS NOTHING

A monk asked, "When a beggar comes, what shall we give him?" The master answered, "He is lacking in nothing."

## 5. THE TRUE MAN NOT A MAN

A monk asked, "Who is the man who finds no mate in the whole universe?" "He is not a man!" the master answered.

## 6. "WHO ARE YOU?"

A monk asked, "Who is the Buddha?" The master fired back, "Who are you?"

## 7. AT A FUNERAL PROCESSION

At the funeral of one of his monks, as the abbot joined the procession, he remarked, "What a long procession of dead bodies follows the wake of a single living person!"

## 8. HOW CHAO-CHOU LAUGHED OVER HIS DEFEAT

Nothing could be more interesting than to watch two great masters of Ch'an tease each other and pull each other's legs. When Chao-chou visited the master Ta-tz'u, he asked the latter, "What can be the body (substratum) of prajñā?" Ta-tz'u just repeated the question, "Indeed, what can be the body of prajñā?" This time the ancient Buddha was caught; he had asked a senseless question! But instead of feeling embarrassed, he burst into a loud guffaw and went out. The next morning, as he was sweeping the courtyard, Ta-tz'u chanced upon him and to tease him asked, "What can be the body of prajñā?" Laying down the sweeper, Chao-chou laughed wholeheartedly and went away. Thereupon Ta-tz'u returned quietly to his room.

### 9. NO WISDOM BY PROXY

A monk besought him to tell him the most vitally important principle of Ch'an. The master excused himself by saying, "I must now go to make water. Think, even such a trifling thing I have to do in person!"

### 10. CH'AN AS AN OPEN SECRET

A monk once asked him, "What is Chao-chou?" Obviously he was not asking about the city of Chao-chou, but about the distinctive features of the master's Ch'an. But the master answered him in terms of the city, "East gate, west gate, south gate, north gate." His Ch'an is like an open city, which can be approached from all directions. There is nothing esoteric about his teaching. Every person with an ordinary mind can enter the city through any of its gates.

But this does not mean that the gates are always open. There is a time for opening the gates, and there is a time for closing them. When they are closed, it is said that no external force, not even the combined forces of the whole universe, can break through. Such then is Chao-chou's Ch'an—an open secret!

# CHAPTER VIII

# Outstanding Masters in the Lineage of Shih-t'ou:

## Tao-wu, Lung-t'an, Te-shan, Yen-t'ou, and Hsüeh-feng

The five masters whom we are going to treat in this chapter are important not only because they form a continuous bridge between Shih-t'ou, on the one hand, and Yün-men and Hsüan-sha on the other, but because each of them was highly original and had some fresh insights to contribute to the whole tradition of Zen.

Tao-wu of the T'ien-huang temple (748–807) was born of a Chang family in Wu-chow, Chekiang. When he was fourteen, he felt a vocation to be a monk. As his parents would not hear of it, Tao-wu reduced his diet until he became dreadfully thin and weak. Finally his parents relented and gave their permission. He was professed in his mid-twenties in Hangchow, and was noted for his extreme asceticism. Then he went to Yu-hang to visit Ching-shan Tao-ch'in (d. 792), who was an outstanding Ch'an master in the lineage of the Fourth Patriarch Tao-hsin and Niu-t'ou Fa-jung. It was Ching-shan who first initiated Tao-wu into Ch'an. After serving Ching-shan for five years, he went to visit Ma-tsu, who confirmed him in his insights. After he had spent two summers with Ma-tsu, he went to visit Shih-t'ou, asking, "After one is freed of dhyāna and prajñā, what Dharma can one show to others?" Shih-t'ou said, "In my place there being no slaves, what is there to be freed from?" "How is this to be verified?" Tao-wu further inquired. Shih-t'ou asked back, "Can you grasp at the empty and void?" "Well," said Tao-wu, "this [ungraspability] does not begin today." Then Shih-t'ou asked, "When, I wonder, did you come from that place?" "I am not a man of that place!" was Tao-wu's answer. Shih-t'ou said, "I knew long ago where you came from." Tao-wu replied, "How can you, Master, bring this false charge against me without concrete evidence?" "Your body itself is the present evidence!" said Shih-t'ou. "Be that as it may," said Tao-wu, "my question still is how to teach the posterity." Shih-t'ou fired back, "Tell me *who* is the posterity?" At this Tao-wu was suddenly enlightened and began to understand thoroughly what his two previous masters had communicated to him.

Tao-wu's way of teaching can be gathered from how he dealt with his disciple Lung-t'an (d. first part of the ninth century). Lung-t'an came from a poor family, who made their living by selling pastry. Tao-wu knew him as a boy and recognized in him great spiritual potentialities. He housed his family in a hut belonging to his monastery. To show his gratitude, Lung-t'an made a daily offering of ten cakes to the master. The master accepted the cakes, but every day he consumed only nine and returned the remaining one to Lung-t'an, saying, "This is my gift to you in order to prosper your descendants." One day, Lung-t'an became curious, saying to himself, "It is I who bring him the cakes; how is it then that he returns one of them as a present to me? Can there be some secret meaning in this?" So the young boy made bold to put the question before the master. The master said, "What wrong is there to restore to you what originally belonged to you?" Lung-t'an apprehended the hidden meaning and decided to be a novice, attending upon the master with great diligence. After some time, Lung-t'an said to the master, "Since I came, I have not received any essential instructions on the mind from you, Master." The master replied, "Ever since you came, I have not ceased for a moment to give you essential instructions about the mind." More mystified than ever, the disciple asked, "On what points have you instructed me?" The master replied, "Whenever you bring me the tea, I take it from your hands. Whenever you serve the meal, I accept it and eat it. Whenever you salute me, I lower my head in response. On what points have I failed to show you the essence of the mind?" Lung-t'an lowered his head and remained silent for a long time. The master said, "For true perception, you must see right on the spot. As soon as you begin to ponder and reflect, you miss it." At these words, Lung-t'an's mind was opened and he understood. Then he asked how to preserve this insight. The master said, "Give rein to your nature in its transcendental roamings. Act according to the exigencies of circumstances in perfect freedom and without any attachment. Just follow the dictates of your ordinary mind and heart. Aside from that, there is no 'holy' insight."

Lung-t'an later settled in Lung-t'an or the Dragon Pond in Hunan. A monk once asked, "Who will get the pearl amidst the curls of hair?" (Like the "priceless pearl" of the Bible this expression apparently is a symbol for the highest wisdom hidden in the midst of the phenomenal world.) Lung-t'an answered, "He who does not fondle it will get it!" "Where can we keep it?" asked the monk further. Lung-t'an replied, "If there is such a place, please tell me."

A nun asked Lung-t'an as to what she should do in order to become a monk in the next life. The master asked, "How long have you been a nun?" The nun said, "My question is whether there will be any day when I shall be a monk." "What are you now?" asked the master. To this the nun answered, "In the present life I am a nun. How can anyone fail to know this?" "Who knows you?" Lung-t'an fired back.

The famous Confucian scholar, Li Ao, once asked Lung-t'an, "What is eternal wisdom?" The master replied, "I have no eternal wisdom." Li Ao remarked, "How lucky I am to meet Your Reverence!" "Even this it is best to leave unsaid!" the master commented.

Lung-t'an was instrumental in the conversion of Te-shan Hsüan-chien (780–865). Te-shan, born of a Chou family in Cheng-tu, Szechwan, began early as a member of the Vinaya order, steeped in scriptural learning. He made a special study of the *Diamond Sūtra* on the basis of the learned commentaries of the Dharma master Ch'ing-lung. He lectured on this sūtra so frequently that his contemporaries nicknamed him Diamond Chou. Later, hearing about the prosperity of the Zen platform in the south, he became indignant and said, "How many home-leavers have spent a thousand kalpas in studying the Buddhist rituals and ten thousand kalpas in observing all the minute rules of the Buddha. Even then they have not been able to attain Buddhahood. Now, those little devils of the south are bragging of pointing directly at the mind of man, of seeing one's self-nature, and attaining Buddhahood immediately! I am going to raid their dens and caves and exterminate the whole race, in order to requite the Buddha's kindness."

Carrying on a pole two baskets of Ch'ing-lung's commentaries, he left Szechwan for Hunan, where Lung-t'an was teaching. On his way, he encountered an old woman selling pastries, which in Chinese were, and still are, called "mind-refreshers." Being tired and hungry, he laid down his load and wanted to buy some cakes. The old woman, pointing at the baskets, asked, "What is this literature?" He answered, "Ch'ing-lung's commentaries on the *Diamond Sūtra*." The old woman said, "I have a question to ask you. If you can answer it, I will make a free gift of the mind-refreshers to you. But if you cannot, please pass on to another place. Now, the *Diamond Sūtra* says: 'The past mind is nowhere to be found, the present mind is nowhere to be found, and the future mind is nowhere to be found.' Which mind, I wonder, does Your Reverence wish to refresh?" Te-shan had no word to say and went on to Lung-t'an. After he had arrived at the Dharma Hall, he remarked, "I have long desired to visit the Dragon Pond. Now that I am here on the very spot, I see neither pond nor dragon." At that time, the master Lung-t'an came out and said to him, "Yes, indeed, you have personally arrived at the true Dragon Pond." Te-shan again had nothing to say. He decided to stay on for the time being. One evening as he was attending on the master, the latter said, "The night is far advanced. Why don't you retire to your own quarters?" After wishing the master good night, he went out but returned at once, saying, "It's pitch dark outside!" Lung-t'an lit a paper-candle and handed it over to him. But just as he was on the point of receiving the candle, Lung-t'an suddenly blew out the light. At this point, Te-shan was completely enlightened and did obeisance to the master. The master asked, "What have you seen?" Te-shan said, "From now on, I have no more doubt about the tongues of the old monks of the whole world."

Next morning, the master ascended to his seat and declared to the assembly, "Among you there is a fellow, whose teeth are like the sword-leaf tree, whose mouth is like a blood-basin. Even a sudden stroke of the staff on his head will not make him turn back. Some day he will build up my doctrine on the top of a solitary peak."

On the same day, Te-shan brought all the volumes of Ch'ing-lung's commentaries to the front of the hall, and, raising a torch, said, "An exhaustive discussion of the abstruse is like a hair thrown into the infinite void, and the fullest exertion of all capabilities is like a little drop of water falling into an unfathomable gulf." Thereupon he set fire to the commentaries.

This episode is not merely spectacular but profoundly suggestive. It recalls to mind what Lao-tzu has said, "Where darkness is at its darkest, there is the gateway to all spiritual insights. In the present instance, the night was dark enough, but it became infinitely darker after the candle was lit and blown out again. When all external lights were out, the inner light shone in all its effulgence. But, of course, this did not work automatically. It worked in the case of Te-shan because his mind was just at that moment ready for the enlightenment. The little chick was stirring in the egg and trying to break through the shell; and it took just a peck by the hen on the outside to effectuate the breakthrough.

Te-shan's act of burning the learned commentaries and his realization that all discursive reasonings of the philosophers were no more than a hair in the infinite void should remind us of what St. Thomas Aquinas in his last days said to his secretary who was still urging him to continue his writing: "Reginald, I can do no more; such things have been revealed to me that all the writings I have produced seem to me like a straw."

Te-shan was by nature a man of fierce intensity. Before he was enlightened, he had clung fiercely to the letter of the scriptures. When he heard of the prevalence of Zen teaching in the south, he became fiercely indignant, breathing threats and murder against those rebellious "devils." After his conversion, he became fiercely iconoclastic. Nothing short of the absolutely real and true could satisfy him; and *that* he had discovered in the pitch darkness of the happy night, namely, his true self. Everything else was to him nothing but rubbish. It is in this light that we should read some of his shocking utterances, such as: "I see differently from our ancestors. Here there is neither patriarch nor Buddha. Bodhidharma is an old stinking barbarian. Śākyamuni is a dry toilet strip. Mañjuśrī and Samantabhadra are dung-heap coolies. *Samyak-sambodhi* and subtle perception are nothing but ordinary human nature freed of fetters. Bodhi and nirvāṇa are but dead stumps to tie the donkeys to. The twelve divisions of the scriptures are only registers of ghosts, sheets of paper fit only for wiping the pus from your ulcers and tumors. All the 'four fruitions' and 'ten stages' are nothing but demons lingering in their decayed graves, who cannot even save themselves."

In dealing with his disciples, Te-shan resorted to the rod as frequently as Lin-chi resorted to the shout, as evidenced by the current saying, "Te-shan's rod, Lin-chi's shout." Once Te-shan announced to his assembly, "If you speak rightly, I will give you thirty blows. If you speak wrongly, I will also give you thirty blows." When Lin-chi heard about this utterance, he said to his friend Lo-p'u, "Go to ask him why the one who speaks rightly should be given thirty blows. As soon as he begins to strike, catch hold of his rod and push it against him. See what he will do." Lo-p'u acted accordingly. As soon as he put the question, Te-shan started to strike him, and he caught hold of the rod and made a violent thrust against him. Thereupon, Te-shan returned quietly to his room. When Lo-p'u came back to report to Lin-chi, the latter said, "From the very beginning I have had my doubts about that fellow. Be that as it may, do you recognize the true Te-shan?" As Lo-p'u fumbled for an answer, Lin-chi gave him a beating.

In his last illness, Te-shan still remained the radical nondualist that he was. Someone asked him, "Is there still the one who is never sick?" Te-shan said, "Yes, there is." "Tell me something about this never-sick one," the visitor persisted. The master cried, "Oya, oya!" signalling intense pain. The one who is sick is identical with the one who is never sick!

Te-shan had only a few disciples, of whom two stood out: Yen-t'ou Ch'üan-huo (828–887) and Hsüeh-feng I-ts'un (822–908). In spiritual gifts, Yen-t'ou was superior to Hsüeh-feng. Yen-t'ou's mind was sharp as a razor. He never deferred to anyone, not even Te-shan and T'ung-shan. One day as he came to see Te-shan, no sooner had he stepped into the door than he asked, "Is it holy or profane?" As Te-shan shouted, Yen-t'ou did obeisance. Later someone related the incident to Tung-shan, the latter remarked, "Anyone else than Yen-t'ou would have found it hard to respond so well." When Yen-t'ou heard of this compliment, he said, "The old man of Tung-shan is very insensible to have passed such an erroneous judgment. He does not know that on that particular occasion, in acting the way I did, I was uplifting him (Te-shan) by one hand while pinching him by the other hand."

In asking, "Is it holy or profane?" Yen-t'ou was, of course, referring to that state in which there is no more distinction between the holy and profane. In shouting at the question, Te-shan made him understand that he saw eye-to-eye with him. In doing obeisance, he was on the one hand showing his delight at the master's reaction, but on the other hand he was testing how he would react. But poor Te-shan sat like an idol and accepted unsuspectingly a homage which was meant for the merely "holy!"

Yen-t'ou's radical transcendentalism finds an illustration in another episode. As he was chatting with his friends Hsüeh-feng and Ch'in-shan, Hsüeh-feng suddenly pointed at a basin filled with plain water. Ch'in-shan remarked, "When the water is clear, the moon appears." Hsüeh-feng said, "When the water is clear, the moon disappears." Yen-t'ou said nothing but, kicking off the basin, went away.

In this episode, it is clear that Ch'in-shan's approach is positive, while Hsüeh-feng's is negative. But what is the big idea of kicking off the bowl? Probably, Yen-t'ou wished by his act to indicate the need of transcending both the positive and negative. Yen-t'ou often spoke of the "last word," which, in his view, few Zen masters understood. Can it be that his kicking in this case is the last word? Anyway, he very seldom if ever allowed another to say the last word.

Hsüeh-feng's mind did not work as quickly as Yen-t'ou's; but by virtue of his utter sincerity, humility, patience, and selflessness, he became one of the greatest teachers in the whole history of Zen. His great quality, so rare among Zen masters, was that he was willing to allow others to say the last word and to express his wholehearted approval and delight when it was said by another. If Yen-t'ou had a more brilliant mind, Hsüeh-feng had a greater soul. Like the patient hen, he hatched out many a brilliant disciple, including Yün-men and Hsüan-sha, the spiritual grandfather of Fa-yen. Thus, two important houses of Zen were descended from Hsüeh-feng, while Yen-t'ou did not have much of a progeny.

However, it cannot be denied that while both Hsüeh-feng and Yen-t'ou were disciples of Te-shan, the former treated the latter as his elder brother and came to his ultimate enlightenment through his help. Once Hsüeh-feng was traveling with Yen-t'ou. When they arrived at the county of Ao-shan in Hunan, they were caught in a snowstorm and could not proceed. Yen-t'ou took it easy and slept away his days, while Hsüeh-feng spent his days in sitting and meditating. Ony day, he tried to rouse Yen-t'ou from sleep by shouting, "Elder brother, get up!" Yen-t'ou answered, "Why should I?" Hsüeh-feng was vexed and murmured, "In this present life why am I so unlucky to be traveling with a fellow like this, who just drags me down like a piece of luggage. And since we have arrived here, he has been doing nothing but sleeping!" Yen-t'ou shouted at him, saying, "Shut up and go to sleep! Every day you sit cross-legged on the bed. How like an idol in the soil-shrine of a common village! In the future you will be bedeviling the sons and daughters of good families!" Hsüeh-feng, pointing to his own breast, said, "Here within me I feel no peace. I dare not deceive myself." Yen-t'ou said that he was very much surprised to hear him speak like this. Hsüeh-feng repeated again that he really felt an inner restlessness. Then Yen-t'ou asked him to relate to him his perceptions and experiences and promised to sift the genuine from the spurious. Hsüeh-feng told him how he had got an entrance into Zen at the feet of the master Hsien-kuan, how he was inspired by reading the gāthā that Tung-shan had composed after his enlightenment, and finally how he asked Te-shan about the Vehicle beyond all vehicles, how Te-shan responded to his question by striking him with his rod, saying, "What are you talking about?" and how he felt at that moment like a tub whose bottom had fallen out. At this, Yen-t'ou shouted, saying, "Haven't you heard that he who enters by the door is not the treasure of his own house?" Hsüeh-feng asked, "From now on what shall I do?" Yen-t'ou said, "Hereafter, if you want to spread broadcast the great teaching, let everything flow from your own bosom and let it cover and permeate the sky and the earth!" At these words, Hsüeh-feng was thoroughly awakened. After he had done his obeisance, he rose and cried ecstatically, "Elder Brother! Today at Ao-shan I have truly attained the Tao!"

Hsüeh-feng later became an abbot, with a community of fifteen hundred monks under him. Once a monk asked him what he had learned from Te-shan. He replied, "I went to him empty-handed and empty-handed I returned." The truth is, as he pointed out, that "no one really gets anything from his master." This reveals that Hsüeh-feng was as transcendental in his outlook as any of the great masters. On the other hand, his duties as a teacher of so many monks compelled him to accommodate himself to their needs. He had to keep the sword in the scabbard. When someone asked him, "What happens if the arrow reveals its sharp head?" he said, "The brilliant archer misses his aim." Thus, it seems that he had taken seriously to heart the Taoist lesson of toning down the dazzling splendor of one's light. However, he knew as well as anybody that attachment to one particular method would blind the eyes of a beginner. Once a novice besought him to point out to him a definite entrance into Zen. He replied, "I would rather have my body pulverized into dust than run the risk of blinding the eyes of a single monk!"

Hsüeh-feng was quick to recognize the superior qualities of another. He admitted his inferiority to the master Huang Ni-p'an, saying, "I live within the three worlds: you are beyond the three worlds." He called Kuei-shan the "ancient Buddha of Kuei-shan" and Chao-chou the "ancient

Buddha of Chao-chou." When the master San-sheng asked him, "When the golden-scaled fish had gone through the net, what food does it feed on?" Hsüeh-feng replied, after the style of old masters, "I will tell you after you have come out from the net." San-sheng remarked, "How strange it is that the guardian of fifteen hundred men does not even recognize the point of a question!" Hsüeh-feng apologized, "This old monk is too preoccupied with his duties as an abbot." On another occasion, as both Hsüeh-feng and San-sheng were participating in the regular manual work of the community in the field, they saw a monkey. Hsüeh-feng remarked, "Everyone has an antique mirror in him; so does this monkey." San-sheng said, "How can the eternally nameless manifest itself as an antique mirror?" Hsüeh-feng answered, "Because flaws have grown on it." San-sheng again charged him with not understanding the meaning of words. Hsüeh-feng again apologized for his preoccupation with his duties.

Obviously, Hsüeh-feng knew his rubrics as well as San-sheng; but when he was speaking of the "antique mirror" and the flaws gathering on it, it was for the ears of the beginners. That he knew what he was doing is clear from another incident. Once he asked a visiting monk where he came from, to which the latter answered, "From the master Fu-ch'uan." Now Fu-ch'uan meant "sunken boat." So Hsüeh-feng made a pun of his name, saying, "There is still much to do in ferrying over the sea of birth and death, why should he sink the boat so soon?" The monk, knowing not what to say, returned to report to Fu-ch'uan, who remarked, "Why didn't you answer that *that one* is beyond birth and death?" The monk came back to Hsüeh-feng and spoke as taught. Hsüeh-feng said, "These words are not yours." The monk admitted that it was Fu-ch'uan who had taught him to say so. Hsüeh-feng said, "I have twenty blows of the rod for you to bring to Fu-ch'uan, reserving twenty blows for myself. This has nothing to do with you."

Fu-ch'uan erred by leaning to the transcendent, while Hsüeh-feng erred by leaning to the immanent. But did Lao-tzu not say, "Know the bright, but cling to the dark?" Hsüeh-feng knew the other shore, but kept to this shore. Oh the trials and agonies of a teacher!

# CHAPTER IX

# Kuei-shan Ling-yu:
## Founder of the
## Kuei-yang House

Kuei-shan Ling-yu (771–853), a disciple of Pai-chang, was the first to found a house of his own. His enlightenment came about in a most unexpected way. One day, as he was waiting upon Pai-chang, the latter asked him to poke the stove, to see whether there was any fire left in it. Kuei-shan poked but found no fire. Pai-chang rose to poke it himself and succeeded in discovering a little spark. Showing it to his disciple, he asked, "Is this not fire?" Thereupon Kuei-shan became enlightened.

This hidden spark of fire may be regarded as the symbol of Kuei-yang Ch'an. By a queer coincidence, the enlightenment of Yang-shan, Kuei-shan's disciple who was destined to be his cofounder of the house, occurred as a result of a dialogue in which the master mentioned the power of the divine spark. On that occasion, Yang-shan's question was about the abiding place of the true Buddha. In reply, Kuei-shan said, "By the ineffable subtlety of thinking without thinking, turn your attention inwards to reflect on the infinite power of the divine spark. When your thinking can go no farther, it returns to its source, where nature and form eternally abide, where phenomenon and noumenon are not dual but one. It is there that abides the suchness of the true Buddha."

The nonduality of the phenomenal and the noumenal corresponds, it seems to me, exactly to Lao-tzu's "mysterious identity" of the *miao* and the *chiao* (the outer and inner). The spiritual spark which is hidden within us corresponds to Lao-tzu's "subtle light" (*wei-ming*) or "inner vision" (*hsuan-lan*).

While both Lin-chi and Kuei-shan were of Taoist affiliations, by temperament Lin-chi was akin to Chuang-tzu, but Kuei and Yang had something of the mellowness and quietness of Lao-tzu.

When a monk asked, "What is Tao?" Kuei-shan replied, "Mindlessness is Tao." The monk said, "I do not comprehend." "All you need is to apprehend the one who does not comprehend!" The monk again asked, "Who is the one who does not comprehend?" Kuei-shan answered, "He is none other than yourself." He further taught, "I wish to see all men now living know how to experience directly their selfhood. Know that the one who does not comprehend is precisely your mind, precisely your Buddha. If you gain bits of knowledge and information from the outside, mistaking them for Ch'an and Tao, you are quite off the mark. This kind of learning is like dumping dross upon your mind rather than purging it of dross. Therefore, I say it is not Tao at all." In the light of this conversation, we can understand clearly what Lao-tzu meant when he declared that "the practice of Tao consists in daily losing."

One of the most significant contributions of the Kuei-yang house to the understanding of Ch'an is the distinction that Yang-shan brought out between Tathāgata Ch'an and Patriarch Ch'an. Once Yang-shan visited his junior co-disciple Hsiang-yen Chih-hsien, and, wishing to test his attainment in Ch'an, asked him to state some of his recent apperceptions. Hsiang-yen composed a gāthā:

> *Last year's poverty was no real poverty:*
> *This year's poverty is poverty indeed.*
> *Poor as I was last year,*
> *I still possessed enough ground to stand an awl on.*
> *This year I am so poor*
> *That I do not even have an awl.*

Yang-shan, however, remarked, "From this I can only say, dear brother, that you have attained the Tathāgata Ch'an. As to the Patriarch Ch'an, you do not seem to have dreamed of it yet." Hsiang-yen then improvised another gāthā:

> *I have an innate aptitude*
> *To look at him by a twinkle.*
> *If anyone does not understand this,*
> *Let him not call himself a śrāmanera!*

This time, Yang-shan was delighted, and reported to Kuei-shan, "I am happy to find that my younger brother Chih-hsien has already attained the Patriarch Ch'an."

If we compare the two gāthās, we should be able to see the distinction between the two orders of Ch'an. The first represents already a high degree in spiritual life, but it belongs still to the stage of faith, meditation, and asceticism, in which one deliberately ponders and applies the precepts and counsels as found in the scriptures. This is called the Tathā-gata Ch'an. The second gāthā is a spontaneous articulation of a direct insight into the inner man who is one's true self. This is what Yang-shan called the "personality stage" as against the "faith stage." It belongs to the order of infused contemplation, a pure spiritual perception without any mixture of conceptual, rational, and ethical elements. The second line— "To look at him by a twinkle"—is the vital core of the gāthā. The original Chinese for "him" here is yi, which corresponds to t'a, na-kuo or "that one" and tz'u or "this." All these terms are used by the Ch'an masters to point to the mysterious self.

Although the inner self is the pivotal point of all houses of Ch'an, it is to the credit of Kuei-yang that it highlighted the divine spark within us by which we can "look at him in a twinkle" and identify ourselves with him. The divine spark or mystic insight is called chi, while the true self is a subsistent being or t'i. All our actions and words after our enlightenment are the functionings or yung of the true self. The true self stands in the same relation to Tao as the ātman to Brahmā.

Another valuable contribution of the Kuei-yang House is that on the one hand it sticks firmly to the axiom of instantaneous enlightenment, but on the other hand it insists upon the necessity of gradual cultivation. Once a monk asked Kuei-shan, "After a man has attained an instantaneous enlightenment, must he still cultivate his spiritual life?" Kuei-shan's answer to this important question is the locus classicus of the union of instantaneous enlightenment and gradual cultivation, which has since become the prevailing doctrine among Buddhist philosophers. It is therefore worth quoting at length:

If a man is truly enlightened and has realized the fundamental, and he is aware of it himself, in such a case he is actually no longer tied to the poles of cultivation and noncultivation. But ordinarily, even though the original mind has been awakened by an intervening cause, so that the man is instantaneously enlightened in his reason and spirit, yet there still remains the inertia of habit, formed since the beginning of time, which cannot be totally eliminated at a stroke. He must be taught to cut off completely the stream of his habitual ideas and views caused by the still operative karmas. This [process of purification] is cultivation. I don't say that he must follow a hard-and-fast special method. He need only be taught the general direction that his cultivation must take. What you hear must first be accepted by your reason; and when your rational understanding is deepened and subtilized in an ineffable way, your mind will of its own spontaneity become comprehensive and bright, never to relapse into the state of doubt and delusion. However numerous and various the subtle teachings are, you know intuitively how to apply them—which to hold in abeyance and which to develop —in accordance with the occasion. In this way only will you be qualified to sit in the chair and wear your robe as a master of the true art of living. To sum up, it is of primary importance to know that Ultimate Reality or the bedrock of reason does not admit of a single speck of dust, while in innumerable doors and paths of action not a single law or thing is to be abandoned. And if you can break through with a single stroke of the sword without more ado, then all the discriminations between the worldly and the saintly are annihilated once for all, and your whole being will reveal the truly eternal, in which reigns the nonduality of universal reason and particular things. This is indeed to be the Bhutatathatā Buddha.

Kuei-shan must have been a born teacher. He was so wise, mellow, and patient in guiding his disciples to attain their perfect enlightenment. One day, as Yang-shan, who was not yet completely enlightened, was picking tea leaves, Kuei-shan said to him, "We have been picking tea leaves all day. I have only heard your voice but have not seen your form. Show your original form that I may see it." Thereupon Yang-shan shook the tea tree. But the master said, "You have only realized the function, not yet the self-substance [being]." "How would you do it, Master?" asked the disciple. The master made no answer but remained silent for a long while, till the disciple interjected, "The master has only realized the self-substance, but not the function." The master only said, "I will release you from twenty strokes of the staff incurred by you."

Of course, the inner self, whether you call it the "self-nature," as the Sixth Patriarch did, or "original face" and "self-substance," is invisible and therefore cannot be shown directly. In shaking the tree, Yang-shan obviously meant to point at his inner self by means of its functioning. But most Ch'an masters preferred to evoke it by silence or retiring quickly. Here Yang-shan did not commit a serious error. But when he said that his master had only realized his inner self without realizing its function, his error was a substantial one. As function is implicit in substance, there can really be no substance without function. This was why the master thought his disciple deserved twenty strokes of his staff, which however he was willing to remit.

This leads us to another charming characteristic of the Kuei-yang Ch'an. The masters of this house, so far as the records show, seldom resorted to beating or even shouting in training their disciples. The only instance of a somewhat violent treatment happened to Yang-shan. One day, Kuei-shan said to his assembly, "Ah, so many persons have only got great potentialities, which have not flowered into great actions." Yang-shan did not understand and went to ask the prior of a monastery below the mountain, saying, "The abbot taught thus, and so what could be his meaning?" The prior requested him to repeat the question. As Yang-shan was beginning to repeat it, the prior stamped upon him so that he fell on the ground. When he returned to the mountain, he reported his experience to Kuei-shan. This so tickled the master's sense of humor that he broke into loud laughter.

Anyway it is doubtful if the said prior belonged to the House of Kuei-yang. So far as Kuei-shan was concerned, he was only humorous enough to laugh over his disciple's painful experience, but apparently not enough of an athlete to administer the kicking or beating.

Kuei-shan's paternal mildness was, however, only a veneer for the fire-eater and iconoclast underneath. One day as Kuei-shan was sitting, Yang-shan came into his room. The master said, "My son, say something immediately; only do not enter the shadowy realms." By this he meant that his disciple should utter an insight without however being glued to mere words and concepts. Yang-shan, sensing the master's meaning, replied, "I do not even formulate my creed." The master asked, "Do you believe in a creed, which you refuse to formulate, or is it that you really believe in no creed and therefore you have nothing to formulate?" Yang-shan answered, "Whom else can I believe than my inner self?" The master said, "In that case, you are a śrāvaka of a set mind." Yang-shan replied, "I see no Buddha." Finally, Kuei-shan asked, "In the forty rolls of the *Mahāparinirvāṇa Sūtra*, how many words are the Buddha's and how many the demon's?" Yang-shan's answer was: "All words belong to the demon!" The master was so delighted by this answer that he said to his disciple, "Hereafter, nobody will be able to do anything to you!"

This reminds me of what Justice Holmes once said to me, "In any system of philosophy its basic ideas are comparatively simple and easy to understand, but words are the devil!" If only we do not forget that "words are the devil," we should be able to enjoy reading without any danger of being entangled in the intricate network of words and concepts.

It seems to me that Yang-shan is even more subtle than his master. One day the two were out in the fields. Kuei-shan remarked, "Those fields are higher than these." Yang-shan said, "No, these are higher than those." "If you don't believe my observation," said Kuei-shan, "let us stand at the middle point and look at the two sides from there." Yang-shan replied: "It is not necessary to stand at the middle any more than stick to either side." The master then suggested, "Let us then gauge the relative heights by reference to the water level, for nothing is more even than water." To this the disciple replied, "But water has no fixed level either. In a higher place, it forms a higher level, and in a lower place, a lower level. That's all." The old man let the conversation drop at that.

The style of the House of Kuei-yang has a charm of its own. It is not as steep and sharp-edged as the houses of Lin-chi and Yün-men, nor as close-knit and resourceful as the House of Ts'ao-tung, nor as speculative and broad as the House of Fa-yen. But it has a greater depth than the others. The story of the enlightenment of Hsiang-yen is quite typical. Hsiang-yen was originally a novice under Pai-chang; he was exceptionally brilliant and quick-witted, strong in analytical power and logical acumen, and versed in the scriptures. But he was not initiated into Ch'an. At the death of Pai-chang, he made himself a disciple of Pai-chang's senior disciple Kuei-shan. Kuei-shan said to him, "I hear that when you were with our late Master Pai-chang, you could give ten answers to a single question.

. . . This shows your remarkable intelligence and ingenuity, which enables you to understand ideas and unfold their consequences. Now the question of birth and death is the most fundamental of all. Try to tell me something about your state before you were born of your parents." This question plunged his mind into a thick fog. He did not even know what to think. Returning to his room, he made a feverish search in all the books that he had read for something appropriate to say in answer to the question; but he could not find a single sentence that could be used. So he sighed to himself, saying, "As the saying goes, a painted cake satisfies not the hunger." After that, he pressed his master time and time again to break the secret to him by speaking explicitly. Every time, Kuei-shan said, "If I should expound it explicitly for you, in future you will reproach me for it. Anyway, whatever I speak still belongs to me, and has nothing to do with you."

In his despair, Hsiang-yen burnt all his books, saying, "In this life I will not study the Buddha dharma any more. Let me become a mendicant monk ever on the move from one place to another." He took leave of his master weeping. His wandering brought him to the ruins of a temple in Nan-yang associated with the memory of Master Hui-chung. There he made his temporary abode. One day as he was mowing and cutting the grass and trees, he tossed at random a piece of broken tile, which happened to hit a bamboo tree, causing it to emit a crisp sound. Startled by the unexpected sound, he was suddenly awakened to his true self not born with his birth. Returning to his cell, he bathed himself and lit incense to pay his long-distance obeisance to Kuei-shan, saying, "O Venerable Abbot, how great is your compassion! I am grateful to you more than to my parents. If you had broken the secret to me then, how could I have experienced the wonderful event of today?"

I sometimes wonder how many promising talents have been nipped in the bud, simply because their master had overdone their explanation of a subject, whose mastery depends by its very nature upon an experiential realization. Great as Kuei-shan was in what he expressed, he was greater in what he left unsaid.

The House of Kuei-yang lasted only for five generations. But certainly its spirit is not dead, and many of its profound insights have become property of all students of Ch'an. I myself have found great delight in the subtle humor and quiet conversations between master and disciple. For example, in a certain year, Yang-shan, after his summer retreat, came to pay a visit to his master Kuei-shan. The master asked, "My son, I have not seen you for the whole summer. What works did you accomplish down there?" Yang-shan: "Well, I have tilled a strip of land and planted a basket of seeds." The benign master said, "Then you have not passed this summer in idleness." Yang-shan in turn asked the master what he had been doing during the summer. Kuei-shan said, "Taking a meal at midday, sleeping in the night." "So you too, Master, have not passed this summer in idleness." Having said this, it came home to him how ironic the words sounded; so he stretched out his tongue, as some people do when they have unwittingly committed a faux pas in social intercourse. Noting his disciple's embarrassment, Kuei-shan said reproachfully, "My son, why should you deal such a fatal blow to your own life?" To feel embarrassed for having made a remark which is in perfect accord with the Ch'an scale of values is to show that one's outlook is still somewhat mixed with the utilitarianism of the worldlings; it is to forget, at least momentarily, the one thing necessary, being still unconsciously nostalgic for activities which are really much ado about nothing. Certainly there was no occasion for stretching the tongue, and just as certainly there was occasion for the reproach. The words of reproach were pretty severe, but they were spoken in a mild and humorous manner. Still waters run deep.

In the later utterances of Yang-shan, after he had become abbot, we can see how deeply imbued he was with the spirit and teachings of Kuei-shan. The following passage, taken from one of his conferences, is a veritable epitome of the style and thought of the Kuei-yang House:

Let each and every one of you turn the light inwards upon himself and not try to memorize my words. Since time without beginning, you have turned your back upon the light and run after darkness. The habits of erroneous thinking are so deep-rooted in you that it would be extremely difficult to uproot them overnight. This is why one is compelled to resort to the use of make-believe expedients, in order to strip you of your crude ways of thinking. This is on a par with what a parent sometimes would do in order to stop his little child from crying— giving him some yellow leaves, making believe that they are precious coins. It's also like a man setting up a store stocked with all kinds of goods for daily use as well as articles of gold and jade, to accommodate customers of different abilities. As I have often said, Shih-t'ou's is a gold shop, while mine is a general store, selling all and sundry. If someone wishes to buy rat's excrement, I will sell him rat's excrement; and if he wishes to buy an article of pure gold, I will sell him an article of pure gold. . . . But business depends on the demand. If there is no demand, there is no business. If I deal only with the essence of Ch'an, I would be left all alone. Even a single companion would be hard to get, to say nothing of a community of five or seven hundred monks. If, on the other hand, I talk about things of east and west, people would come in flocks pricking up their ears to catch every bit of my tales. That would be like showing an empty fist to little children pretending that there are candies in it. This is just humbug. Now let me tell you in all plainness: Do not divert your mind to the holy things, rather direct it to your self-nature and cultivate yourself with your feet solidly on the ground. Do not desire the "three gifts of vision" and the "six supernatural powers." Why? Because these are only accidentals of holiness. The one thing essential now is to recollect your mind to attain the fundamental, the very root of your being. Having arrived at the root, you need have no worry about the accidentals. In time you will find that you are self-provided with all these accidental gifts and powers. On the other hand, so long as you have not got at the root, you will not be able to acquire such gifts and powers through study and learning.

# CHAPTER X

# Tung-shan Liang-chieh:
## Founder of the
## Ts'ao-tung House

Ts'ao-tung House of Ch'an was founded jointly by Tung-shan Liang-chieh (807–869) and his disciple Ts'ao-shan Pen-chi (840–901). It has been called Ts'ao-tung rather than Tung-ts'ao, not because the disciple was more important than the master, but because the mountain where the disciple later resided as abbot was named by him Ts'ao-shan in honor of the Sixth Patriarch, who used to reside in Ts'ao-ch'i. Hence the name Ts'ao-tung.

Tung-shan was born into a Yü family of Kuei-chi in present Chekiang. In his tender years he joined a Buddhist monastery as a novice. The master taught him to recite the *Pan-jo Hsin-ching (Prajñā Hridaya Sūtra)*; but when he came to the sentence: "There is no eye, ear, nose, tongue, body, or mind," he suddenly put his hand on his face and asked his master, "I do have eyes, ears, nose, tongue, and so forth; how, then, can the sūtra say that there are no such things?" The master was amazed by this unexpected question and began to marvel at the boy's matter-of-factness.

This little incident is quite significant. The boy did not show any precocity in spiritual understanding. But at least he did show that independence of mind which is so indispensable to a seeker of Truth. Ordinary pupils of those days were all too apt to assume that nothing found in the sacred scriptures could be wrong; but the young Tung-shan refused to be hoodwinked by any man or any book. This evidently was what made the master marvel and say, "I am not the teacher for you!"

He was professed in his early twenties. As usual, his profession was

followed by a period of journeying to different centers of Buddhist learning and calling on different masters for their instructions. The first one
whom Tung-shan visited was Nan-ch'üan, the beloved disciple of the late
Ma-tsu. The visit happened to fall on the eve of an anniversary of Ma-tsu's
decease. In a regular gathering, Nan-ch'üan asked his monks, "Tomorrow
we are going to make offerings to Ma-tsu. I wonder if Ma-tsu will come.
What do you think?" The whole community remained silent. Only Tung-
shan came forward and said, "He will come as soon as he finds his
companion." Profoundly impressed by the young visitor, Nan-ch'üan remarked, "Although this man is still a youth, he is excellent material to
carve and polish." "Let not the Venerable Abbot," said Tung-shan, "debase
a free man into a slave!" Here again he showed his spirit of independence
and, besides, some idea of the inner self, which cannot be carved and
needs no polishing.

He next visited Kuei-shan (771–853), and wished him to enlighten
him on the question of whether it is true that the inanimate things expound the Dharma, and, if so, how is it that we do not hear their expounding. After some discussions, Kuei-shan finally said, "The mouth
which my parents gave me will never explain it to you." Somewhat puz-
zled, he asked Kuei-shan whether he knew another lover of Tao whom he
could consult. At Kuei-shan's recommendation, Tung-shan went to see
Yün-yen (782–841), to whom he put the question point-blank, "When the
inanimate beings expound the Dharma, who can hear it?" "The inanimate
can," was the immediate reply of Yün-yen. Tung-shan again asked, "Do
you hear?" "If I did," said Yün-yen, "you would not hear my expounding of
the Dharma." Tung-shan was still skeptical as to whether the inanimate
beings could really expound the Dharma. Yün-yen then raised his dust
whisk, asking, "Do you hear it?" "No, I do not hear," Tung-shan answered.
Thereupon Yün-yen said, "If you do not even hear my sermon, how can
you expect to hear the sermon of the inanimate beings?" And he added,
"Have you not read in the *Amitābha Buddha Sūtra*: 'Streams, birds, and trees
are all chanting Buddha and Dharma?'" At that point Tung-shan was made
aware of the truth, and composed a gāthā to record his experience:

> *How wonderful! How wonderful!*
> *The inanimate expounding the Dharma—*
> *What an ineffable truth!*

*If you try to hear it with your ears,*
*You will never understand it.*
*Only when you hear it through the eye,*
*Will you really know it.*

Yün-yen asked him, "Are you happy now?" His answer shows his usual candor: "I do not say that I am not happy, but my happiness is like that of someone who has picked up a bright pearl from a heap of garbage." The bright pearl referred, of course, to the new insight; as to the heap of garbage, very probably he had in mind the remnants of old habits which, as he confessed, were still in him.

Later when Tung-shan bade farewell to his master, the latter remarked affectionately, "After this separation, it will be hard for us to see each other." "Rather it will be hard for us not to see each other!" replied the disciple. Again he asked the master, "After you have completed this life, what shall I say if anyone asks, can you still recall your master's true face?" The master remained silent for a long while and then replied, "Just *this one* is." This set the disciple to musing. Finally, the master said, "In carrying out this charge, exercise your utmost circumspection and care."

While on his journey, Tung-shan continued to muse on the cryptic words of the master: "Just *this one* is." Later on in crossing a stream, he happened to see his own reflection in the water, and right on the spot he was thoroughly awakened to the real meaning of "Just *this one* is." He epitomized the experience in a gāthā:

*Do not seek him anywhere else!*
*Or he will run away from you!*
*Now that I go on all alone,*
*I meet him everywhere.*
*He is even now what I am.*
*I am even now not what he is.*
*Only by understanding this way*
*Can there be a true union with the Self-So.*

The term I have rendered here as "self-so" is *ju-ju,* which is the same as *chen-ju,* the Chinese for the Sanskrit Bhutatathatā. It is "self-subsistent suchness," "thusness," or "eternal that." It corresponds to the eternal Tao of the *Tao-te Ching,* to the Brahmā in Hinduism, and to the "I-Am-That-I-Am" of the Old Testament. The most significant couplet of this remarkable gāthā is:

> *He is even now what I am:*
> *I am even now not what he is.*

Clearly there is a subtle distinction between the "I" and the "he." He is I, but I am not he. This is like saying that God is more myself than myself, although I am not God. There is the same relation between the "I" and the "he" as between atman and Brahmā, and between the true man of Tao and eternal Tao.

This gāthā is one of the most precious gems, not only in Buddhism, but in the spiritual literature of the whole world. It presents a vision, a living experience, with authenticity written all over its face. Transparent yet profound, it reminds us of Tu Fu's:

> *"How limpid the autumn waters, and with no bottom."*

In this gāthā, you still see the same old independent and matter-of-fact Tung-shan with his vision lifted to a new height. He is alone and yet in company. He has attained oneness, yet it is a oneness not unrelieved by a refreshing diversity. His ethereal vision does not prevent him from walking on solid ground. And his contemplation of the eternal self-so has led him back to the here and now.

When his wandering took him to Le-tan, he saw the assembly leader Ch'u, who used to say:

> *Oh, how wonderful, how wonderful!*
> *The ineffable realms of Buddha and Tao!*

Tung-shan remarked, "I would not ask about the realms of Buddha and Tao. I only wish to know the man who is speaking of the realms of Buddha and Tao." Further on, he said, "Buddha and Tao are but names and words; why don't you resort to the true doctrine?" When Ch'u asked, "What does the true doctrine teach?" Tung-shan replied, "When you have got at the idea, forget about the words." This was a quotation from the book of Chuang-tzu. It is remarkable that Tung-shan should have introduced a quotation from Chuang-tzu. This bespeaks his catholicity and reveals the close affinity between Ch'an and Tao.

Around 860, when he was in his early fifties he became an abbot on Tung-shan Mountain in present Chiang-hsi. (Like so many other cases he has been called by the name of the mountain where he taught.) On an anniversary of Yün-yen's decease, a monk asked Tung-shan, "Abbot, when you were with Yün-yen, what particular instructions and directions did you receive from him?" Tung-shan replied, "Although I was in his community, he neither directed nor instructed me." "This being the case," asked the monk, "why do you make offerings to him?" "Well," said the abbot, "I revere my late master not for his virtue and learning, but because he did not break the secret to me." Then the monk asked him whether he agreed with all the teachings of his late master. "I accept half and reject half," the abbot replied. "Why not accept the whole?" the monk asked, and the abbot explained, "If I did, I should be unworthy of my late master." Evidently, his growing age had not lessened his spirit of independence. In fact, it was a part of Ch'an traditions that a disciple must prove smarter than his master before the latter could transmit the lamp to him.

When a monk asked, "On cold days and hot days, where can we betake ourselves to avoid the coldness or the heat?" the abbot asked back, "Why don't you go to a place where there is neither coldness nor heat?" "What kind of place is it?" "When it is cold, you are frozen to death. When it is hot, you are roasted to death." This dialogue serves to show what a patient and subtle teacher Tung-shan was. In his hands, even a silly question could be turned into a springboard for the ocean of mystical wisdom.

Tung-shan was equable in temper, never resorting to shouts or beatings. Nor did he resort to the mind-teasing *kung-ans*. His dialogues are simple yet profound. They are like olives: the more you chew at them the better they taste. For instance, a monk asked him whether it was true that the late master Yün-yen had once said, "Just *this one* is." The abbot answered, "Yes." "Do you believe that he knew that *there is*?" asked the monk again. The abbot replied, "If he did not know that *there is*, how could he speak of it as he did? If, on the other hand, he knew that *there is*, why did he force himself to speak of it at all?" "This one" of course refers to the true self, and "there is" (in Chinese, *yu*) is a common expression in Ch'an literature, to designate pure being or reality. Strictly speaking, neither the true self nor pure being could be expressed in words. On the one hand, one is aware that the true self or pure being *is*; on the other hand, it is essentially inexpressible in words, and even the phrase "this one" is already an intruder. This, I imagine, is what Tung-shan meant to suggest to

the mind of his questioner. But being a great master of the Ch'an peda-
gogy, he refrained from stating his views plainly and resorted to the use of
questions in order to stimulate his pupil to think and find the answer for
himself. One answer that a student finds for himself is worth more than a
hundred answers hammered into his head by a teacher.

Anyone who deals with the teachings of Tung-shan and his house will
soon notice the doctrine of the "five positions of prince and minister."
This doctrine and others like it are not of central importance in the
teaching of Tung-shan's school. They are merely expedient means or ped-
agogical schemata for the guidance of the less intelligent students. It is
regrettable that historians of Ch'an have a tendency to treat these inci-
dentals as essentials and to ignore the true essentials altogether.

With this necessary reminder, let me give a brief account of the doctrine of "five positions." (In fact, there are various ways of formulating
them. Tung-shan has one way, while Ts'ao-shan has another.) As Tung-
shan presented them, the five positions are (1) the noumenal hidden
under the phenomenal, (2) the phenomenal pointing to the noumenal, (3)
the noumenal entering consciously into the phenomenal, (4) the two
arriving at a harmony, and (5) reaching the heart of the harmony.

These five positions were meant to indicate the progressive stages or
degrees of spiritual life and enlightenment. In the first stage, the student is
more or less unaware of the noumenal in him and directs his attention to
the phenomenal. Instead of being the host that he virtually is, he remains
a guest. But as in reality the noumenal and the phenomenal form a continuous whole or, in the words of Lao-tzu, a "mysterious identity," even a
one-sided attention to the phenomenal and a serious study of its laws and
interrelations may turn out to be a useful preparation for soaring into the
heights and diving into the depths. Besides, no one can study the phenomenal for long without becoming gradually aware of the part that his
mind plays and contributes. The discovery of the subjective element in
the objective is the beginning of self-discovery. So, too, on the moral
plane, one begins by behaving conformably to the prevailing customs of
his community, regarding them as sacred and universally applicable to all
men everywhere. But as he grows in experience he comes to discover that
the familiar is not necessarily right, nor the unfamiliar necessarily wrong.
Bewildered for a moment by the phenomenon of conflicting moral standards, he is inevitably driven to turn inwards to himself and to seek

guidance in reason and conscience. In this way, he becomes more and more aware that essentially he is a free man rather than a slave. But on all planes, the old habits die hard.

Tung-shan's characterization of this first "rank" is as follows:

> *The noumenal hidden under the phenomenal!*
> *In the dusk of early evening, before the moon has risen,*
> *It is little wonder if you fail to recognize the person you meet.*
> *Dimly, dimly, you approach him as a stranger with your habitual*
> *suspiciousness.*

In the second stage, we see the phenomenal moving to the noumenal. It is a centripetal movement. The light has dawned in you, and as you see your old friend clearly, you have no more dim fears and suspicions bred in you by painful experiences in the past, when you used to be betrayed by people whom you foolishly took for friends but who turned out to be thieves and robbers. You are disillusioned with the world of illusions and at the same time awakened to the real and immutable. This stage is marked by the crucial experience of enlightenment or *satori*. Tung-shan's poetic characterization of it is both clear and interesting:

> *The phenomenal moving to the noumenal!*
> *The dawn has come to the surprise of an old woman,*
> *And she chances upon an antique mirror, in which she sees*
> *Clearly and distinctly her own face, so different from all the images she*
> *had formed of herself!*
> *From now on, she will no longer ignore her own head*
> *And grasp at its mere shadows.*

Having been enlightened in the second stage, a man becomes what he really is, a true man, a free man, a host and a prince. He is now definitely in the "personality stage." He may be called a "noumenal man." Now, let the noumenal man come back to the phenomenal world to work and teach for the sake of his fellow beings. This third stage is called "coming from the noumenal." The man who thus comes is in the world but not of it. Tung-shan put it thus:

> *Coming from the noumenal!*
> *In a cloud of dust he follows a secret road beyond the reach of dust.*

*He excels in keeping unsaid things tabooed at present.*
*Yet he says more than the most eloquent tongues of the past.*

In other words, coming from the noumenal, he realizes how impossible it is to convey in words things he has personally experienced and intimately known to persons who are still in the first stage, and how misleading it would be to them if he were to offer them some neat and easily memorized formulas in lieu of the real thing. This is why the Ch'an masters have mostly followed the via negativa and an esoteric approach far from the beaten track. Sometimes, they resort to interesting parables and very original and striking figures of speech. Even shouts and beatings and nonsensical answers to sensible questions have been preferred to cut-and-dried definitions and systematic presentations, which would only create an illusion of certainty and lull people to sleep. The Ch'an master, at least the greatest among them, had only one aim in mind: to rouse the dormant potentialities of the pupils, to make them think for themselves and be the men that they are. As to whether they have used the best means is another question.

When an enlightened man has penetrated deeply into the phenomenal world, he feels more at home in the world than in the third stage till he realizes that kleśa is nothing else than bodhi. He comes to know experientially what he already realized in his intellect, that the phenomenal and the noumenal are essentially one. He comes to see that both the noumenal and the phenomenal belong to the realm of relativity, and not the Absolute. It stands to reason that the source, the "mysterious whole," from which, as Lao-tzu pointed out, both the *miao* (the noumenal) and the *chiao* (the phenomenal) spring out, is prior to and greater than either of them. Actually the noumenal and the phenomenal constitute one single stream flowing from the Ultimate Source. The very words *noumenal* and *phenomenal* are but tags invented by the human mind, and therefore there are no real distinctions between them. The enlightened man is not just his noumenal self but an integral whole of the noumenal and the phenomenal. Therefore, he does not aspire to the noumenal, but to something infinitely higher and deeper at the same time, the ne plus ultra. This point will be clearer to us if we read carefully Tung-shan's characterization:

*The noumenal and the phenomenal coming together!*
*There is no need to avoid their crossed swords!*

*The experienced soldier blooms like the magical lotus amidst fire,*
*While all the time his heroic wishes pierce beyond the skies.*

In the final stage, one reaches the heart of the union of the noumenal and the phenomenal. At the heart, the union turns into a unity. In the fourth stage, there is still the aspiration soaring beyond the cosmos. That stage may therefore be called "meia-cosmic." This stage, on the other hand, is "trans-meta-cosmic." Having soared to the transcendental, the man must now return to this noumenal-phenomenal world. In the fourth stage, he was heroic; in the present stage, he finds heaven on earth, and to him even the most ordinary things in life are heavenly. As Tung-shan put it:

> *Lo, he has arrived at supreme unity!*
> *Beyond the "is" and the "is not."*
> *Who dares to follow the rhymes of his poetry?*
> *Let others aspire to the extraordinary!*
> *He is happy to return home and sit amidst ashes!*

"To sit amidst ashes" is to be enveloped in complete darkness. That this should have been put by Tung-shan at the very summit of such a wonderful pilgrimage of the spirit may at first sight appear rather strange if not disappointing. What an anticlimax it would seem to be! But to anyone who is acquainted with the testimonies of great mystics of the world, it would be surprising if his final finding were different from what he actually found and recorded. Here his remarkable matter-of-factness has stood him in good stead even in the rarefied sphere of high mysticism. He is in the company of Lao-tzu, Chuang-tzu, Plotinus, Meister Eckhart, and John of the Cross. "Knowing yet unknowing is the highest," Lao-tzu had declared, and all the masters of Dark Truth have echoed him. Tung-shan's charcoal or ashes is but a symbol of Dark Truth. On another occasion, he referred to it in these words: "Something there is: it is the prop of the sky above and the earth below, it is black like lacquer, it is perpetually in movement and activity." This sounds like a riddle. Actually it is more than a riddle, it is none other than Tao, the mystery of mysteries.

Tung-shan has given us another somewhat different sketch of the five stages, under a new set of names: (1) *hsiang*, or admiration, attraction, or aspiration, (2) *feng*, or willing submission, (3) *kung*, or fruition, (4) *k'ung kung,* or multiple fruition, and (5) *kung kung,* or the fruition of fruition. Evidently, this was a chart for the spiritual direction of his disciples.

In the initial stage of hsiang, the master must be the kind of person whose conduct and wisdom can inspire love and admiration in his disciples, so that they too may aspire to his ideals. Tung-shan poetized this stage thus:

> *All holy rulers have patterned themselves upon Emperor Yao,*
> *Who treated his people with respect and humility.*
> *Whenever he passed by crowded markets and streets,*
> *He was hailed by all his people for his benevolent government.*

In the political world, this would be the peak of achievement. But in the spiritual order, this is but the beginning, the initial attraction.

In the stage of feng, the disciple is expected to embrace wholeheartedly sober meditation and strict discipline. The first fervor must now be turned into a steady fire. Tung-shan poetized it thus:

> *"For whom have you stripped yourself of your gorgeous dress?"*
> *"The cuckoo's call is urging all wanderers to return home!"*
> *Even after all the flowers have fallen, it will continue its call*
> *In the thickets of wood among the jagged peaks.*

This stanza needs a little annotation. In the first line we find the novice already started on the lifelong job of living, of being himself. He has cleansed himself of all his colorful adornments. For whom has he done it? His answer is found in the second line: he has done so certainly not because the master has pressed him, but simply because a mysterious voice has been urging him to return home. This mysterious voice is symbolized by the cuckoo's cry. In the poetical lore of China, the cuckoo's note sounds like *ch'ui kuei* (time to return home), so that on hearing it the wanderer becomes homesick. But whose voice is it? It might be the voice of a brother, a sister, a lover, a friend, or even a parent. Anyway, it is the voice of someone very intimate to you, who has a selfless concern about you, warning you against your aimless wanderings which, to put it moderately, can lead you nowhere. It is not a stern voice speaking categorically, but a gentle voice like the refreshing breeze in a hot summer day. It is all the more irresistible for its tenderness. But whose voice is it?

The disciple in this stage, however, is more interested in the message than in the messenger. He is still in the "faith stage," not yet in the "personality stage." The message is the call to return home. But monks have called themselves home-leavers. Is the cuckoo calling them to return to the homes they have left? That's impossible. Then where is the home the voice is calling them to return to? The home is within you. Recollection is the beginning of the interior life.

In the last two lines, the veteran master is telling the novices they are not the only wanderers who need to be reminded of the home, for in a sense even the most advanced in the life of the spirit are still on the way. This prospect does not make the novice falter: rather, it consoles him by making him realize that in his journey home he is not alone but in good company.

This leads us to the third stage, the stage of first fruition. This is a period of rest and delight. The rest is well earned, but the delight is a surprising boon. Tung-shan's poem itself breathes rest and delight:

> The withered tree flowers into a new spring far, far away from time's
>     kingdom.
> The hunter of the unicorn rides backwards on a jade white elephant.
> Carefree, he makes his lofty home now beyond the myriad peaks,
> Where clear moon and pure breeze fill him with happy days.

This scene is too beautiful and quiet! Any comment on my part would only soil it. Only the second line needs a little elucidation. The jade white elephant symbolizes the Tao in motion and operation. The unicorn is the Tao as the ultimate goal. Now the pursuer of Tao has entered on the path of fruitful passivity, letting the Tao direct the course instead of trying to direct the course of Tao. The "reverse ride" evokes the idea of a childlike trustfulness, which is the soul of the passive way.

Now we come to the stage of reinforced fruition. In the preceding stage, it was the flowering of the withered tree that created a spring for itself; and it was in the clouds that the man made his home. In the present stage, we find the new spring spreading to the three realms, as the following stanza shows:

> There is no conflict between the Buddhas and all the living beings.
> The mountains are of themselves high as waters are of themselves low.
> All distinctions in kind or in degree—what do they prove?
> Wherever the partridge cries, flowers of all kinds are blooming afresh!

This stanza may be called a poetic epitome of Chuang-tzu's marvellous essay on "The Leveling of All Things." Tung-shan has elsewhere declared, "Only he who knows that there is a man beyond Buddha can participate in this discourse." When a monk asked him who that "Buddha-transcending man" is, the master answered, "Not Buddha." In the eyes of that man, there could be no important difference between all the Buddhas and other beings. This is the message of the first line. In the second line, the keynote is in the words "of themselves." It is none of your business that the mountains are high and the waters are deep. You are not called upon to interfere with their intrinsic qualities. You are not even warranted in passing judgment upon them or making any discriminations between them. Who are you to judge another's servants? Or, rather, what entitles you to turn subjects into objects of your judgment? Do not render to another what you would not like to have rendered to yourself.

But since you are now free of discriminating tendencies and habits, you are like the partridge which calls all kinds of flowers into blooming afresh.

The last and fifth stage is called "the fruition of fruition." Let us recall that in the third stage you came to fruition alone, and in the fourth you and the world came to fruition together. But Tung-shan would not stop even there! Like a lark in the morning, he continues to soar till he can soar no more. Nor can he report in positive terms his experience this time:

> *As soon as your antennae begin to stir, it is already an intolerable misery.*
> *The slightest intention to pursue Buddhahood is a cause for shame.*
> *In the endless empty eons nobody has ever intimately known*
> *That which journeyed south visiting fifty-three enlightened ones.*

What an agonizing ideal of perfection is here presented! Even the hardly felt first motions of self-complacency and self-seeking are to be nipped in the bud. However, the tension of the first couplet is relieved in the second couplet. If we do not have a clear and intimate knowledge of our true self, we can console ourselves with the fact that nobody else since the beginning of time has actually known him. Or perhaps he does not stand in front of us to be an object of our knowledge? Then he is not for us *to know* but for us *to be.*

The very fact that Tung-shan should have placed this stanza at the summit of spirituality shows that he is of the same mind with Lo-han Kuei-ch'eng who was to declare, "Unknowing is the greatest intimacy!"

In this connection, let me quote what Thomas Merton has written on Chuang-tzu. "Chuang-tzu," he writes, "looked on life as a whole—and as a mystery—that could not be grasped merely in a clear doctrine, with logical explanations of the ways things are, implemented by orderly social customs and patterns of behaviour. He reached out for something more, something which could not be expressed, and yet could be *lived:* the ineffable Tao" (introduction to *The Way of Chuang-tzu*, in manuscript). As Tung-shan was in the lineage of Shih-t'ou, whose affinity with Chuang-tzu is well known, it is little wonder that these words from Merton on Chuang-tzu seem to fit Tung-shan so well.

Tung-shan's ultimate ideal transcends even enlightenment. As he wrote:

> *Wonderful is the eternal reality*
> *Beyond delusion and enlightenment.*

It is beyond all intermutabilities or polarities, such as host and guest, the noumenal and the phenomenal, silence and speech, the via positiva and the via negativa, action and nonaction, subitism and gradualism, motion and rest, the inner and the outer. To illustrate the subtlety of his thought, a single sample will suffice:

> *"True eternity emerges in an endless flow."*

Many of his subtlest ideas are to be found in his long gāthā which he presented to his disciple Ts'ao-shan on transmitting the Dharma seal to him. However, these ideas belong to speculative philosophy, not to mystical realization. For they are mostly idealistic aspirations, not experiential insights like those embodied in the gāthā on the occasion of his enlightenment. In the gāthā to Ts'ao-shan, the most interesting couplet is found near the conclusion:

> *Keep your good deeds hidden and your function secret;*
> *That you may appear as a stupid and dull-witted man.*

From this you can see what a practical and shrewd teacher Tung-shan was! Not only the mystical insights of Lao-tzu but also his practical roguishness seems to run in the blood of this great master of Ch'an!

Superficially, his constant recurrence to the five stages of spiritual life might seem to run counter to the spirit of his great ancestor Ch'ing-yüan, who had no use for stages and degrees. Yet, we should remember that in the hands of Tung-shan they were avowedly used as expedients of teaching. So long as they are regarded as temporary devices, they have their proper place in eternal reality. It is only when they are mistaken for eternal categories that they become as obtrusive as a sore finger.

Tung-shan was above all a great teacher with his attention wholly on the needs of his disciples. He remained a selfless teacher up to the very end of his earthly life. The scene of his last days is most touching. Sometime in the spring of the year 869, he fell sick. A monk asked him, "While you are sick, is there still someone who is never sick?" He replied, "There is." "Does the never-sick one look at you?" "Rather it is for this old monk to look at him." "How do you look at him?" "When this old monk is looking, I see no sickness anywhere." This was a Ch'anish way of saying that the never-sick one is none other than his true self. To put it in another way, only his *nirmāṇakāya* (transformation form) is sick, while his *dharmakāya* remains healthy and whole and, being unborn, cannot die. When he felt it was time for him to go, he had his head shaved, took a bath, put on his robe, rang the bell to bid farewell to the community, and sat up till he breathed no more. To all appearances he had died. Thereupon the whole community burst out crying grievously as little children do at the death of their mother. Suddenly the master opened his eyes and said to the weeping monks, "We leavers of homes are supposed to be detached from all things transitory. In this consists true spiritual life. To live is to work, to die is to rest. What is the use of grieving and moaning?" He then ordered a "stupidity-purifying meal" for the whole community. Sensing that their beloved master meant to leave them after that liturgical meal, they were not in a particular hurry to eat it. So they took seven days to prepare it. The master participated in the meal with them. After the meal, he said to them, "Please make no fuss over me! Be calm, as befitting a family of monks! Generally speaking, when anyone is at the point of going, he has no use for noise and commotion." Thereupon he returned to the abbot's room, where he sat up as in meditation till he passed away. It is interesting to see how he kept his spirit of independence and matter-of-factness right up to the end.

# CHAPTER XI

# Lin-chi I-hsüan:
## Founder of the Lin-chi House

In Lin-chi I-hsüan we encounter a man utterly down to earth, a solid character and an eager pursuer of truth. He came from a Hsing family in present Shantung. We do not know the year of his birth, although it is fairly certain that he died in 866 or the following year. Perhaps it was in the early years of the ninth century that he was born.

From the standpoint of natural endowment, Lin-chi was a typical northerner. As a young monk he was an earnest and plodding pilgrim in the way of perfection, with pietist inclinations. Even though his enlightenment was sudden, he had had to work toward the point the hard way.

He was already a fully ordained monk when he began to feel an attraction for Ch'an. Probably in his twenties he joined the community of the master Huang-po in what is today the province of Anhwei. At that time Mu-chou Tao-ming was the leader of the community. He was impressed by the purity of Lin-chi's character and conduct and kept an eye on him for a long time. When he thought that the time had come, he approached Lin-chi, asking, "How long has Your Reverence been here?" "Three years," replied Lin-chi. "Have you ever presented a question to the abbot?" "No. I have never done so because I do not even know what to ask." "Why don't you ask the abbot to explain to you the essential principles of Buddhism?" Following the suggestion, Lin-chi went to put the question before the abbot. Hardly had he finished with his question when Huang-po struck him with his staff. When Lin-chi came back, Mu-chou asked him, "How did he answer the question?" Lin-chi told him what had happened, adding that he really could not make heads or tails of the abbot's unaccountable action. Mu-chou again egged him on to repeat the question. Lin-chi did as before, and once again he was beaten. Mu-chou pressed him for the third time, and, believing that he might have better luck, Lin-chi asked the question for the third time, but he was beaten for the third time. Thereupon Lin-chi made up his mind that he had had enough of this nonsense and that it was time for him to leave the place for good. Even then he did not lose either his temper or his manners. He confided his decision to Mu-chou, saying, "I appreciate your instigating and urging me to ask about the Buddha dharma. Repeatedly the abbot has deigned to bestow his beatings upon me. I only regret that due to some obstructive karma of my own making I have not been able to comprehend the profound doctrine. There's nothing left for me to do but to leave." Mu-chou said, "Before you go away, it is proper that you should take leave of the abbot." Lin-chi bowed and retired. In the meantime, Mu-chou lost no time in coming to the abbot, whispering to him, "The monk who asked the questions, although he is still young, is an extraordinary man. When he comes to take leave, please receive him tactfully. In the future he is destined to be a towering tree, which will cast its salutary shadows upon mankind." When Lin-chi came to take leave of the abbot, the latter said, "You need not go to other places. Just go to the river bank at Kao-an to consult Ta-yü, and I am sure he will tell you everything."

When Lin-chi came to Ta-yü, the latter asked where he had come from, to which he answered that he had come from Huang-po's place. Ta-yü then asked, "What instructions have you received from Huang-po?" Lin-chi replied, "Three times I inquired about the essentials of the Buddha dharma, and three times I was beaten. I don't know whether or not I had committed any fault." Ta-yü said, "The fact is that Huang-po had treated you with the compassionate heart of an old woman, bent upon releasing you once for all from bondage and distress. And yet you have come here to ask me whether you are not at fault!" Lin-chi was thoroughly enlightened at these words. Then he said, "So after all there is not much to Huang-po's Buddha dharma!" Ta-yü grasped him, saying, "You bed-wetting imp! Only a moment ago you were still asking whether you might not be at fault. And now you are so bold as to say that there is not much to Huang-po's Buddha dharma. What truth do you see? Tell me right away!" Lin-chi did not speak, but punched Ta-yü below the ribs thrice. Ta-yü pushed him away, saying, "After all, your master is Huang-po, not me. Why should I be involved?"

After taking leave of Ta-yü, Lin-chi went back to Huang-po. When the latter saw him come back, he remarked, "This fellow comes and goes, goes and comes. When will there be an end to all this?" Lin-chi said, "Only because of the impetuous compassion of an old woman!" Then he reported his trip and everything Ta-yü had said. Huang-po: "That old windbag Ta-yü! I will beat the daylights out of him when he comes here." Lin-chi: "Why wait? Now is the time for beating." And he gave Huang-po a slap on the face. Huang-po said, "What a mad fellow he is to pluck the whiskers of a tiger!" Lin-chi uttered a shout. Huang-po ordered him to be led away to the conference in the hall.

One day during the time set apart for manual labor, the abbot too came out with a hoe in his hand. Looking back he saw Lin-chi was following along without a mattock. "Where is your hoe?" Huang-po asked. "Someone is carrying it." Huang-po said, "Come here, I want to exchange some ideas with you about something." When Lin-chi had come near, Huang-po stood the hoe upon the ground, saying, "This thing alone, nobody in the world is capable of handling and raising it." Obviously he was using the hoe as a pointer to the great function of teaching and transmitting the lamp of Ch'an. Lin-chi, quick to perceive the master's meaning, immediately snatched the hoe from his hands, and, holding it erect as the master had done, said, "How is it that this thing has fallen into my hands?" A symbolic way of saying that in a mysterious manner the charge was now in his hands. Thereupon Huang-po retired to the temple, remarking, "Today there is already someone to invite the whole community to work in the fields." That is to say, as he found Lin-chi ready to assume the role of the host, he could safely retire.

Lin-chi joined the others in manual labor. As he was digging the ground, he saw Huang-po coming again. So he stopped work, leaning against his hoe. Meaning to test his disciple once more, Huang-po remarked, "This fellow must be tired." Lin-chi said, "I have not even raised the hoe, how could I be tired?" As Huang-po raised his cane to strike him, the latter caught hold of its other end and thrust it backwards with such force that the master fell to the ground. Huang-po called for the deacon of the monastery to help him up. As he was helping him up, the deacon said, "Abbot, how can you tolerate the rudeness of this mad fellow?" No sooner was Huang-po on his feet again than he struck the deacon! At the same time, Lin-chi kept hoeing and digging the ground, saying, "While people are being cremated in all quarters, I am being buried alive here." This was a tremendous utterance, the first authentic roaring, as it were, of a young lion. It was tantamount to declaring that his old conventional self was now dead and buried, with only the true self living in him; that this death may and should take place long before one's physical decease; that it is when this death has taken place that one becomes one's true self which, being unborn, cannot die.

From that time on, there could no longer be any doubt in Huang-po's mind that his disciple was thoroughly enlightened, destined to carry on and brighten the torch of Ch'an. Lin-chi continued to stay with Huang-po or, at any rate, near about for a considerable period of time, before he became the rector of the Lin-chi Monastery in present Hopeh. It is most interesting to see how Huang-po and his newly enlightened disciple teased each other and tried to outwit each other like two boxers in a sparring match. One day Lin-chi was taking a nap in the hall. When the master saw him, he tapped the couch with his staff. Lin-chi lifted his head and, seeing that it was none other than the abbot, went to sleep again. The abbot, after giving another tap on the couch, went on. Finding the leader of his community sitting in meditation, he said to him, "The young fellow down there is seated in meditation, how is it that you are indulging in wild fancies here?" The leader said, "Oh, this old fellow, what is he doing?" The abbot, tapping the seat once, went out. But what a strange lesson he had given! Sleeping is sitting in meditation, and sitting in meditation is indulging in wild fancies!

On another occasion seeing that Lin-chi was planting pine trees, the master asked, "What's the use of planting so many pine trees in the depths of the mountain?" Lin-chi replied, "In the first place, they will beautify the scenery of the mountain temple. In the second place, they will set up standards and patterns for posterity." This said, he punched the ground thrice with his hoe. Huang-po teased him by saying, "Even so, you have already received thirty blows from me." Lin-chi again punched the ground thrice and then heaved a long sigh. Huang-po finally remarked, "Our family tradition will bloom forth in your generation."

Halfway through a summer retreat, Lin-chi climbed Huang-po Mountain to see the abbot. Finding him reading a sūtra, he teased the abbot by remarking, "I had expected to see a *man*, but I have found an old monk with the black pupils of his eyes blindfolded!" After staying a few days, he wished to return to the summer retreat. Huang-po said, "Having broken the retreat, why don't you stay on till the end of the summer?" Lin-chi: "I came up here just to pay my abbot a brief visit." The abbot struck him and drove him away. After walking a few miles, he began to doubt if he should have left so abruptly, so he returned to spend the summer with the abbot. Then he took leave again. The abbot asked him where he was going, he answered, "If not to the north of the river, then to the south of the river." Huang-po raised his staff to strike, but Lin-chi caught hold of it and gave the abbot a slap. The abbot broke into a loud laughter and called an attending monk to bring him the late master Pai-chang's Ch'an baton and hassock. Apparently, he intended to transmit these signals of authority to Lin-chi. But Lin-chi called after the attendant, saying, "Bring fire with you!" Huang-po said, "Not so! You just carry these with you, that in the future you may sit and teach to break the tongues of all men."

Before his enlightenment, Lin-chi, as we have seen, tended to be timid and pietistic. After his enlightenment the iconoclast in him came to the fore. One day as he was visiting the stupa of Bodhidharma, the guardian monk asked him, "Do you wish to pay your reverence first to the Buddha or first to the patriarch?" "I do not want to pay my reverence to either!" was Lin-chi's reply. This naturally scandalized the guardian, who queried, "What enmity is there between your Venerable Self and the Buddha and the patriarch?" Lin-chi shook his sleeves and went out.

This attitude was not merely temperamental but based upon his inner convictions, as will be seen from his conferences. For example, he said, "Followers of the Tao! It is for the pursuit of truth that we have left our homes. Take this mountain monk for instance. At first I concentrated my attention upon the strict disciplines of the Vinaya school; and I too was an earnest student of the sūtras and *śāstras*, hoping therein to find truth. Only later did I come to realize that all those rules, ceremonies, and books are nothing but expedients for the salvation of the world like medical prescriptions for the cure of the sick. Consequently I abandoned them once for all, and gave myself to the direct quest of truth and the pursuit of Ch'an. Later I was fortunate enough to meet a great enlightened master. Only then was the Tao Eye opened in me, so that I could recognize the attainments of the old sage monks of the world, and I could easily discern the false from the authentic. But no one is born wise and understanding. Everybody must go through serious study and personal experience, must be subjected to severe drills and trials, before he can hope to come to an actual awakening in his own heart someday. Followers of the Tao! If you wish in like manner to get a genuine insight, the most important thing is not to be misled by others. If you encounter anywhere anyone who impedes your vision, quickly get rid of him. When you encounter a Buddha, kill the Buddha. When you encounter a patriarch, kill the patriarch. When you encounter an arhat, kill the arhat. When you encounter your father and mother, kill your father and mother. When you encounter your kith and kin, kill your kith and kin. Only in this way can you arrive at your ultimate liberation. Then you will be non-attached to anything, thoroughly independent and free, thoroughly yourself."

All this murderous sounding talk of killing need alarm no one. The pursuit of truth and self-realization was, with Lin-chi, the one important thing; and it is understandable that he should have regarded anything or anyone lying in the way as something that must be ruthlessly brushed aside. For him, the problem of life is veritably "To be or not to be," and only when one is free and unattached to anything or anyone short of the ne plus ultra can one begin *to be*. Far from being irreligious his iconoclasm really springs from an authentic religious spirit.

The focal point of his philosophic vision is the "unconditioned true man." He never wearied of stressing reliance on one's self, but this self is not the temporary individual, subject to all the contingencies of life, but the true self who is never born and therefore does not die, who is beyond time and space, who is one with the Tao. So long as a man identifies himself with his temporary self alone, he remains a slave. Once he is awakened to the true man within him, he arrives at his true selfhood and becomes free.

In one of his regular discourses, he said to his assembly, "In your red fleshly heart, there is a true man of no title, constantly going out and coming in through your forehead. Whoever has not yet come to this realization should try to perceive it." At that moment a monk came forward, asking, "What is a true man of no title?" Lin-chi came down from his Ch'an couch and grasped the monk, saying, "Speak, speak!" As the monk was considering what to say, the master pushed him away, remarking, "What a dry toilet strip is this true man of no title!" So saying, he returned to the abbot's room.

The meaning of all this will be plain, if we remember that the monk who asked that question was still thinking of the true man as a stranger and therefore was far from realizing his selfhood. Essentially a free man, he remained a slave by identifying himself with his temporary self, thereby degrading himself to the state of a lifeless and worthless object like a dry toilet strip.

There is a strange coincidence between Lin-chi's notion of the "true man" and Emerson's notion of the "aboriginal Self." Like Lin-chi, Emerson advocated self-reliance or self-trust and insisted that the self to be trusted is not the individual ego but a fundamental self. Let me introduce here a quotation from Emerson's "Self-Reliance," which is perhaps too familiar to be understood in its true light but which, I hope, will reveal its perennial freshness when read in the strange context of Ch'an:

> The magnetism which all original action exerts is explained when we inquire the reason of self-trust. What is the aboriginal Self, on which a universal reliance may be grounded? What is the nature and power of that science-baffling star, without parallax, without calculable elements, which shoots a ray of beauty even into trivial and impure actions, if the least mark of independence appears? The inquiry leads us to that source, at once the essence of genius, of virtue, and of life, which we call Spontaneity or Instinct. We denote this primary wisdom as Intuition, whilst all later actions are tuitions. In that deep force, the last fact behind which analysis cannot go, all things find their common origin. For, the sense of being which in calm hours rises, we know not how, in the soul, is not diverse from things, from space, from light, from time, from man, but one with them, and proceeds obviously from the same source whence their life and being also proceed.

That "aboriginal Self," that "science-baffling star, without parallax, without calculable elements," corresponds, to my mind, exactly to Lin-chi's "true man of no title" whom he sometimes calls "independent man of the Tao" (*wu-i tao-jen*) or simply "this man" (*tz'u jen*). Everywhere in his recorded talks and acts, he was pointing to this "star without parallax," sometimes directly, at other times in a more roundabout way. He kept a constant watch, season in, season out, for the "least mark of independence" in his monks, although most of the time he was disappointed. He saw in each and every one of them the "aboriginal Self" waiting with patient eagerness for any opportunity to break through the shell of the little ego, so that, released himself, he could have a free hand in releasing the ego from its self-imposed bounds of ignorance and craving. Yet, what a pathetic sight it must have been for Lin-chi to see that most of his pupils, impervious to their original freeborn state, seemed to be willing to remain snugly in slavery. Turning their back upon intuition, they would rather pay tuition for worthless "tuitions." Carrying within them the very "mother of Buddha," they turned their eyes outwards to seek an external Buddha. Why should these seekers, Lin-chi often wondered, have left their households, only to belong to another household? Underneath all his roughness there was a burning compassion, which was all the more inevitable because it was not blind but enlightened. In this light, we can easily see that all his shouts and beatings actually sprang from the fountain of his compassionate heart.

There is a popular saying in Ch'an circles: "Only when you have the actual experience of bringing up your children will you realize and remember gratefully the kindness of your parents." This was how Lin-chi felt toward his master Huang-po. He once said to his assembly, "In the pursuit of truth, you should not try to avoid the risk of losing your lives. I was staying with my late master Huang-po for twenty years. Once I asked thrice about the essentials of Buddhism, and thrice he deigned to rain blows upon me with his staff, which I felt as acutely as if I were pierced by a thorny log. Now I yearn for another beating of that kind, but who is there to do the beating?" At the moment a monk came forward from the crowd, saying, "I can do the beating!" Lin-chi handed over his whisk to him, but he hesitated to receive it. So this time again, the master had to give the beating. There is no shirking of responsibility.

Frequent as was his resort to the rod, Lin-chi had nevertheless been noted in later generations as the master of shouts, as is evident in the well-known saying: "Te-shan's beatings, Lin-chi's shouts." It is not without reason that he has been considered a specialist in shouting, seeing that he developed a philosophy of shouting. He classified shouts into four main categories. As he once expounded to a monk, "Sometimes a shout is like the sword of Vajrarāja; sometimes a shout is like a lion crouching on the ground; sometimes a shout is like a sounding rod for testing the grasses; sometimes a shout is not used as a shout." After stating these categories, he asked the monk, "How do you understand this?" As the monk was fumbling for an answer, the master shouted. I suppose that this shout belongs to the first category, because it was meant to cut off the monk's chain of thoughts which would lead nowhere.

But, as so often happens with any community, when a master takes a special delight in a certain means, it is apt to be institutionalized as a result of the slavish imitation on the part of the students. So Lin-chi's students all practiced shouting in and out of season without understanding its philosophy and its proper application. The situation became so annoying that Lin-chi had to call a halt to all the noise. "You all imitate my shouting," he said, "but let me give you a test now. One person comes out from the eastern hall. Another person comes out from the western hall. At their meeting, they simultaneously shout. Do you possess enough discernment to distinguish the guest from the host? If you have no such discernment, you are forbidden hereafter to imitate my shouting."

Shouting, then, is not the important thing. The important thing is to recognize the host and to be one. Who is the host? None other than your true self. As Lin-chi told his assembly, "If you wish to be free and untrammeled in the world of births and deaths, going out and abiding, recognize right now the man who is listening to my sermon, who is above shape and form, not rooted or planted in any place, nor abiding in any abode. Yet he is very much alive and alert, responding readily to all situations with his unlimited resourcefulness, performing his function according to the circumstances without being pinned down to any. He eludes your embracing and evades your seeking. Hence he may be called the 'Great Secret.' " Time and time again he referred to this mysterious listener, the "independent man of the Tao," who is at the same time the "mother of all the Buddhas." He is not only the listener, but also the speaker. "Right now this man is clearly before our eyes with a brightness uniquely his own, listening to my speech; this man moves freely in all places, penetrating into all directions, and equally at home in all the three realms. He can enter any milieu without being affected by its peculiar features. In a single instant he soars into the *dharmadhātu*. Encountering a Buddha, he talks Buddha; encountering a patriarch, he talks patriarch; encountering an arhat, he talks arhat; encountering hungry demons, he talks in their language too. In teaching and transforming all animate beings, no thoughts or desires of theirs are alien to him; yet he remains pure and calm everywhere, with his light piercing into all corners, seeing all things as one."

If Lin-chi were living today, he would have said with Thomas Merton, "What can we gain by sailing to the moon if we are not able to cross the abyss that separates us from ourselves?" In fact, the whole meaning of his teaching consists precisely in crossing this abyss. For the "independent man of the Tao" is none other than your real self. True, you have your body, which is compounded of the four great elements. But for Lin-chi, "It is not this compound of the great four that is listening to my sermon, although the true listener can make use of the physical body. If you possess this insight, you will enjoy untrammeled freedom in your goings about and restings." Nor should you loathe your body. The enlightened man is the integral man, not a bodiless man. He need not undertake extraordinary actions either. On the contrary, after enlightenment, all the ordinary actions become the actions of the true man. Nor do you need to think extraordinary thoughts. Lin-chi often quoted the saying of Nan-ch'üan: "Tao is nothing but the ordinary mind." "Followers of Tao!" Lin-chi said, "the way of Buddhism admits of no artificial effort; it only consists in doing the ordinary things without any fuss—going to the stool, making water, putting on clothes, taking a meal, sleeping when tired. Let the fools laugh at me. Only the wise know what I mean." Again he said, "The truly noble man is a man of no concern and no ado. Don't try to be clever and ingenious. Just be ordinary." We are all originals, if only we are just what we are. If on the other hand we strain deliberately to be original, we thereby lose our originality.

Lin-chi was deeply steeped in the Taoism of Lao-tzu and Chuang-tzu. Whatever his substantive beliefs might be, his mode of thinking is essentially Taoist. His doctrine of *wu-shih* (nonconcern) and *wu-ch'iu* (non-seeking) is on all fours with Lao-tzu's doctrine of *wu wei* (non-ado). He declared, "To seek Buddha is to lose Buddha; to seek Tao is to lose Tao; to seek the patriarch is to lose the patriarch." The greatest treasure, the independent man of the Tao, is within you, is yourself; therefore to seek it outside is to miss it. And since it is yourself, you need not seek it even within you, for it is the seeker himself, not the object sought. In other words, your true self is always the subject, never an object.

Around the question of subject and object, Lin-chi worked out four different ways of dealing with four different grades of potentialities. "Sometimes I would snatch away the subject while leaving alone the object; on other occasions, I would snatch away the object while leaving alone the subject; on still other occasions, I would snatch away both the subject and the object; finally, in some cases, I would leave both the subject and the object untouched."

These four propositions seem to represent the methods of dealing with people in four different stages in the life of the spirit. In the first stage, a person has a distorted view of things because of his subjective hopes and fears and prejudices. These subjective elements of the little ego must be purged before one can attain at least a normal objectivity, so that he will no longer see human beings as trees walking. In the second stage, people of normal vision, who see mountains as mountains and rivers as rivers, must be reminded of the part that their own mind contributes to the appearance of things, and that what they naively take for objectivity is inextricably mixed with subjectivity. Once aware of subjectivity, one is initiated into the first stages of Ch'an, when one no longer sees mountains as mountains and rivers as rivers. In the third stage, the student of Ch'an is made to realize that even the balanced vision of things as a blend of the subjective and the objective still belongs to the field of empirical reality, the realm of relativity. At this juncture, he must be lifted to a higher plane, from which he will see the subject and the object in the phenomenal world as flowing from one and the same source, the mind, which is the absolute subject. This is what Lin-chi meant by "snatching away both the subject and the object." In the final stage, having identified oneself with the true self, and with one's mind sufficiently subtilized by the trainings and experiences in the previous stages, one can safely return to the world of phenomena and enjoy mountains as mountains and rivers as rivers, well knowing that all such terms are to be taken for what they are worth and to be understood as symbols rather than rigidly defined concepts. This may be called a twice-born realism, as distinguished from the naive realism of the first stage.

It is only in the last state that one can be called an "independent man of Tao" or an "unconditioned true man," who can go anywhere "without leaving his house." Like Chuang-tzu, Lin-chi spoke of the true man as one who "can enter into fire without being burned and plunge into water without being drowned." It is obvious that neither Chuang-tzu nor Lin-chi could have meant the physical man, but a man's true self, an eternal spirit not subject to the vicissitudes of the phenomenal world. It is about this spirit that Lin-chi was speaking when he said, "When expanded, it fills the whole dharmadhātu; when recollected, it does not set up itself as something of the size of the finest hair. It is self-evidently the solitary light, and it is lacking in nothing. Since it is neither perceptible to the eye nor audible to the ear, what kind of a thing can it be called? As an ancient put it, 'To say that it is like anything is to miss it altogether.' Just see it for yourself; what else can there be? It is vain to talk about it." Like the Tao, the true self cannot be articulated in words.

The fact that Lin-chi saw eye-to-eye with Lao-tze and Chuang-tzu on so many points does not detract from his originality. The important question is not whether he was the first man to have such insights, but whether these insights represented his genuine convictions. In my view, Lin-chi was one of the most original spirits among the pursuers of Tao who spoke directly from their hearts. His utterances are as spontaneous as the spurts from a powerful geyser. He was a well-read man, versed not only in Buddhist literature but also in Taoist classics. But whatever he had assimilated from his learning became an integral part of a vital philosophy of his own. From the following quotation, which may be regarded as an epitome of his philosophy, it is easy to discern the strands of Taoism and Buddhism, but at the same time it is not hard to feel that the whole passage presents a mode of thinking refreshingly new.

The true follower of Tao does not grasp at the Buddha, nor at bodhi-sattvas, nor at the arhats, nor at the exceeding glories in the three realms. In his transcendental independence and untrammeled freedom, he adheres to nothing. Even if the universe should collapse, his faith would not falter. Should all the Buddhas from the ten heavens appear before him, he would not feel the slightest elation. Nor would he experience the slightest fear, should all the demons come out from the three hells. How can he be so calm? Because he sees the fundamental voidness of all things, which are real only to those still subject to change but not to the immutable. The three realms are only a manifestation of the mind, and the ten thousand things arise from consciousness. What then is the use of grasping at a dream, an illusion, a flower in the air? Only the one person who is right now before your very eyes listening to my discourse is authentically real. He can enter into fire without being burned and plunge into water without being drowned. The three hells would be turned into a pleasure garden for him. Ministering unto the hungry ghosts and beasts, he accepts no reward. What makes such a state possible? The law of non discrimination! If you should love the saintly but hate the worldly, you will never cease to be engulfed in the sea of birth and death. Afflictions and trials (kleśa) exist because you are mindful of them. But if you are not mindful of them, how can they disturb you? Spare yourself the vain labor of discriminating and grasping at appearances and in a single instant you will realize Tao with spontaneous ease.

From the above quotation, we can see how right Dr. D. T. Suzuki was when he wrote that Ch'an "is the offshoot of Taoist thought grafted onto Indian speculation as formulated by native Buddhist scholars." In fact, Ch'an is "the synthesis of Taoism, Confucianism, and Buddhism applied to our daily life as we live it." Suzuki has further brought out the intimate relation between the wisdom of Chuang-tzu and the spirit of Ch'an on the one hand, and, on the other hand, Ch'an's significant contribution by way of implementing the effective transmission of the essential insights common to Tao and Ch'an. Here is what Suzuki says: "What, however, is the distinctly characteristic hallmark of Zen is its insistence on the awakening of pratyamajñā. Pratyamajñā (Sanskrit) is an inner perception deeply reaching the core of one's being (hsin or hridaya). This corresponds to Chuang-tzu's 'mind-fasting' or 'mind-forgetting' or 'clear as the morning' (chao-che). In the Chuang-tzu, however, this existence is more or less casually treated, while in Zen it is the most essential discipline. Modern Japanese Zen has achieved great development around this point."

One of Lin-chi's strong points lay precisely in his resourcefulness as a pedagogue. Without this resourcefulness, he could never have founded the House of Lin-chi, which is still alive and shouting today. It is not likely that he actually intended to found such a house or school of Ch'an; but there can be no question that his proficiency as a teacher stood him in good stead in laying the foundations of a vital tradition.

We have already dealt with his interesting philosophy of shouting and his formulation of the four propositions which he applied to the four levels of potentialities. Although he despised ingenuity, he was nevertheless extremely ingenious himself. Perhaps, he was ingenuously ingenious, being inventive with open eyes. Enlightened master as he was, he felt free to use ingenious methods and subtle distinctions as convenient *upāya* without being entangled in them. But there is no telling how many of his less intelligent epigones in the later generations have been entrapped in them and failed to break through. Take for instance one of his utterances: "In promoting the vehicle of our school, let every sentence contain three mystic doors and each mystic door three essentials; and you should know what is merely an expedient means and what is the real end, what is the fundamental vision and what is merely its function." Now, Lin-chi himself did not tell what exactly the "three mystic doors" and "three essential points" were. This very silence has tempted many later students of Ch'an, whether of his own school or of another school, to offer their own interpretations; and they have been at loggerheads with one another. Up to the present time, it remains an unsettled kung-an. Some insist that the three mystical doors are (1) mystery relating to the *kāya* (body), (2) mystery of expression, and (3) mystery beneath mystery. The three essential points have been interpreted as (1) true substance without ego, (2) great method without method, and (3) no setting up of inner and outer. A contemporary upasaka, Lu K'uan-yü, in his *Zen and Ch'an Teaching: Series Two*, writes: "The three profound doors are: spiritual body or substance; its object of aim; and its expression, speech or sentence. Each profound door has three vital stages or states which are preliminary, intermediate and final. Therefore, in order to attain Buddha wisdom, a Ch'an practiser should pass through nine vital stages of three profound doors. Lin-chi, who had succeeded in passing through all of them, made an analysis of his achievement which he now revealed to his students."

If this interpretation is true, Lin-chi would be like a rat placed in a maze having three doors one after another, with three secret buttons attached to each door. In order to come out of the maze, the poor rat must be able to touch the right button successively for nine times! To my mind this could never have been the meaning of Lin-chi. It is out of tune with the whole spirit of Ch'an, as I understand it. Fen-yang Shan-chao seems to have come closer to the spirit of Ch'an in his summary gāthā:

*The three mystical doors and the three essential points*
*Are in actuality hard to divide and distinguish.*
*If you get the idea, you must forget the words:*
*This is the simple way to approach the Tao.*
*All phenomena are clearly comprehended in one sentence:*
*At the feast of "double-nine," the chrysanthemums bloom afresh.*

It must never be forgotten that the fundamental insight of Lin-chi is the perception or awareness of the true man of no position, degree, or title as one's real self. All expedient methods and discursive formulas are of secondary importance and temporary utility. It is ironic that later students of Ch'an have paid more and more attention to things of secondary importance to the neglect of the one thing necessary. This is, no doubt, the reason why Ch'an has not been able to keep its original vitality. For once you mistake the kung-an for a puzzle to be solved by intellectual acumen, you will be glued to it as a fly to the flypaper. The great masters of Ch'an have invariably used the kung-an to drive you to the wall, so that in your intense agony you may open your inner eye and see that the hopeless labyrinthine maze you are in is nothing but a nightmare, which disappears as soon as you awake. Let the reader ponder a significant anecdote of the great master Nan-ch'üan. One day, Governor Lu Hsüan put a tricky question to Nan-ch'üan: Once an ancient reared a gosling in a bottle. As the gosling grew big, it could not get out of the bottle through its narrow neck. Now, you must not break the bottle, nor injure the gosling. How are you going to get it out?" Nan-ch'üan called, "Your Excellency!" As Lu responded, "Yes!" the master said, "It's out already!" Lu thereupon became aware of his true self.

One wonders how Lin-chi himself would have felt about the erudite commentaries and long-winded speculations on his "three mystical doors" and "three essential points." I should not be surprised if he should consign all of them to the privy and shouted the gosling out of the bottle.

"Followers of Tao," he once said to his assembly, "do not take the Buddha for the Ultimate (ne plus ultra). As I look at him, he is still like the hole in the privy. As to the bodhisattvas and arhats, they are all cangues and chains to keep you in bondage. . . . Virtuous ones! Do not deceive yourselves! I care nothing for your expertise in interpreting the sūtras and

śāstras, or for your high positions in the world, or for your flowing eloquence, or for your intelligence and wisdom; I only care for your true and
authentic insight and genuine perception. Followers of Tao! Even if you
were able to expound a hundred sūtras and śāstras, you would still be no
match for a simple and humble monk with no concern for anything."

# CHAPTER XII

# Yün-men Wen-yen:
## Founder of the
## Yün-men House

Ch'an masters, like other men, may be divided into two types. Some are slow-breathers, others are fast-breathers. Of the founders of the five houses of Ch'an, Kuei-shan, Tung-shan, and Fa-yen belong to the slow-breathers, while Lin-chi and Yün-men, belong to the fast-breathers. Of these two, Lin-chi breathes fast enough, but Yün-men breathes faster still. Lin-chi's way is like the blitzkrieg. He kills his foes in the heat of the battle. He utters shouts under fire. When the lion roars, all other animals take cover. No one can encounter him without his head being chopped off by him. It makes no difference whether you are a Buddha, a bodhisattva, or a patriarch, Lin-chi will not spare you if he should chance to encounter you. So long as you bear a title or occupy any position, Lin-chi will send out his "true man of no title" to kill you off in the split second. So terrible is Lin-chi! But more terrible is Yün-men!

Lin-chi only kills those whom he happens to encounter. Yün-men's massacre is universal. He does away with all people even before they are born. To him the "true man of no title" is already the second moon, therefore a phantom not worth the trouble of killing. Yün-men seldom if ever resorts to shouts or beatings. Like a sorcerer he kills by cursing. His tongue is inconceivably venomous, and what makes the case worse, he is the most eloquent of the Ch'an masters.

Yün-men is a radical iconoclast. In one of his sermons to his assembly, he related the legend that the Buddha, immediately after his birth, with one hand pointing to heaven and the other pointing to earth, walked around in seven steps, looked at the four quarters, and declared, "Above heaven and below heaven, I alone am the Honored One." After relating the story, Yün-men said, "If I were a witness of this scene, I would have knocked him to death at a single stroke and given his flesh to dogs for food. This would have been some contribution to the peace and harmony of the world."

Vimalakīrti fared no better with him. One day, beating the drum, he announced, "Vimalakīrti's realm of wonderful joy is shattered to pieces. Bowl in hand, he is now heading toward a city in Hunan to beg for some gruel and rice to eat."

It seems as though Yün-men had no respect for any person. He once quoted these words: "He who hears the Tao in the morning can afford to die in the evening." Everybody knows that it was Confucius who had uttered these words; but Yün-men did not even mention his name and merely commented airily, "If even a worldly man could have felt like that, how much more must we monks feel about the one thing necessary to us?"

Nor was Yün-men more polite with himself than with others. For instance, he said to his assembly, "Even if I could utter a wise word by the hearing of which you attain an immediate enlightenment, it would still be like throwing ordure on your heads." This is to say that even if the master had done all that could have been expected of him and even if his words had been instrumental to their awakening, still the end can never justify the means. To Yün-men, any speech, however legitimate from the worldly point of view, is out of place in regard to the eternal Tao. He seems to be obsessed with the primary insight of Lao-tzu: "The Tao that could be expressed in words is not the eternal Tao." As Yün-men was interested in nothing else than the eternal Tao, what use could he have for mere words? That is why whenever he had to make a conference he always apologizes for his speaking at all. The beginning of his very first sermon as the abbot of Ling-shu Monastery is typical:

Do not say that I am deceiving you today by means of words. The fact is that I am put under the necessity of speaking before you and thereby sowing seeds of confusion in your minds. If a true seer should see what I am doing, what a laughingstock I would be in his eyes! But now there is no escape from it.

The great paradox about Yün-men is that, on the one hand, he had an extraordinary gift of eloquence, while on the other hand he had a phobia for the word, as if every word were an intruder into the sacred ground of the inexpressible Tao. What a tension this must have created in his mind! Fortunately, he hit upon a happy solution of this tension with another paradox. The man who has realized his self can "stand unharmed in the midst of flames." So "even if he talks all day, in reality nothing cleaves to his lips and teeth, for he has actually not spoken a single word. Likewise, although he wears his clothes and takes his meals every day, actually he has not touched a single grain of rice nor put on a single thread of silk."

The keenness of his mind reached an agonizing degree. He seemed to be sensitive to every motion of his own mind, and his self-knowledge enabled him to discern the thoughts and feelings of others. From the same source of sensitivity have sprung many a piercing insight into the secrets of spiritual life. For instance, he said, "Each of us carries a light within him, but when it is looked at it is turned into darkness." Here is a profound insight whose authenticity is beyond question.

Yün-men was conscious that his way was the narrow way. He appealed only to the highly intelligent. His house has been characterized by all students of Ch'an as steep and abrupt. He himself wrote a poem descriptive of the style of his Ch'an:

> Steep is the Mountain of Yün-men, rising straight upward,
>     Leaving the white clouds down below!
> Its streams, dashing and eddying about, allow
>     No fish to linger around.
> The moment you step into my door, I already know
>     What kind of ideas you've brought with you.
> What's the use of raising again the dust
>     Long settled in an old track?

Such, then, is the style and aura of the man, into whose life and teachings we are going to peep, with an undaunted spirit! We are told that one day Yün-men put his hands into the mouth of a wooden lion and cried at the top of his voice, "Help, help! I am bitten to death." Now we are going to put our hands into Yün-men's mouth, but there is no reason for fear. Even if we should meet with the same terrible experience of being bitten by a lion, we could still survive as he did.

Yün-men Wen-yen (d. 949) was born into a Chang family in Chia-hsin of Chekiang. Most probably, his family was in the pinch of extreme poverty, and he was placed when a mere boy by his parents in the hands of the Vinaya master Chih-ch'eng of the K'ung-wang temple as a novice. He was noted for his exceptional intelligence, especially for his natural gift of eloquence. As soon as he was of age, he had his head shaved and was duly ordained. He continued to wait upon his master for a few more years, during which period he delved deeply into the Vinaya branch of Buddhist scriptures. All this learning, however, did not satisfy his deeper needs. He felt that it did not throw any light on the most vital problem of his own self. Hence he went to see the Ch'an master Mu-chou, the disciple of Huang-po, hoping for the necessary instructions. But as soon as Mu-chou saw him, he slammed the door in his face. When he knocked at the door, Mu-chou asked from inside, "Who are you?" After he had told him his name, Mu-chou asked, "What do you want?" Yün-men replied, "I am not yet enlightened on the vital problem of my own self, and I have come to beg for your instructions." Mu-chou opened the door but, after a quick look at him, shut it again. In the following two days, Yün-men knocked and met with the same experience. On the third day, as soon as the master opened the door, Yün-men squeezed in. The master grabbed him, saying, "Speak! Speak!" As Yün-men fumbled for something to say, the master pushed him out, saying, "A Ch'in-time relic of a drill!" and shut the door so quickly that it hurt one of Yün-men's feet. This initiated him into Ch'an. At Mu-chou's recommendation, he went to see Hsüeh-feng (822–908).

As he arrived at the village below the mountain where Hsüeh-feng was, he met a monk and asked him, "Is Your Reverence going up the mountain today?" As the monk said that he was going up, Yün-men asked him whether he would be willing to bring a timely message to the abbot but present it as his own. The monk having consented to do so, Yün-men said, "After your arrival at the monastery up there, as soon as you see the abbot entering the hall and the assembly gathered together, go forward at once, clasp your hands, and, standing erect before him, say: "O poor old man! why does he not take off the chain from his neck?!" The monk did exactly as he had been told to do, but Hsüeh-feng sensed immediately that those words were not his own. Coming down from his seat, he grabbed him firmly, saying, "Speak! Speak!" As the poor monk knew not what to say, Hsüeh-feng pushed him away and said, "Those words are not yours." At first he still insisted that they were his own words. But the relentless master called for his attendants to come with ropes and sticks. Frightened out of his wits, the monk confessed, "They are not my words. It was a monk from Chekiang I met at the village who taught me to speak thus." Then the abbot said to his community, "Go, all of you, to the village below to greet the one destined to be the spiritual guide of five hundred persons and invite him to come."

The next day Yün-men came up to the monastery. On seeing him, the abbot said, "How could you arrive at your present state?" Yün-men said nothing but just lowered his head. Right from that moment, he saw eye-to-eye with the master. He stayed several years with Hsüeh-feng, under whose guidance he delved more and more deeply into the profundities of Ch'an, until the master transmitted to him the Dharma seal.

Yün-men then journeyed forth to visit the luminaries of different quarters, leaving profound impressions everywhere. Finally he went to Ling-shu, where the master Chih-sheng was abbot. Now, Chih-sheng had been the abbot of Ling-shu for twenty years; but, for a reason known only to himself, he kept the assembly leader's seat vacant all this time, although from time to time he did speak, rather mysteriously, of someone destined to be his assembly leader. On the day when Yün-men was to arrive, the abbot suddenly ordered his monks to strike the bell and go out of the outermost gate of the monastery to welcome the assembly leader. The whole community went out, and, lo and behold, there arrived Yün-men!

After the demise of Chih-sheng, the prince of Kuang ordered Yün-men to be the abbot of Ling-shu. At his inauguration, the Prince came in person to attend the meeting, saying, "Your humble disciple begs for your instruction." "Before your eyes," said the new abbot, "lies no other road." To Yün-men there is only one road, not many roads. But what is the one road he had in mind? In the answer to this crucial question lies the touchstone of all his philosophy.

Once Yün-men quoted a saying from Ma-tsu: "All words belong to the school of Nāgārjuna, with 'this one' as the host." He then remarked, "An excellent saying! Only nobody asks me about it." At that moment a monk came forward and asked, "What is the school of Nāgārjuna?" This called the abbot's ire upon him, "In India, there are ninety-six schools, and you belong to the lowest!" In Ma-tsu's saying, the important point is obviously "this one," while the school of Nāgārjuna is merely a window dressing. Ma-tsu could have mentioned any other school without changing the living meaning of the sentence. But the foolish monk took the accidental for the essential, and left out the essential entirely. For Yün-men, as for Ma-tsu, the one thing necessary is the realization of "this one" who is none other than everybody's own self. This is not only the one goal but also the one road, for the simple reason that there is no road to lead to the self outside of itself.

"This one" who is your true self is complete in itself and "lacking in nothing." Time and time again, Yün-men asked his assembly, "Are you lacking in anything?" Time and time again, he reminded them that only one thing is essential, that all other things are of no concern to them, that in this vital matter they must rely on themselves, for no one else can take their place. All his sermons were like the signs of a dumb person trying to hint at what is in his mind. The following discourse is as typical as any:

> My duty compels me to attempt the impossible. Even in telling you to look directly into yourself and to be unconcerned about other things, I am already burying the real thing under verbiage. If you proceed from thence and set out in quest of words and sentences, cudgeling your brains over their logical meanings, working out a thousand possibilities and ten thousand subtle distinctions, and creating endless questions and debates, all that you will gain thereby is a glib tongue, while at the same time you will be getting farther and farther away from the Tao, with no rest to your wandering. If *this thing* could really be found in words, are there not enough words in the Three Vehicles and the twelve divisions of scriptures? Why should there be a special transmission outside the scripture? And if you could get at it by studying the various interpretations and learned commentaries on such terms as *potentiality* and *intelligence*, then how is it that the saints of the ten stages who could expound the Dharma as resourcefully as the clouds and rain, should still have incurred the reproach that they only saw the self-nature vaguely as through a veil of gauze? From this we can know that to follow the intentions and vagaries of your mind is to be separated from your self as far as the earth from the sky. But if you have really found your true self, then you can pass through fire without being burned, speak a whole day without really moving your lips and

teeth and without having really uttered a single word, wear your clothes and take your meal every day without really touching a single grain of rice or a single thread of silk. Even this talk is but a decoration on the door of our house. The important thing is your experiential realization of this state.

Yün-men has been noted in the Ch'an circles for his "one-word barrier." However, this is merely one of his tactics in rousing the dormant potentiality of his disciples and should not be regarded as an essential element of his vision. Some students of Ch'an have thought that his one-word answers have no rational bearing whatever on the questions. They tend to make a cult of irrationality. I believe that this is a wrong approach, as wrong as to make a cult of rationality. The truth is that Yün-men, like all great masters of Ch'an, had moved beyond the rational and irrational. His answers were his spontaneous reactions to the questions. They were at least occasioned by them, and in this sense and to this extent they did have a bearing on the questions. Not only were they occasioned by the questions, but also they were each directed to the questioner, whose spiritual state and needs the master had sensed intuitively from the very question he had raised. If, therefore, they had no logical bearing on the questions, at least they had a vital bearing on the persons asking those questions.

Here I will present a cluster of Yün-men's one-word answers together with the questions that had called them forth. I shall refrain from any more comments, leaving the reader to shift for himself.

QUESTION:   What is the right Dharma Eye?
ANSWER:     All-comprehensive!

QUESTION:   How do you look at the wonderful coincidence between the chick tapping inside its shell and the hen's pecking from outside?
ANSWER:     Echo.

QUESTION:   What is the one road of Yün-men?
ANSWER:     Personal experience!

QUESTION:   One who is guilty of patricide can repent and vow to amend his life before Buddha. But if he has killed the

Buddha and the patriarchs, before whom can he repent and make the promise to amend?

ANSWER:     Exposed!

QUESTION:   What is Tao?

ANSWER:     Go!

QUESTION:   Where our late teacher (Ling-shu) remained silent when a question was put to him, how shall we enter it in the epitaph?

ANSWER:     Teacher!

There is no particular magic in the "one-word barrier of Yün-men." One word or many words, there is always the barrier for you to break through. It is just one of his ways of evoking the incommunicable.

As another means of his teaching, Yün-men used his staff as a pointer to "this one" or the true self, who is identical with the Absolute. We must always keep this in mind in reading some of his utterances which on their surface may sound like the braggings of a magician waving his wand. Let me give some instances. One day, Yün-men held up his staff before his assembly and declared, "This staff has transformed itself into a dragon and has swallowed up the whole cosmos. Where then have the mountains, rivers and the immense earth come from?" On another occasion, holding up his staff, he sang aloud, "Lo and behold! the old fellow Śākya has come here!" On still another occasion, he abruptly asked his audience, "Do you want to make the acquaintance of the patriarchs?" Pointing at them with his staff, he announced, "The patriarchs are capering on your heads! Do you want to know where their eyes are? Their eyes are under your feet!"

Once he asked a deacon, "What did the ancients wish to indicate by raising and lowering a dust whisk?" The deacon replied, "To reveal the self before the raising and after the lowering." This evoked from him a hearty approval, which he so rarely gave.

Sometimes, he dispensed with his staff and pointed to the self more directly, as where he said, "Buddhas innumerable as specks of dust are all in your tongue. The scriptures of the Tripiṭaka are all under your heels." This insight is, according to Yün-men, only one of the entrances to the self. The self being beyond space and time, it is nowhere and yet it is manifested everywhere and in all things. Therefore, to try to find him only in the innermost recesses of your mind is to miss him. On this point, Yün-men saw eye-to-eye with his great contemporary Ts'ao-shan. He once asked Ts'ao-shan, "What is the best way of being intimate with this Man?" The latter replied, "Don't seek intimacy with him esoterically and in the innermost recesses of your mind." Yün-men asked again, "What follows if we don't?" Ts'ao-shan answered, "Then we are truly intimate with him." Yün-men exclaimed, "How true! How true!"

It makes no difference whether he was influenced by Ts'ao-shan. What is certain is that Yün-men's final vision transcended the esoteric and the exoteric, the inner and the outer. He came to see the Absolute in all things and in all places. "Within the cosmic order, amidst the universe, there is a mysterious gem hidden in the depth of a visible mountain." Yün-men used these words of Seng-chao to hint at the immanence of the Absolute. But immediately he added, "It [the mysterious gem] carries a lantern into the Buddha hall and puts the three entrance doors of the monastery on the lantern. What is it doing?" Having no answer from the assembly, he gave the answer himself, "Its mind veers according to the course of things." After a moment of silence, he added, "As the clouds arise, thunder starts."

Now, that there is an invisible gem in the midst of the phenomenal world is comparatively easy to comprehend. But what could he mean when he said that the invisible gem is carrying a lantern into the Buddha hall and putting the three doors of the monastery on the top of the lantern? This phenomenal absurdity was obviously meant to lift the minds of his hearers to the transcendence of the Absolute.

The answer that he gave to his own question evokes still another aspect of the Absolute—how it functions in the phenomenal world. The lantern symbolizes the spirit of Ch'an. The three entrance doors stand perhaps for the Three Vehicles (the śrāvaka, the pratyekabuddha, and the bodhisattva). Putting them together on the lantern is reducing and uniting them into the One Vehicle as spoken of by the Sixth Patriarch. At first the Three Vehicles had each arisen to answer the needs of men. Likewise the One Vehicle has arisen to meet the needs of new men. This is what Yün-men meant when he said that the Absolute, when applying its mind to the phenomenal world, veers according to the course of things, and its operation here is as spontaneous as its operation in the natural world: "As clouds arise, thunder starts."

This leads us to the famous "three propositions of the House of Yün-men." Although these three propositions were first formulated and brought together as a continuous series by Yün-men's disciple Te-shan Yüan-mi (who flourished in the latter part of the tenth century), the ideas were implicit in the teachings of the master. The three propositions are:

1. Permeating and covering the whole cosmic order.

2. Cutting off once for all the flow of all streams.

3. Following the waves and keeping up with the currents.

All these three refer ultimately to the Absolute. They represent its three aspects as we view it, forming, as it were, a dialectical series. Looking at its immanent aspect, we find that it permeates and covers the whole of the cosmos and all its parts. In its transcendent aspect, it is infinitely higher than the cosmos, alone and peerless, in no way approachable by any being in the world. This is what is suggested by the phrase "Cutting off once for all from the flow of all streams." But in the end we see the great return. For, in its functioning in the world, it follows the waves and keeps abreast of the currents of the time.

In the sayings of Yün-men, we can find apt illustrations of each of the three phases. For instance, he quoted his late master Hsüeh-feng's saying: "All the Buddhas of the past, present, and future are turning the great wheel of the Dharma over the blazing fire." Then he commented on it, saying, "Rather the blazing fire is expounding the Dharma to all the Buddhas of the three times, and they are standing on the ground and listening." He saw the Absolute in the fire, in the grain of sand, and even in the smallest speck of dust. He saw it near and far, in himself and in the yonder polestar. This illustrates the first proposition.

Yün-men was once invited to a vegetarian feast held in the palace. A court official asked him, "Is the fruit of Ling-shu ripe yet?" Yün-men asked back, "In what years, according to your view, could it ever be said to be unripe?" This was one of the most delightful repartees for which he was famous. But did it answer the officer's question? Apparently what the officer wished to know was how his work as the abbot of Ling-shu (which is the Chinese for the "holy tree") was progressing, whether the "holy tree" had produced any ripe fruit in the form of enlightened disciples. But instead of answering the question, the abbot used it as a springboard to leap from time to eternity by equating the fruit of the holy tree with the eternal Tao or, perhaps, with "this one." Only in the realm of time can you speak of progress, of birth, growth, ripening, and decay, which are entirely inapplicable to the realm of the Absolute. This was Yün-men's way of lifting the mind of the questioner from the phenomenal to the supraphenomenal, and it is a clear instance of "cutting off once for all the flow of all streams." Another interesting instance is where he was asked by a monk who had just finished the summer retreat how he should answer if anybody should ask him about his prospects ahead. The abbot's reply was, "Let everyone step backwards!" Instead of thinking of forging ahead in the phenomenal world, the abbot wanted him to return where there is no progress, where "the pure wave cannot be reached by any route."

Yün-men's mind seemed to be particularly in its element in dealing with this transcendental aspect of the Absolute. One of the most beautiful and pregnant of his utterances was his lightning-like answer to the question: "What happens when the tree has withered and its leaves dropped?" All that he uttered was a phrase of four words: "T'i lu chin-feng!" (Body bared to golden wind). The phrase carries a dual meaning. On the natural plane, it means, of course, that the trunk of the tree is exposed nakedly to the breath of autumn. On the spiritual plane, it suggests that the dharmakāya or the true self in its purity is now in its natural element— eternity. The phrase is clear like a crystal, evoking the autumn sky without a speck of cloud, which in turn lifts our hearts to the empyrean of pure light.

It would be interesting to compare this cameo-like phrase with Tung-shan's

> *"The withered tree flowers into a new spring far, far beyond the realm of time."*

What different types of landscapes they present to us! In Tung-shan we find the cordial warmth of a mild spring day. In Yün-men we find the refreshing coolness and transparent limpidity of a moonlit night in autumn. Yet both of them were spiritual giants, with their minds soaring beyond the orbits. Heaven, therefore, must be a house of many mansions to be the home of so many different types of excellence.

Now, an outstanding trait of Ch'an common to all the five houses is the idea that in the life of the spirit you will never reach a point where it is no longer possible for you to take another step upward. Even if you had climbed to the crest of a mountain, you must still go upward by coming down to the plains. Even if you had reached the other shore, you still must advance farther by returning to this shore to live the life of a man who is truly a man. You must shed off whatever esoteric habits you may have acquired previously, and become all things to all men. After having cut off the flow of all streams, you are now to keep yourself in constant flux and be perfectly at home in it.

The striking thing about Yün-men is that in soaring to the transcendent sphere he shoots like a rocket straight up without making any circles like the eagle, and yet when he comes down to the earth, he wants us to veer with the wind and to follow all the waves, tides, currents, eddies, swingings back and forth of the river of life. For this is how the eternal Tao functions in the world.

When he was asked, "What is Tao?" Yün-men uttered just one word, "Go!" This word is so pregnant in meanings that it is impossible to pin him down to a definite connotation. But in the context of his whole teaching, it would not be too far off the mark to say that one connotation he had in mind is "Go your way free and unencumbered, doing everything as befitting your state without being attached to particular methods or to the results of your doing. Do your work and pass on."

He was deeply convinced that "true emptiness does not destroy the existential realities" and that "the formless is one with the world of forms." He assured a prominent lay disciple of his that there is no difference between the lay and the cleric in the matter of self-realization, quoting a passage from the Lotus sūtra in support of his conviction that all activities by way of ministering unto the existential needs of oneself and others are in no way incompatible with the nature of reality. Of course, different states of life entail different duties, and everyone must put his feet solidly on the ground and walk steadily in the path of duty. This is much better than to indulge in wild fancies and empty speculation. To the enlightened man, "Heaven is heaven, earth is earth, mountain is mountain, river is river, monk is monk, and layman is layman." He discouraged all theoretical and epistemological inquiries as a waste of one's precious time. The important thing is to be one's self.

Once you have become your self, you are freed from all the inhibitions and fears bred by the ignorance and cravings of your ego. Then you will be happy when you work, happy when you play, happy to live, and happy to die. When a monk asked the master, "Who is my self?" he answered, "The one who roams freely in the mountains and takes his delight in the streams." This might not be descriptive of the state of the questioner, but certainly revealed the beautiful inner landscape of Yünmen himself. In fact, one of his happiest utterances was: "Every day is a good day!"

# CHAPTER XIII

# Fa-yen Wen-i:
## Founder of the
## Fa-yen House

The House of Fa-yen was founded by Fa-yen Wen-i (885–958). It was the last of the five houses to be established. Although it was short lived, yet its influences have been far reaching. In order to understand and appreciate its characteristic features, we should remember that it stretched its roots deep into the traditions, not only of Chinese Buddhism, but also of Chinese culture in general. It is in the lineage of Ch'ing-yüan, one of the two outstanding disciples of the Sixth Patriarch Hui-neng. Fa-yen was in the ninth generation after Hui-neng, and among his intermediary ancestors were such spiritual giants like Shih-t'ou, Te-shan, Hsüeh-feng Hsüan-sha, and Lo-han Kuei-ch'eng, whose disciple Fa-yen was.

Let us recall that Shih-t'ou's enlightenment was occasioned by his reading of the *Chao-lun*, a book written by Seng-chao, an outstanding disciple of Kumārajīva. Seng-chao was well steeped in the philosophy of Lao-tzu and Chuang-tzu; and his book constituted an effective synthesis of Buddhist and Taoist thought. His whole system was built upon the mystic identity of the noumenal and the phenomenal, as taught by Lao-tzu in the first chapter of the *Tao-te ching*. From Chuang-tzu he assimilated the mystic insight into the nonduality of the self and the world, making his own what Chuang-tzu had said: "Heaven and earth spring from the same root as myself, and all things are one with me."

When Shih-t'ou, in reading the *Chao-lun*, arrived at the sentence: "Who but the sage can realize that all things are one with himself?" he exclaimed, "The sage is selfless, and therefore to him there is nothing that is not himself. The dharmakāya is formless, where can the distinction between the self and the other come in? The round mirror reflects ineffably the shapes of all things; and the world of phenomena springs from the hidden fountain of the noumenon and becomes visible. As there is no duality between the knowing and the known, how can there be any talk of going and coming? Oh, what a supreme vision is unfolded by those words!"

Unlike the other houses of Zen, whose approach to Supreme Reality is mainly through an experiential realization of the inner self, the house of Fa-yen, while not neglecting the true man in us, arrived at the same goal of ne plus ultra by opening its eyes to the unlimited horizons of the cosmos. In its vision, all things in the universe speak of the Absolute and lead to him. An anecdote about Hsüan-sha, one of the most important forebears of this house, may serve as a good illustration of this point. One day he was scheduled to discourse to his assembly; but as he arrived at the platform, he heard the twittering of a swallow outside the hall. Thereupon he remarked, "What a profound discourse on reality and a clear exposition of the Dharma!" And he retired from the platform as though signifying that his sermon was done.

That all things, including even the insentient, speak of the Dharma or Law has nothing new or strange about it. The National Teacher Hui-chung, who was one of the immediate disciples of Hui-neng, had defended this doctrine very effectively. A monk asked him, "An ancient Worthy once declared:

> 'Green, green the emerald bamboos!
> They belong, one and all, to the dharmakāya.
> Lush, lush, the yellow flowers!
> They belong, one and all, to the prajñā.'

Some do not agree with this, saying that it represents an erroneous view. Others think it a true insight, unfathomable in its profundity. How do you regard it?" Hui-chung said, "This is probably the vision of Vis-vabhadra and Mañjuśri, beyond the faith and conception of the mediocre and literal-minded. But it is in perfect accord with the ultimate message of all the Mahāyāna scriptures. For example, the Avatamsaka says:

> 'The Buddhakāya fills the whole dharmadhātu,
> Manifesting itself universally to all beings.

*It responds to their every wish and need according to their karmas,*
*While at the same time never leaving the Bodhi seat.'*

Now, since the emerald bamboos are not outside the dharmadhātu, can it be said that they do not belong to the dharmakāya? Again, in the Wisdom sūtras, we find: 'Just as the forms and colors are without limit, so is the *Prajñā* without limit.' Now, since the yellow blossoms do not lie beyond the world of forms and colors, can it be said that they do not belong to the *Prajñā*? But it is hard for men of no understanding to make out the sense of these truths."

This strain of speculative contemplation was assimilated by the house of Fa-yen, and became its dominant trait. Instead of focusing its attention on the inner self, it attempted to transcend both the subject and the object and to aspire after the mysterious beyond. Compelled to use language, it designated this beyond as mind or spirit (*hsin*), the unique fountainhead from which spring the three realms and all things in them. It is beyond the subjective and the objective, beyond unity and multiplicity, beyond identity and difference, beyond the inner and the outer, beyond the universal and the particular, beyond the noumenal and the phenomenal. In one word, it is beyond all attributes. This being the case, the method that this house adopted was of necessity the via negativa and the way of unknowing.

So far we have only presented the background of the Fa-yen Ch'an. Let us now proceed to look into the teachings of its founder and his heirs in the few generations it was destined to last.

Fa-yen Wen-i was a native of Yü-hang in present Chekiang, born into a Lu family. He joined a monastery early in his childhood. At first he studied under the outstanding Vinaya master Hsi-chüeh in the famous Yü-wang temple (named after Asoka) in present Ningpo. A lover of learning, he not only studied the Buddhist scriptures but also steeped himself in the Confucian classics. Urged by a mystic impetus stirring in him, he went southward to Fu-chou (Foochow) to seek instruction from a Ch'an master there, but his mind was not opened, and hence he took to the road again. As he was passing by the monastery of Ti-tsang, he was caught in a snowstorm, so that he had to stop over for a while. As he was warming himself by the stove, the abbot Lo-han Kuei-ch'eng asked him, "What is the destination of your present trip?" "I am only a pilgrim," he answered.

"What is the meaning of your pilgrimage?" asked the abbot. "I don't know," was the reply. "Unknowing is the closest intimacy," came the cryptic remark of the abbot. When the snow had stopped, he took leave of the abbot, who accompanied him to the door, and asked him, "You say that the three realms are nothing but mind, and all dharmas nothing but consciousness. Now tell me, is that stone out there in the courtyard within your mind or outside your mind?" "Within my mind," he replied. At this the abbot said, "O you wanderer, what makes it so necessary for you to travel with a stone on your mind?" Fa-yen was taken aback by this remark, and, laying down his bag, he decided to stay longer with the abbot in order to settle his doubts. Every day he presented his new views and new reasons to the master; but all that the master commented was, "The Buddha dharma is not like that." At the end of a month, Fa-yen said to the master, "I have exhausted my stock of words and reason." The master said, "As regards the Buddha dharma, everything is a present reality." At the hearing of these words Fa-yen was greatly enlightened.

Later when Fa-yen became an abbot, he used to say to his assembly, "Reality is right before you, and yet you are apt to translate it into a world of names and forms. How are you going to retranslate it into its original?" Learned as he was, he warned his monks against mere learning. Since reality is right before us, it can only be perceived by direct intuition, and reflection and reasoning will only blindfold our eyes.

Fa-yen once quoted an old master Ch'ang-ch'ing's well-known verse: "In the midst of myriad phenomena the solitary body (dharmakāya) reveals itself"; and asked Tzu-fang, a former disciple of Ch'ang-ch'ing, how he understood it. Tzu-fang just raised his dust whisk; but Fa-yen said, "How can you understand it in this way?" "What is your view?" asked Tzu-fang. Fa-yen asked back, "What are the myriad phenomena anyway?" "Well," said Tzu-fang, "the ancients did not brush aside the myriad phenomena." Fa-yen was quick with his repartee, "Since the solitary body reveals itself in the very midst of the phenomenal world, what need is there to talk about brushing aside or not brushing aside?" At this Tzu-fang was instantaneously enlightened.

Once a monk asked, "In what way must one expose oneself to Tao so as to be in tune with Tao?" Fa-yen asked back, "When have you ever exposed yourself to Tao without being in tune with it?"

It does not seem likely that the monk who asked that question had ever

exposed himself to Tao. The question itself reveals that he was still playing Tao instead of letting Tao play. The master's subtle counter question
should have awakened him to his error; however, still unenlightened, he
proceeded to ask, "But what can you do when the six senses are incapable
of appreciating the subtle voice of truth?" Obviously he was trying to pass
the buck to the senses. But the master, not to be hoodwinked, said, "They
are all your own children!" There was no shirking of responsibility. The
master then proceeded to point out to him, "You say that the six senses do
not apprehend the subtle voice of truth. Is it the ear that is at fault, or is it
the eye? But if fundamental reality truly *is*, how can it be negated (even
though the six senses have no perception of it)? As the ancients said, 'To
leave the senses is to be attached to the senses, and to leave names and
letters is to be attached to names and letters.' This is why the *devas* of the
thoughtless heaven fell in a single day back to their original state of
ignorance and delusion after eighty thousand *mahākalpas* of self-cultivation
and mortification. This was bound to happen, seeing that they did not
have an authentic insight into fundamental reality."

Once confirmed in this authentic insight, you no longer look at things
through your fleshly eyes but the eye of that fundamental reality itself.
This eye is called the Dharma Eye (Fa-yen) or, as Fa-yen himself used to
call it, the Tao Eye. Once he put a question to his monks, "When the 'eye'
[the channel] of a wellspring gets stuck, it is because it is filled up with
sand. Now, when the Tao Eye is not opened, what is obstructing it?"
Getting no answer from the assembly, he answered it himself, "The ob-
struction lies in the eye!"

This does not mean that our natural eyes have no use. They are quite
useful, so long as they do not try to fill the place of the Tao Eye. In the
Tao Eye of Fa-yen, all things have their place and function and their
relative reality in the one fundamental reality, so long as we take them for
what they are—expedients and intermediary stages. For him, Buddha is
not the Ultimate, only a name created for expediency. On the other
hand, in the Ultimate there are no more stages or states. Once a monk
asked, "What is the state of one reality." Fa-yen replied, "If it is a state,
there cannot be the one reality."

Fa-yen was realistic through and through, empirically as well as meta-
physically. That he was a metaphysical realist is clear from his explicit

emphasis on the fundamental reality beyond all attributes. His empirical realism is to be found in the operational way he defined things. For instance, when he was asked what is the mind of the ancient Buddhas, he said, "It is that from which flow compassion and joyful giving." When asked what is the right and true way, he answered, "That which I have vowed, once and again, to teach you to walk on." Again, when a monk asked, "It has been said, 'All the worthies and sages of the ten quarters belong to *this* school.' Now, what is exactly *this* school?" His answer was, "That to which all the worthies and sages of the ten quarters belong."

Although Fa-yen was an immensely learned man, well versed in the traditional teachings, yet he never became a slave to learning and book knowledge. It seems that all learning was grist to the mill of his own mind. He frequently quoted the wise sayings of the ancients, but in his lips they became integral parts of his own discourses. He never took the means for the end, and the end was always to lead his hearers to them-selves and ultimately to the eternal Tao which is beyond words and con-ception. Everywhere he directed the attention of his monks to the here and now. When a monk asked about the ancient Buddhas, he remarked, "Even now there are no barriers." That is, no barriers between you and the Fundamental Reality. When another monk asked how to conduct himself in the twenty hours of the day and night, he said, "Let each step tread on it." That is, on the path of Tao. When he was asked what was the secret aim of all the Buddhas, he said, "You also have it in yourself." On another occasion, a monk said to him, "I am not asking about the pointer, I only wish to know what is the moon?" The master answered him with a counterquestion, "Who is the pointer that you do not ask about?" Another monk then asked, "I am not asking about the moon; I only wish to know who is the pointer." "The moon," said the master. The monk protested, "I was asking about the pointer; why did you answer me with the moon?" The master replied, "Because you were asking about the pointer!" In other words, the moon, like everything else in the universe, is but a pointer to the supreme mystery. In the words of Chuang-tzu, "The whole cosmos is but a pointer."

When Fa-yen was the abbot of the Ch'ing-liang temple in present Nanking, he was on very intimate terms with the lord of southern T'ang, Prince Li Ching (916–961). One day when they had finished with their

spiritual discussions, they went together to look at the blooming peonies.
At the request of the prince, Fa-yen hit off a poem on the spot:

> Donned in felt, I commune secretly with the blooming bush,
> With feelings peculiarly my own.
> Just this day, my hairs have begun to turn white:
> Last year, the flowers looked redder than these.
> Their tender beauty is going the way of the morning dew;
> Their fragrant breath is evaporating into the evening breeze.
> Why must we wait for their wilting and falling
> Before we can realize the evanescence of life?

From this we can say that Fa-yen was not only a philosopher and a
scholar, but a poet. The second couplet is a very original imitation of Tu
Fu's well-known lines:

> Tonight the dew has begun to whiten into frost:
> The moon is bright only in the homeland.

Technically, Fa-yen's poem leaves nothing to be desired. But one wonders
at its sad tone and misses the cheerful spirit and untrammeled freedom of
some of the great masters like Nan-ch'üan, Chao-chou, and Yün-men.
Can the blooming peonies ever fade and fall? Or can the swallow that
Hsüan-sha heard ever cease to twitter, anymore than the flock of wild
swans that Ma-tsu saw can ever fly away? Was Fa-yen not an enlightened
master and an apostle of the here and now, to whom every day should be
the best day? Could he possibly be one of the worldlings who, as Nan-
ch'üan said, look at the flowers as in a dream?

My answer to all these queries is that the poem was not meant to
articulate his deepest thoughts but to administer a salutary medicine to his
royal disciple, who, it is recorded, understood the master's meaning immediately. In fact, Fa-yen was noted for his exceptional qualities as a
spiritual guide, and he has been compared to a skillful medical doctor who
knows how to apply the proper remedies to various patients. He was at
once enlightened and practical.

That the above poem did not reveal his interior landscape will be
crystal clear from another poem, which was obviously written to amuse
himself:

*A bird in a secluded grove sings like a flute.*
*Willows sway gracefully with their golden threads.*
*The mountain valley grows the quieter as the clouds return.*
*A breeze brings along the fragrance of the apricot flowers.*
*For a whole day I have sat here encompassed by peace,*
*Till my mind is cleansed in and out of all cares and idle thoughts.*
*I wish to tell you how I feel, but words fail me.*
*If you come to this grove, we can compare notes.*

This lovely poem puts Fa-yen in the company of Tao Yüan-ming and Wang Wei. It is a spontaneous leap of mind in the eternal breaking out into sound.

At bottom, Fa-yen was a mystic. His was not a natural or cosmic mysticism, but a metacosmic one. Although as a keen student of the Avataṃsaka sūtras, he was intensely interested and well versed in the doctrine of six basic attributes of being and their interpenetration, he did not identify the phenomenological universe of attributes with the Ultimate Reality or Being, which is entirely devoid of all attributes. For him Fundamental Reality is Formless Void. This is clearly shown in a dialogue Fa-yen had with his disciple Yung-ming Tao-ch'ien. The first time Tao-ch'ien came to call, the master asked him what sūtras he was reading. Learning that he was reading the *Hua-yen ching*, the master asked, "The six attributes of being: the universal and the particular, the same and the different, the positive and the negative—in what part of the *Hua-yen ching* is this subject treated?" Tao-ch'ien replied, "It is treated under the section on 'The Ten Stages.' But logically speaking, the six attributes are universally applicable, since every dharma, whether in the mundane sphere or in the supramundane, possesses the six attributes." The master then asked, "Does śūnyatā or Formless Void possess the six attributes?" The newcomer was baffled by the question and did not know what to say. The master said, "Suppose you ask me the same question; I will give you my answer." Tao-ch'ien accordingly asked, "Does the Formless Void possess the six attributes?" "Formless Void!" was the immediate answer from the master, and the disciple's mind was suddenly opened to enlightenment. Jumping about for joy, he paid his obeisance in gratitude. When the master asked him how he understood it, his immediate answer was "Formless Void!" And the master was delighted.

After the master's death (958), Prince Li Ching conferred on him the posthumous title of Ta Fa-yeh Ch'an-shih (Great Ch'an Master of the Dharma Eye) and named his stupa Wu Hsiang (the Formless).

Among his immediate disciples, T'ien-t'ai Te-shao (891–972) was the most prominent. We cannot go into the details of his teaching. Suffice it to quote here a gāthā he wrote when he was abbot of a temple on Mount T'ung-hsüan-feng:

> Over the crest of the T'ung-hsüan-feng,
> The human world is no more.
> Nothing is outside the Mind;
> And the eye is filled with green mountains.

It is said that this gāthā was heartily approved by Fa-yen. Perhaps, it would have been the answer to the question posed by his late master Lo-han about the stone and the mind. The stone is certainly not in the human mind or eye; but just as certainly it is not outside the Mind transcendent to the world.

Te-shao is important also as the master of Yung-ming Yen-shou (904–975), who came to be one of the greatest Buddhist writers China has produced. He was a man of speculative genius and a great systematizer. His Tsung-ching lu is a monumental work of a hundred volumes, purporting to be a presentation of the principles of Zen. But as a matter of fact, Yen-shou was fundamentally an eclectic, absorbing ideas and materials from all sources, in order to buttress the principles of Zen or what he regarded as such. Although his book is of considerable value as an interpretation of Mahāyāna Buddhism in general, yet, as far as the school of Zen is concerned, it did more disservice than service. It is ironic that the school of Ch'an which had started with such leading ideas as "a special transmission outside of the scriptures" and "no setting up of or dependence on words and letters" should have ended by producing such a long-winded treatise. Of course, it did not kill Zen but it certainly hastened the extinction of the House of Fa-yen, of which Yen-shou was a member. The spirit of Ch'an is fundamentally inimical to the spirit of systematization and eclecticism, of which Yen-shou happened to be an embodiment. The fact is that Yen-shou's dominant passion was to unify the school of Zen and the school of the Pure Land, holding, in the apt words of a modern historian, "that invocation of the Buddha's name, reciting the sūtras, and observing

the precepts should accompany Ch'an's meditation." But the tragedy is
that when Zen is wedded to a particular set of practices and rituals, it
loses independence and ceases to be itself, although it is not to be denied
that this wedding enlivened the Pure Land school.

However, it cannot be said that Yen-shou did not have any spark of
Zen in him. Some of his dialogues and gāthās reveal his great potentialities as a Zen master. The reader will find the following gatha delightfully
refreshing:

> You wish to know the spirit of Yung-ming Zen?
> Look at the lake in front of the gate.
> When the sun shines, it radiates light and brightness.
> When the wind comes, there arise ripples and waves.

What a simple and charming picture it presents, and at the same time how
pregnant with insight! There is a time for peaceful contemplation; there is
a time for dynamic action; and all the time the lake remains itself.

Yen-shou belonged to the third generation of the House of Fa-yen,
which was yet to last for two more generations. In both the third and the
fourth generations, there were still a galaxy of masters, showing that the
spirit of Fa-yen was still running in their blood. I will only mention a
couple of examples here. One was Hang-chou Hung-shou, whose enlightenment was occasioned by hearing the sound of a piece of firewood
falling on the ground. The gāthā he wrote on that occasion was a direct
and simple utterance of his own mind and at the same time embodies an
insight typical of the House of Fa-yen. I need not reproduce it here,
because it is quoted by Chu Hsi (1130–1200) in a passage which I intend
to present at the end of this chapter.

The other delightful personality I wish to mention is Hang-chou Wei-
chen (986–1049), who was noted for his congenial humor and easy-going
philosophy of life. Evidently, he was steeped in the Confucian classics,
especially the Analects. Now, Confucius had once said, "People speak of
ritual, ritual! Does ritual merely mean jades and silks? People speak of
music, music! Does music merely mean the bells and drums?" Wei-chen,
mimicking the style of Confucius, said, "People speak of Buddha, Buddha!
Does Buddha merely mean portraits and images? People speak of monk,
monk! Does a monk consist merely in dignified vestments?" But he never
talked about Zen. Once somebody took him to task, saying, "Are you not

called a Zen master? Yet you have never spoken about Zen!" The master said, "Why should I waste my words? Besides, I am too lazy to resort to ingenious and devious methods of presentation. So I can only rely upon the endless phenomena of nature to expound and play out day and night the truths of Ch'an. Speech easily comes to an end, but this agency of nature is inexhaustible, and that's why it is called the Creator's limitless treasury." This is the last word of the last of the Fa-yens.

The significance of the House of Fa-yen for Chinese philosophy in general lies in the fact that of all the schools and sects of Buddhism it seems to be the most congenial to the minds of Confucian scholars. It is not for nothing that Chu Hsi, the leading Neo-Confucian philosopher of the Sung period, and one of Buddhism's severest critics, should have picked out the teachings of the House of Fa-yen for his unstinted praise in a conversation with one of his disciples. Here is what he said:

There is a certain current in Buddhist thought which is very similar to our Confucian traditions, as where they say:

*"Something there is, which preceded heaven and earth:*
*Without form, without sound, all alone by itself.*
*Yet it has the power to be the master of all things,*
*Not subject to decay in the course of the four seasons."*

Or take this:

*"Plop, there it is! Nothing else than that which,*
*Devoid of matter, fills all corners of the universe!*
*Mountains, rivers, the entire world,*
*One and all, they manifest the body of the Dharma king."*

Or take this:

*"To the man who is intimately aware of Creative Mind,*
*There is not an iota of matter throughout the whole earth."*

Just think what marvellous insights these are! How could the ordinary Confucian scholars of today hope to measure up to those men of high vision? What wonder if they are beaten to the ground? Now, the above insights represent the essential points of the house founded by the Ch'an master Fa-yen. But contemporary students of Ch'an are of one accord critical of these principles, on the ground that they "contain some rational element" and "fall into the beaten track," thus "hindering the perception." The Ch'an of today consists mostly of "Three catties of hemp," "Dry toilet strip," and sayings of that sort. Only such expressions, they maintain, do not fall into the beaten track or the path of reason. Miao-hsi, for example, is of this opinion, though at times he seems to reverse his own views.

From this excerpt, it is clear that Chu Hsi was a sincere and open-minded seeker of truth, not a sentimental defender of the old traditions. It remains for me to add some necessary comments which have occurred to my mind in reading through the passage. The first gāthā quoted by Chu Hsi was originally uttered by the famous Fu Ta-shih in the sixth century, whose lively personality and profound teachings exercised an uplifting influence on the school of Zen which was to come later, and who is regarded as one of its important precursors. The said gāthā was probably a frequent subject of discussion in the House of Fa-yen, although I have seen only one reference to it in the extant literature. There could be no question that the idea embodied in the gāthā constituted the sinew and marrow of Fa-yen's doctrine. But when Chu Hsi said that this was similar to "our Confucian traditions," I think he made a hasty statement, for the gāthā was evidently of Taoist inspiration. However, by Chu Hsi's time Confucianism had very probably assimilated most of the fundamental insights of Lao and Chuang.

The second gāthā quoted by Chu Hsi was uttered by Hung-shou, to whom we have referred in a preceding page. As to his third quotation, I have not been able to trace it to its source.

Chu Hsi's unreserved appreciation of the Zen of Fa-yen House bespeaks the catholicity of his mind, and his strictures against the exaggerated tendencies toward irrationalism manifested in some Ch'an students were called for. But if he had delved into the traditions and origins of the other houses as he had done with the House of Fa-yen, it is likely that he would have found in them much that was "similar to our Confucian traditions." Perhaps, everyone of us is more or less preconditioned in his predilections. This is true not only in matters of taste, but to some extent also in purely intellectual pursuits. Lu Hsiang-shan, for example, would have been impressed by things which left Chu Hsi cold.

CHAPTER XIV

# Epilogue:
# Little Sparks of Zen

## 1. TIME AND ETERNITY

One of the most frequently reiterated couplets in Chinese Zen literature is:

> *An eternity of endless space:*
> *A day of wind and moon.*

This brings us, as it were, to the dawn of creation. Nothing stirs the
heart and mind of man more profoundly than to be reminded of the first
quivering of time in the womb of eternity. An infinite void, utterly silent
and still. In a split second there came life and motion, form and color. No
one knows how it happened. It is a mystery of mysteries. But the mere
recognition that mystery exists is enough to send any man of sensitive
mind into an ecstasy of joy and wonder.

Herein is the secret of the perennial charm of Basho's haiku:

> *An old pond.*
> *A frog jumps in:*
> > *Plop!*

The old pond corresponds to "An eternity of endless space," while the
frog jumping in and causing the water to utter a sound is equivalent to "A
day of wind and moon." Can there be a more beautiful and soul-shaking
experience than to catch ageless silence breaking for the first time into
song? Moreover, every day is the dawn of creation, for every day is

unique and comes for the first time and the last. God is not the God of the dead, but of the living.

## 2. A DAY OF WIND AND MOON

Shan-neng, a Zen master of the Southern Sung, gave a meaningful comment on the couplet:

> *An eternity of endless space:*
> *A day of wind and moon.*

"Of course," he said, "we must not cling to the wind and moon of a day and ignore the eternal Void. Neither should we cling to the eternal Void and give no attention to the wind and moon of the day. Furthermore, what kind of a day is it? Other people complain of its extreme heat. But I love the summer day, because it lasts so long. Warm wind comes from the South, and a comfortable coolness is born around the temple and the terrace."

## 3. AUSPICIOUS SIGN

A monk asked the master Ch'u-hui Chen-chi as he appeared for the first time as an abbot, "I hear that when Śākyamuni began his public life, golden lotus sprang from the earth. Today, at the inauguration of Your Reverence, what auspicious sign may we expect?" The new abbot said, "I have just swept away the snow before the gate."

## 4. THE FUN OF BEING LAUGHED AT

Po-yün Shou-tuan was studying under Yang-ch'i. He was a most earnest student but had little sense of humor. Once Yang-ch'i asked him under whom he had studied before. Shou-tuan replied, "Master Yueh of Ch'a-ling." Yang-ch'i said, "I hear that he came to his enlightenment when he slipped and fell in crossing a bridge, and that he hit off a very wonderful gāthā on the occasion. Do you remember the wording?" Shou-tuan recited:

> *There is a bright pearl within me,*
> *Buried for a long time under dust.*
> *Today, the dust is gone and the light radiates,*
> *Shining through all the mountains and rivers.*

On hearing this, Yang-ch'i ran away laughing. Put out by the master's strange reaction, Shou-tuan could not sleep for a whole night. Early in the morning he went to the master and asked him what it was in his former teacher's gāthā that had caused him to laugh. The master said, "Did you see yesterday the funny antics of the exorcists?" "Yes," Shou-tuan replied. "In one respect you rather fall short of them," said the master. Disconcerted once more, Shou-tuan asked, "What do you mean?" The master said, "They love to see others laugh, but you are afraid to see others laugh!" Shou-tuan was enlightened. Only then did he realize what Aelred Graham calls the "importance of being not earnest."

### 5. THE OPEN SECRET

Huang-lung Tsu-hsin was on intimate terms with the famous man of letters Huang Shan-ku (1045–1105). One day, Shan-ku besought Huang-lung to give him a secret shortcut to Zen. Huang-lung said, "It is just as Confucius put it: 'My dear pupils, do you really think that I am hiding anything from you? In fact, I have hid nothing from you.' What have you thought of these words?" As Shan-ku fumbled for an answer, Huang-lung interjected, "Not this, not this!" Shan-ku felt greatly frustrated. One day, as he accompanied Huang-lung in strolling on the mountain, the cinnamon trees were in full bloom in the valleys. Huang-lung asked, "Do you perceive the fragrance of the cinnamon?" "Yes, I do," replied Shan-ku. Huang-lung said, "You see, I have hid nothing from you!" Shan-ku was enlightened, and did obeisance, saying, "What a grandmotherly heart Your Reverence has got!" Huang-lung smiled and said, "It is my only wish to see you arrive home."

### 6. CUTTING THE GORDIAN KNOT

The masters of Zen often resort to the trick of putting their students in a dilemma from which there is apparently no outlet. When T'ien-i was studying under Ming-chüeh of Ts'ui-feng, the latter made an enigmatic statement: "Not this, not that, not this and that altogether!" That set T'ien-i a-wondering. As T'ien-i was reflecting on this, Ming-chüeh drove him out by beating. This happened several times. Later, T'ien-i was put in charge of carrying water. Once the pole on his shoulder suddenly split so that the pails fell to the ground pouring out all the water. At that very moment he was awakened to his self-nature and found himself out of the dilemma.

Hsiang-yen Chih-hsien once posed a similar question to his community: "The whole affair is like a man who hangs on to a tall tree by his teeth, with his hands grasping no branch and his feet resting on no limb. A man under the tree suddenly asks him, 'What is the significance of Bodhidharma coming from the West?' If he does not answer, he fails to respond to the question. But if he answers, he falls and loses his life. Now what must he do?"

At that time, the elder Chao of Hu-t'ou happened to be in the assembly. He stood forth, saying, "Let us not ask about the man who is already on the tree. Can you tell me something about him before he has climbed up the tree?" Hsiang-yen burst into loud laughter.

I-tuan, one of Nan-ch'üan's great disciples, said to his assembly, "Speech is blasphemy, silence a lie. Above speech and silence there is a way out."

Fa-yün of the House of Yün-men said to his assembly, "If you advance one step, you lose sight of the principle. If you retreat one step, you fail to keep abreast of things. If you neither advance nor retreat, you would be as insensible as a stone." A monk asked, "How can we avoid being insensible?" "Veer and do the best you can," replied the master. The monk: "How can we avoid losing sight of the principle and at the same time keep abreast of things?" The master: "Advance one step and at the same time retreat one step."

### 7. THE WAY UPWARD

Zen masters are soaring spirits. However high a state they have attained, they never cease to speak of the "way upward." But it is interesting to note that at a certain point, the only way to go upward is by descending to the earth. Thus, when a monk asked the master Chi-ch'en, "What is the way upward?" the latter replied, "You will hit it by descending lower."

This makes me think of St. John of the Cross, who wrote:

> By stooping so low, so low,
> I mounted so high, so high,
> That I was able to reach my goal.

Despite all the differences of undertones and overtones between the two, it is intriguing to note the identity of the paradoxical form in which their insights were presented.

St. John of the Cross is a master of paradoxes. For instance, this:

> *In order to arrive at having pleasure in everything,*
> *Desire to have pleasure in nothing.*
> *In order to arrive at possessing everything,*
> *Desire to possess nothing.*
> *In order to arrive at being everything,*
> *Desire to be nothing.*
> *In order to arrive at knowing everything,*
> *Desire to know nothing.*

All these paradoxes have their counterparts in the philosophy of Lao-tzu and Chuang-tzu. As Chuang-tzu puts it, "Perfect joy is to be without joy." Lao-tzu says:

> *The sage does not take to hoarding.*
> *The more he lives for others, the fuller is his life.*
> *The more he gives the more he abounds.*

Again:

> *Is it not because he is selfless*
> *That his self is realized?*

Finally, according to Lao-tzu, to know that we do not know is the acme of knowledge.

## 8. THE DUMB PERSON

A Chinese proverb says, "When a dumb person eats *huanglien* (a bitter herb used for medicine), he feels the bitterness but has no one to tell it to." The Zen masters have a knack of touching up a popular saying for their own purposes. Yang-ch'i, for example, said, "When the dumb person has got a dream, to whom can he tell it?" Hui-lin Tz'u-shou was even more ingenious, as you will see from the following dialogue:

> *Monk: When a man realizes that there is but does not know how to*
> *express it, what is he like?*
> *Tz'u-shou: He is like a dumb person eating honey!*

*Monk: When a man, who actually does not realize that* there is, *yet talks glibly about it, what would he be like?*
*Tz'u-shou: He is like a parrot calling people's names!*

### 9. HOW TAO-SHU COPED WITH A MONSTER

Tao-shu, a disciple of Shen-hsiu, was living on a mountain with a few pupils. There frequently appeared to him a strange man, simple in clothes but wild and boastful in speech. He could take on the appearance of a Buddha, a bodhisattva or an arhat or whatever he had a fancy to. Tao-shu's pupils were all amazed; they could not make out who that wizard was and what he was after. For ten years his apparitions continued. But one day he vanished away, never to return.

Tao-shu said to his pupils, "The wizard is capable of all kinds of tricks in order to bedevil the minds of men. My own way of coping with them is by refraining from seeing and hearing them. His tricks, however multifarious, must come to an end someday, but there is no end to my non-seeing and non-hearing!"

As another master has put it, "What is inexpressible is inexhaustible in its use."

### 10. A MOTLEY BODHISATTVA

The Bodhisattva Shan-hui, better known as Fu Ta-shih, born in 497, was one of the most extraordinary figures in Buddhism and an important precursor of the school of Zen. Once he was invited by Emperor Wu of Liang (who reigned from 502 to 549) to give a lecture on the *Diamond Sūtra*. No sooner had he ascended to the platform than he rapped the table with his rod and descended. The poor emperor was simply lost in amazement. Yet Shan-hui asked, "Does Your Majesty understand?" "I don't understand at all," replied the emperor. "But the Ta-shih has already finished his sermon!" Shan-hui remarked.

On another occasion, as Shan-hui was delivering a sermon, the emperor arrived, and the whole community rose to show their respect. Only Shan-hui remained seated without any motion. Somebody took him to task, saying, "Why don't you stand up when His Majesty has come?" Shan-hui said, "If the realm of the Dharma is unsettled, the whole world would lose its peace."

One day, wearing a Buddhist cassock, a Taoist cap, and Confucian shoes, Shan-hui came into the court. The emperor, amused by the motley attire, asked, "Are you a Buddhist monk?" Shan-hui pointed at his cap. "Are you then a Taoist priest?" Shan-hui pointed to his shoes. "So, you are a man of the world?" Shan-hui pointed to his cassock.

Shan-hui is said to have improvised a couplet on the occasion:

> With a Taoist cap, a Buddhist cassock, and a pair of Confucian shoes,
> I have harmonized three houses into one big family!

If, as Suzuki so well says, Zen is the "synthesis of Taoism, Confucianism, and Buddhism applied to our daily life as we live it," the tendency was already prefigured in Fu Ta-shih.

Two gāthās from Fu Ta-shih have been frequently quoted by Zen masters. One reads:

> Empty-handed, I hold a hoe.
> Walking on foot, I ride a buffalo.
> Passing over a bridge, I see
> The bridge flow, but not the water.

The other reads:

> Something there is, prior to heaven and earth,
> Without form, without sound, all alone by itself.
> It has the power to control all the changing things;
> Yet it changes not in the course of the four seasons.

## 11. "I HAVE LOST MYSELF"

When Chuang-tzu wrote "Wu Shang ngo" ("I have lost myself"), he meant that his real self had got rid of his individual ego. Self-realization through self-loss is the universal message of all religion and wisdom. Lose and you will gain. Be blind and you will see; be deaf and you will hear. Leave home and you will find home. In one word, die and you will live. Life is a perpetual dialogue between wu and ngo.

## 12. LEAVING HOME FOR HOME

Buddhist monks call themselves proudly "home-leavers." It is indeed not a small thing to leave your dear ones at home and wander forth all alone in search of Tao. Once a great prince told the Zen master Tao-ch'in of

Ching-shan that he was thinking of being a home-leaver. "What?" said the master, "It takes a full-grown man to leave home. This is not something that the generals and prime ministers can undertake!"

Yet many Zen masters have spoken of enlightenment in terms of *return home.* I don't know how many times they have referred to Tao Ch'ien's "Song of Returning Home." The following poem by the Zen master Ying-yüan is typical:

> *The cold season is coming to an end,*
> > *And Spring is arriving!*
> *Untethered buffaloes and oxen are*
> > *Jumping all around.*

> *The shepherds have cast away their whips.*
> *Too lazy to blow their holeless flute,*
> *They clap their hands and laugh boisterously.*
> *"Homeward, Homeward, Homeward Ho!"*
> *They sing as they go.*
> *Entering the thickets veiled with mists and vapors,*
> *They lie down with their clothes on.*

## 13. PLAYING GOD OR LETTING GOD PLAY?

One of the most significant books of this age of confusion is Dom Aelred Graham's *Zen Catholicism: A Suggestion.* As Dom Aelred sees it, the spirit of Zen lies in letting God play rather than playing God. He shows a profound insight when he says that *satori* (enlightenment) "is the disappearance of the self-conscious me before the full *realization* of the unself-conscious I." It is only after this realization that one no longer plays God, but lets God play.

This state is ineffable, but we find a suggestive picture of it in a beautiful passage from the *Book of Chuang-tzu* in the beautiful version of Thomas Merton:

> *Fishes are born in water,*
> *Man is born in Tao.*
> *If fishes, born in water,*
> *Seek the deep shadow*
> *Of pond and pool,*

*All their needs*
*Are satisfied.*
*If man, born in Tao,*
*Sinks into the deep shadow*
*Of non-action*
*To forget aggression and concern,*
*He lacks nothing*
*His life is secure.*
*Moral: "All the fish needs*
*Is to get lost in water.*
*All man needs is to get lost*
*In Tao."*

## 14. A TASTE OF SUZUKI'S ZEN

It was in the summer of 1959, in Honolulu. The University of Hawaii was holding its third East-West Philosophers' Conference. Among its panel members was Dr. Daisetz Teitaro Suzuki, who was then already eighty-nine. One evening as he was reporting to us the Japanese philosophy of life, I heard him say, "The Japanese live by Confucianism but die by Buddhism." I was struck by this remarkable statement. Of course, I understood what he meant, for this is more or less true also of the Chinese. All the same, I thought that it was an exaggeration, which stood in need of some amendment. So, as soon as he had finished his report, I asked the chairman to permit me to put a question to Dr. Suzuki. Having got the green light, I proceeded, "I was very much struck by Dr. Suzuki's observation that Japanese live by Confucianism but die by Buddhism. Now, a few years ago, I had the pleasure of reading Dr. Suzuki's *Living by Zen*. Is Zen not a school of Buddhism? or can it be that Dr. Suzuki is the only Japanese who lives by Zen? If there are other Japanese living by Zen, then the statement that Japanese live by Confucianism and die by Buddhism would seem to need some revision." The chairman very carefully relayed my question to Dr. Suzuki (because he was somewhat hard of hearing), and the whole panel was agog for his answer. But no sooner had the chairman presented the question than Dr. Suzuki responded with the spontaneity of a true Zen master, "Living is dying!" This set the whole conference table aroar. Everybody was laughing, apparently at my expense. I alone was enlightened. He did not answer the question, but he lifted the questioner to a higher plane, a plane beyond logic and reasoning, beyond living and dying. I felt like giving Dr. Suzuki a slap in order to assure him that his utterance had clicked. But after all, must I not still live by Confucianism?

### 15. AN ENCOUNTER WITH HOLMES'S ZEN

In 1923 I spent my Christmas holidays with my old friend Justice Holmes in Washington. One morning he was showing me around his wonderful private library, which was full of books on art, literature, and philosophy, besides works on law. From time to time he pulled out a book from the shelves and told me what he thought of it. He told me how William James and Josiah Royce used to play hide-and-seek with God; how he had enjoyed the *Golden Bough*; how deeply he was impressed by the works of de Tocqueville, especially his *Ancien Régime*, which he said that I must read in order to keep my idealism from going wild; and so on and forth. Finally, assuming a very serious tone, he said to me, "But my dear boy, I have not yet shown you the best books in the library." "Where do you keep them?" I asked impatiently. He pointed me to some far corner of the room, saying, "There!" When I looked, I found to my greatest amazement an empty shelf! I laughed, saying, "How characteristic of you, Justice! Always looking forward!" Later it occurred to me that Holmes was not merely looking forward but upward. It was only after I had studied the *Tao-te ching*, with its stress on the empty and invisible, that I realized the full purport of Holmes's pointing.

But somehow Holmes's jolly action liberated my mind from the world of conventional inhibitions. One evening as we were, to use his graphic expression, "twisting the tail of the cosmos" together, Mrs. Holmes (who, like Holmes, was in her early eighties and as vivacious as he) came in. As soon as I saw her, I rose to greet her and, in a jeu d'esprit, said to her, "Madame, may I present to you my friend Justice Holmes?" She shook hands with him, saying, "It's a pleasure to know you, Mr. Oliver Wendell Holmes!" Probably that was what she had said more than sixty years ago at their first meeting! At that moment, the three of us looked at one another with an understanding smile. Had William James not said that a philosopher looks at familiar things as if they were strange and strange things as if they were familiar? At that time I had only had a smattering of

Taoism but never had heard of Zen. As I look at it now, it was undoubtedly a genuine case of Zen. There was a sudden meeting of eternity and time. Like those wild geese flying over the heads of Ma-tsu and Pai-chang, this experience has passed but is not gone.

## 16. THE METAPHYSICAL BACKGROUND OF ZEN

Zen is not without a metaphysical basis, although for the most part it remains inarticulate. The essentials of its metaphysics are to be found in the first chapter of *Tao-te ching*:

> *If Tao can be translated into words, it would not be Tao as such.*
> *Any name that can be given it is not its eternal name.*
> *It is nameless, because it is prior to the universe:*
> *Yet it is nameable in the sense that it is "Mother of all things."*
> *In essence, it is a formless void:*
> *In manifestation, it has all shapes and forms.*
> *But both the essence and manifestation are of one and the same origin,*
> *Although they are differently named.*
> *This is what is called mysterious identity.*
> *In the depth of this mystery*
> *Is the door to all ineffable truths.*

The Zennist interpretation of the above can be briefly stated. In the first place, Tao being something fundamentally inexpressible, any talk about it is more or less a tour de force. It cannot be communicated to another. Every one of us must find it in himself by direct intuition. The words of the masters are meant only to provoke the working of this intuition in you, not to infuse it into you. All the names they may call it are only expedient means for awakening you to the Tao in you. Secondly, Tao is beyond names and namelessness. Absolutely, in its suchness, it cannot be named: but relatively to the world of things, it is, as it were, their common mother. Thirdly, it embraces both the noumenal and the phenomenal, which represent but two aspects of Tao, which is their common origin or source. It embraces both, because it transcends both. This unity of transcendence and immanence is the mystery of mysteries. Fourthly, being the mystery of mysteries, it would be utterly vain to try to understand it. Yet we ourselves are mysteries, mysterious members of the mysterious Whole. Although we cannot understand it, we can embrace it.

In fact we live, move, and have our being in it. We can dive into it until we arrive at the door of all wonders. As Merton had discovered long before he had looked into Taoism or Zen, "A door opens in the center of our being and we seem to fall through it into immense depths which, although they are infinite, are all accessible to us; all eternity seems to have become ours in this one placid and breathless contact."

## 17. RIDING AN ASS

According to Ch'ing-yüan, also called Fo-yen, there are two diseases in connection with the practice of Zen. "The first is to ride an ass in search of the ass. The second is to ride the ass and refuse to dismount." It is easy to see the silliness of seeking the ass you are riding. As your attention is turned outwards, you will never look inside, and all your search will be so much ado about nothing. The kingdom of God is within you, but you seek it outside. There is no telling how many troubles in the world have had their origin just in this wrong orientation.

As Ma-tsu has said, "You are the treasure of your own house." To seek it outside is a pathetic endeavor, because you will always be disappointed. For, at the bottom of your heart, you are seeking the real treasure. Although you may be satisfied for a few moments with faked substitutes, in the depths of your subconsciousness, you can never deceive yourself. Leon Bloy has uttered a profound insight when he said, "There is but one sorrow, and that is to have lost the Garden of Delights, and there is but one hope and one desire, to recover it. The poet seeks it in his own way, and the filthiest profligate seeks it in his. It is the only goal." But the tragedy is that, not realizing that the Garden of Delights is within us, we seek it by flying away from it with an ever-increasing speed.

The second disease is even more subtle and difficult to cure. This time, you are no longer seeking outside. You know that you are riding your own ass. You have already tasted an interior peace infinitely sweeter than any pleasures you can get from the external things. But the great danger is that you become so attached to it that you are bound to lose it altogether. This is what Ch'ing-yüan meant by "riding the ass and refusing to dismount." This disease is common to contemplative souls in all religions. In his *Seeds of Contemplation*, Thomas Merton has uttered a salutary warning against precisely the same pitfall:

Within the simplicity of this armed and walled and undivided interior peace is an infinite unction which, as soon as it is grasped, loses its savor. You must not try to reach out and possess it altogether. You must not touch it, or try to seize it. You must not try to make it sweeter or try to keep it from wasting away. . . .

The situation of the soul in contemplation is something like the situation of Adam and Eve in Paradise. Everything is yours, but on one infinitely important condition: that it is all *given*.

There is nothing that you can claim, nothing that you can demand, nothing that you can take. And as soon as you try to take something as if it were your own—you lose your Eden.

In this light, you can appreciate the profound insight of Lung-t'an that the priceless pearl can only be kept by one who does not fondle it.

Ch'ing-yüan's final counsel is, "Do not ride at all. For you yourself are the ass, and the whole world is the ass. You have no way to ride it. . . . If you don't ride at all the whole universe will be your playground."

### 18. THE IMPORTANCE OF HIDDENNESS

Nan-ch'üan once went to visit a village and found to his surprise that the village head had already made preparations to welcome him. The master said, "It has been my custom never to let anyone know beforehand my goings about. How could you know that I was coming to your village today?" The village head replied, "Last night, in a dream the god of the soil shrine reported to me that Your Reverence would come to visit today." The master said, "This shows how weak and shallow my spiritual life is, so that it can still be espied by the spiritual beings!"

The Zen masters set little or no value on the *siddis* (magical powers). This point is well illustrated in the life of Niu-t'ou Fa-yung (594–657). Niu-t'ou came from a scholarly family in the city of Yen-ling in modern Kiangsu. By the time he was nineteen, he was already well steeped in the Confucian classics and the dynastic histories. Soon after he delved into Buddhist literature, especially the prajñā scriptures, and came to an understanding of the nature of śūnyatā. One day he said to himself, "Confucianism sets up the norms for mundane life, but after all they do not represent the ultimate Law. The contemplative wisdom of the *Prajñā* is truly the raft to ford us over to the supramundane." Thereupon he retired into a hill,

studied under a Buddhist master, and had his head shaved. Later he went
to Niu-t'ou Mountain and lived all alone in a cave in the neighborhood of
the Yu-hsi temple. A legend has it that while he was living there, all kinds
of birds used to flock to his hermitage, each holding a flower in its beak,
as if to pay their homage to the holy man.

Sometime during the reign of Chen-kuan (627–650), Tao-hsin, the
Fourth Patriarch of the Chinese school of Zen, looking at Niu-t'ou Mountain from afar, was struck by its ethereal aura, indicating that there must
be some extraordinary man living there. So he took it upon himself to
come to look for the man. When he arrived at the temple, he asked a
monk. "Is there a man of Tao around here?" The monk replied, "Who
among the home-leavers are not men of Tao?" Tao-hsin said, "But which
of you is the man of Tao, after all?" Another monk said, "About three miles
from here, there is a man whom people call the 'Lazy Yung,' because he
never stands up when he sees anybody, nor gives any greeting. Can he be
the man of Tao you are looking for?" Tao-hsin then went deeper into the
mountain and found Niu-t'ou sitting quietly and paying no attention to
him. Tao-hsin approached him, asking, "What are you doing here?" "Contemplating the mind," said Niu-t'ou. "But who is contemplating, and what
is the mind contemplated?" Tao-hsin asked. Stunned by the question, Niu-
t'ou rose from his seat and greeted him courteously, saying, "Where does
Your Reverence live?" "My humble self has no definite place to rest in,
roving east and west." "Do you happen to know the Zen master Tao-hsin?"
"Why do you ask about him?" "I have looked up to him for long, hoping
to pay my homage to him some day." "This humble monk is none other
than Tao-hsin." "What has moved you to condescend to come to this
place?" "For no other purpose than to visit you!" Niu-t'ou then led the
patriarch to his little hermitage. On seeing that it was all surrounded by
tigers and wolves, Tao-hsin raised his hands as if he were frightened. Niu-
t'ou said, "Have no fear! There is still *this one* here!" "What is *this one?*" Tao-
hsin asked. Niu-t'ou remained silent. Some moments later, Tao-hsin
scribed the word "Buddha" on the rock on which Niu-t'ou used to sit.
Gazing at the word, Niu-t'ou showed a reverential awe. "Have no fear,"
said Tao-hsin, "there is still *this one* here." Niu-t'ou was baffled. Bowing to
the patriarch, he begged him to expound to him the essential truth. Tao-
hsin said, "There are hundreds and thousands of dharmas and yogas; but
all of them have their home in the heart. The supernatural powers and

virtues are as innumerable as the sand on the beaches; but all without exception spring from the mind as their common fountainhead. All the paths and doors of śīla, dhyāna, and prajñā, all the infinitely resourceful siddis, are in their integral entirety complete in your mind and inseparable from it. All kleśas and karmic hindrances are fundamentally void and still. All operations of cause and effect are like dreams and illusion. Actually there are no three realms to escape from. Nor is there any bodhi or enlightenment to seek after. All beings, human and nonhuman, belong to one universal, undifferentiated nature. Great Tao is perfectly empty and free of all barriers; it defies all thought and meditation. This Dharma of suchness you have now attained. You are no longer lacking in anything. This is Buddhahood. There is no other dharma besides it. All that you need is to let the mind function and rest in its perfect spontaneity. Do not set it upon contemplation or action, nor try to purify it. Without craving, without anger, without sorrow or care, let the mind move in untrammeled freedom, going where it pleases. No deliberate doing of the good, nor deliberate avoiding of the evil. Whether you are traveling or staying at home, sitting up or lying down, in all circumstances you will see the proper occasion for exercising the wonderful functions of a Buddha. Then you will always be joyful, with nothing to worry about. This is to be a Buddha indeed!"

Niu-t'ou was enlightened. Thereafter he emerged from his life as a hermit and gave himself to the active works of charity and to the expounding of the *Mahāprajñāpāramitā Sūtra.*

Although the "Zen of Niu-t'ou" has been regarded by later Chinese masters as outside the main currents of the school of Zen, his contributions to the elucidation of the philosophy of Nārgājuna are not to be minimized. His main teaching that illumination is to be achieved through contemplation of the Void spread to Japan through Dengyō Daishi (767–822). In China, the "Zen of Niu-t'ou" claimed adherents as late as in the eighth generation after him. Even at present, Niu-t'ou's gāthās are cherished by Buddhists of all schools as an integral part of the Mahāyāna philosophy in China.

Even in the school of Zen, one of the most popular kōans has to do with Niu-t'ou. The question is: How was it that before Niu-t'ou had met the Fourth Patriarch, the birds used to flock to him with flowers in their beaks, while after his enlightenment the prodigy ceased? Of course, all the masters of Zen have of one accord regarded the latter state as incomparably higher than the former state. But everyone has his own way of describing the two states. Shan-ching described the earlier state as "a magical pine tree growing in a wonderland, admired by all who see it," while he likened the latter state to a tree, with "its leaves fallen and its twigs withered, so that the wind passes through it without leaving any music." But the most graphic comment was from the master I of Kuang-te. Of the first state he remarked:

> *When a jar of salted fish is newly opened,*
> *The flies swarm to it buzzing all around.*

Of the second, he stated:

> *When the jar is emptied to the bottom and washed clean,*
> *It is left all alone in its cold desolation.*

Huai-yüeh of Chang-chou spoke of the first state as "Myriad miles of clear sky with a single speck of cloud"; and of the second as "Complete emptiness." To Ch'ung-ao of Lo-feng, in the first state "solid virtue draws homage from the ghosts and spirits"; while in the second state, "the whole being is spiritualized, and there is no way of gauging it."

From the above samplings, one can see clearly the authenticity of the spirituality of Zen. With the sureness of their experiential insight, the Zen masters seem to have hit upon an unerring scale of values in spiritual life. Sensible consolations are not to be despised, but all the same they must be outgrown if one is to advance higher. Desolation is like the unleavened bread which may not taste so sweet but is of vital essence to one's life. There is still another point which is noteworthy. One's internal life must, of course, be hidden from the human eye. This was true of Niu-t'ou even before he had met Tao-hsin, as he was already a hermit. But, as Nan-ch'üan so clearly saw, your internal life must be so hidden that even the demons and angels have no way of espying it.

In the eye of Tao, what appears to be desolation is in reality a garden of flowers. This point has been beautifully articulated by two masters of the House of Yün-men. One was Yüan-ming of Te-shan, whose comment on the first state was:

> *When autumn comes, yellow leaves fall.*

And his comment on the second state was:

*When spring comes, the grasses spontaneously grow green.*

The other was Fa-chin of Yün-men, who spoke of the first state as "fragrant breeze blowing the flowers to fading," and of the second as "showering anew upon fresher and more beautiful flowers."

This indeed is a glorious vision. These masters actually see the desolate land flourishing like the lily!

Any student of comparative mysticism will see in the tradition and spirit of Zen the hallmark of authenticity. It is little wonder that Father Thomas Berry, a profound student of Oriental philosophy and religion, should have called Zen "the summit of Asian spirituality." He certainly knows what he is talking about.

### 19. WHO HAS CREATED GOD?

Once a Buddhist asked me, "God has created everything, but who could have created God?" I said, "That's exactly what I want to know: who could have created God?" And we had a good laugh together.

This question is similar to what Chao-chou asked of Ta-tz'u, "What can be the substance of prajñā?" When Ta-tz'u asked back, "What can be the substance of prajñā?" Chao-chou realized immediately the silliness of his question and burst out laughing.

### 20. THE ROMANCE OF SELF-DISCOVERY

"For me to be a saint means to be myself. Therefore the problem of sanctity and salvation is in fact the problem of finding out who I am and of discovering my true self." This is what Thomas Merton wrote almost twenty years ago, when he had hardly peeped into the works of Chuang-tzu or any of the Zen masters. Yet this practically sums up the whole endeavor of Zen and the Taoists. It is therefore not by chance that he should in the recent years have taken such a genuine interest in Tao and Zen.

To Chuang-tzu, "Only the true man can have true knowledge." Instead of starting from "Cogito, ergo sum," his starting point was "Sum, ergo cogito." Be a true man, and you will have true knowledge. The true man is one who has discovered his true self. Our whole life is a romance, the romance of discovering our true self. Even the fundamental moral precepts such as: Avoid all evil, pursue all good, and purify your mind, are but preliminaries to the finding and being of oneself. Chuang-tzu has summed up this supreme romance of life in a beautiful passage:

> The moral virtues of humanity and justice are only the wayside inns that the sage-kings of old have set up for the wayfarers to lodge for a night. They are not for you to occupy permanently. If you are found to tarry too long, you will be made to pay heavily for it. The perfect men of old borrowed their way through humanity and lodged in justice for a night, on their way to roam in the transcendental regions, picknicking on the field of simplicity and finally settling in their home garden, not rented from another. Transcendency is perfect freedom. Simplicity makes for perfect health and vigor. Your garden not being rented from another, you are not liable to be ejected. The ancients called this the romance of hunting for the *Real*.

Our whole life is, then, a pilgrimage from the unreal to the Real. No romance can be more meaningful and thrilling than this. Because the goal and the process are romantic, there is nothing in life which is not romantic. That's why the Zen masters have so often quoted a significant line from a love poem:

> *In her hands, even the prose of life becomes poetry.*

Many years ago, Justice Holmes wrote me that I must "face the disagreeable" and learn "to tackle the unromantic in life with resolution to make it romantic." The world will not fully realize how this true man of America led me back to the wisdom of the East or, shall I say, to my aboriginal self.

## 21. THE SPIRIT OF INDEPENDENCE

One of the most striking qualities of the Zen masters is their spirit of independence. Single-heartedly devoted to the one thing necessary, they refuse to bow to anything or anyone short of that. As Shih-t'ou declared, "I would rather sink to the bottom of the sea for endless eons than seek liberation through all the saints of the universe!" This is no sign of pride, but rather the part of wisdom. The fact is that no external factor can ever give you freedom. Truth alone makes you free, and you must realize truth by yourself.

There is an interesting anecdote about Wen-hsi disciple of Yang-shan. It is said that when Wen-hsi was serving in the kitchen, Wen-ju (Mañjuśri) often appeared to him. Wen-hsi took up a cooking utensil and drove away the apparition, saying, "Wen-ju is Wen-ju; but Wen-hsi is Wen-hsi!"

In the same spirit, Ts'ui-yen declared:

> The full-grown man aspires to pierce through the heavens:
> Let him not walk in the footsteps of the Buddha!

The Zen masters realize what a superlatively hard task it is to be a full-grown man, what heart-rending trials and backbreaking hardships, what gravelike loneliness, what strangling doubts, what agonizing temptations one must go through before one can hope to arrive at the threshold of enlightenment. That's why they have approached it with all their might and have never been willing to stop short of their ultimate goal.

## 22. THE FUNCTION OF A MASTER

The Zennists are so independent that they have often declared that they have got nothing from their masters. As Hsüeh-feng said in regard to his master Te-shan, "Empty-handed I went to him, and empty-handed I returned." Strictly speaking, this is true. No master would claim to have instilled anything into his disciple. Still, the master does have a necessary function to perform.

When Shih-t'ou visited his master Ch'ing-yüan for the first time, the master asked, "Where do you come from?" Shih-t'ou answered that he was from Ts'ao-ch'i, where the late Sixth Patriarch had been teaching. Then Ch'ing-yüan asked, "What have you brought with you?" Shih-t'ou replied, "That which had never been lost even before I went to Ts'ao-ch'i." Ch'ing-yüan further asked, "If that is the case, why did you go to Ts'ao-ch'i at all?" Shih-t'ou said, "If I had not gone to Ts'ao-ch'i, how could I realize that it had never been lost?"

From this it is crystal clear that although a master cannot actually instill anything into you, he can nevertheless help open your eyes to what you have within you. His instruction may at least serve as a catalyst in your enlightenment.

## 23. POEMS USED BY ZEN MASTERS

The most favorite lines among the Zen masters are Wang Wei's:

*I stroll along the stream up to where it ends.*
*I sit down watching the clouds as they begin to rise.*

I have seen this charming couplet many times in Zen literature. One master made it his own by adding two words to each line:

*Without strolling along the stream up to where it ends,*
*How can you sit down watching the clouds as they begin to rise?*

Wang Chin-huan's famous couplet has also been quoted to evoke the way upward:

*To see farther into the horizons,*
*Let's mount one more flight of stairs.*

But the most interesting instance is Wu-tsu Fa-yen's use of a couplet from a popular love song:

*Time and again she calls for "Little Jade,"*
  *Not that she needs her service.*
*She only wants her sweet bridegroom*
  *To recognize her voice.*

This needs a little explanation. Little Jade was the name of the bride's maid. In old China, when the girl of a well-to-do family was married, she was usually accompanied for the first few days by a handmaid to help her in dressing and undressing. In normal cases, the bridegroom and the bride had never met before their wedding, but usually they fell in love with each other at first sight. In this case, at any rate, she was already in love with her bridegroom, but like other brides she was still too shy to speak directly with the bridegroom, who was perhaps just as shy. To familiarize him with her voice, she called her maid as though she needed her service. When her maid came and asked her if she needed anything, she would reply, "Oh thanks, nothing important!"

But what has all this to do with Zen? The bridegroom stands for the "true man of no title," the inexpressible and inconceivable. You cannot call him, because he has no name. On the other hand, although he has no name and you cannot speak about him, there is no denying that you are in love with him with your whole mind, your whole heart, your whole being. So, even your calling the names of others is nothing but an expression of your love for him. He is the meaning of all your action and speech, which far from distracting you from him, only help you to vent your feeling of love.

Fa-yen's disciple, Yüan-wu, wrote a gāthā in the form of an excellent love poem:

> *The incense in the golden duck is burning out,—*
> *She is still waiting behind the embroidered curtains.*
> *In the midst of flute playing and songs,*
> *He returns intoxicated, supported by friends.*
> *The happy adventure of the romantic youth,—*
> *His lady alone knows its sweetness.*

Zen is so personal a thing that it has often been compared to eating and drinking. This gāthā from Yüan-wu is a lone instance of speaking of Zen in terms of sexual love. But his meaning is clear. He has elsewhere given another beautiful description of satori in terms of landscape: "You gain an illuminating insight into the very nature of things, which now appear to you as so many fairy flowers having no graspable realities. Here is manifested the unsophisticated self which is the original face of your being; here is shown all bare the most beautiful landscape of your birthplace."

### 24. CHUANG-TZU AND THE DHARMA EYE

Liang-shan Yüan-kuan, a member of the House of Ts'ao-t'ung, was once asked by a monk to tell him what is the right Dharma Eye. He answered, "It is in the *Nan Hua!*" Now, *Nan Hua* was the canonical title which had been conferred on the *Book of Chuang-tzu* in 742. This answer must have surprised the monk. So he asked, "Why in the *Nan Hua?*" The master replied, "Because you are asking about the right Dharma Eye!"

As time went on, the fundamental affinity between Chuang-tzu and Zen became more and more widely recognized. A number of Zen masters brought their profound insights into the nature of the Absolute to bear upon Chuang-tzu's philosophy of Tao. For instance, the outstanding Zen master of the Ming period, Han-shan Te-ch'ing (1546–1623) wrote an annotation of the first book of *Chuang-tzu*, which seems to me far more illuminating than Kuo Hsiang's annotation.

Ta-hui Tsung-kao (1089–1163) gave an excellent exposition of Chuang-tzu's idea that Tao is not only beyond speech but beyond silence as well. He made an effective use of this idea in opposing the advocates of what is called "silent contemplation Zen." He was equally opposed to Hua-t'ou Zen, the theory that Zen consists in tackling with the kōan. He went to the extent of burning his master Yüan-wu's *Pi-yen chi.* His notion of Zen corresponds to Chuang-tzu's notion of Tao: it is everywhere and nowhere. In its practical aspect, Zen consists in doing or non-doing in accordance with the fitness of the occasion. There is silence in speech, speech in silence; there is action in inaction, inaction in action. Timeliness is all. If your action is timely it is as though you had not acted. If your speech is timely, it is as though you had not spoken.

All-rounded as his doctrine is, Ta-hui is more speculative than contemplative. He is like a singer whose voice is highpitched and loud; but one feels that it comes from the throat rather than the diaphragm. With the great masters of T'ang, their voice seems to come from the heels. Ta-hui is too brilliant to be profound. It was not for nothing that the Lin-chi Zen after Ta-hui began to decay, just as the Fa-yen Zen began to fade out after Yen-shou.


## 25. GOODNESS AS AN ENTRANCE TO ZEN

The Zennists have usually emphasized intuitive perception of truth as the way to enlightenment. But in my view, not only the sudden perception of truth, but also an unexpected experience of spontaneous goodness, can liberate you from the shell of your little ego, and transport you from the stuffy realm of concepts and categories to the beyond. Whenever goodness flows unexpectedly from the inner self, uncontaminated by the ideas of duty and sanction, there is Zen. I need to give but a few examples of such goodness.

Han Po-yu's mother was of irascible disposition, and when Po-yu was a child, he was often beaten by her with a staff. He always received the beating graciously, without crying. One day, however, when he was beaten, he wept piteously. Greatly surprised, his mother said, "On all former occasions you always received my discipline gladly. What makes you cry today?" Po-yu replied, "In the past I always felt pain when Mom beat me, so that I was secretly comforted that Mom was in vigorous health. Today, I no longer feel any pain. So I am afraid that my dear mom is decaying in energy. How can I help crying?"

Hung Hsiang's father was down with paralysis, and Hsiang attended upon him day and night, serving medicine and helping him to get up on necessary occasions. His father felt that it was unfair to his daughter-in-law to keep her newly married husband away from her even in the night. So he told his son, "I am getting better now. Please go to sleep in your own room. It will be enough to leave a servant to wait on me at night." Hsiang pretended to accede to his father's wishes, but as soon as his father was asleep, he stole into the room and slept beside his bed. In the depth of night, the father was, as usual, under the necessity of getting up. Seeing that the servant was soundly asleep, he attempted to stand on his feet but tottered. Suddenly, Hsiang rose to hold him, keeping him from falling in the nick of time. The father, taken by surprise, asked, "Who are you?" "It's me, Dad!" said Hsiang. Realizing to what heroic lengths his son had gone in his filial love, he embraced him, weeping for gratitude and saying, "Oh God! What a filial child you have given me!" Hung Hsiang was called by his neighbors "Master of Hidden Virtue."

Yang Fu took leave of his parents and went to Szechwan to visit the Bodhisattva Wu Chi. He met an old monk on the way, who asked him, "Where are you going?" Yang Fu told him that he was going to visit Wu Chi and to become his disciple. The old monk said, "It is better to see the Buddha himself than to see a bodhisattva." Yang Fu asked where could he find the Buddha." The old monk said, "Just return home, and you will see someone meeting you draped in a blanket and wearing slippers on the wrong feet. Mark you well: this will be the very Buddha." Yang Fu accordingly turned his way homeward. On the day of his arrival, it was already late in the night. His mother had already gone to bed. But as soon as she heard the knock of her son, she was so excited that she had no time to dress up. Putting on a blanket for an overcoat, and hastily stepping into her slippers right-side-left, she came to the door to welcome him back. On seeing her, Yang Fu was shocked into enlightenment. Thereafter he devoted all his energies to serving his parents and produced a big volume of annotations on the *Classic of Filial Piety*.

It is significant that the last story is found in a Taoist compilation of edifying anecdotes. So we have here a Taoist using the wisdom of a

Buddhist bodhisattva (for the old monk was none other than Wu Chi) for the promotion of Confucian ethics.

Even morality can be beautiful when it springs directly from the pure fountain of the child's heart. It is no less a door to enlightenment than the croak of a frog or the upsetting of a chamber-vessel.

## 26. HAN-SHAN AND SHIH-TE

One of the most cherished poems of the T'ang dynasty was a quatrain by Chang Chi (f. latter part of the eighth century) on "A Night Mooring at Maple Bridge":

> *The moon has gone down,*
> *A crow caws through the frost.*
> *A sorrow-ridden sleep under the shadows*
> *Of maple trees and fishermen's fires.*
> *Suddenly the midnight bell of Cold Mountain Temple*
> *Sends its echoes from beyond the city to a passing boat.*

This poem is redolent of Zen. It seems as though eternity had suddenly invaded the realm of time.

Cold Mountain Temple in the suburbs of Soochow was built in memory of Han-shan Tzu or the "Sage of Cold Mountain," a legendary figure who is supposed to have lived in the seventh century as a hermit in the neighborhood of Kuo-ch'ing Temple on T'ien-t'ai Mountain in Chekiang. He was not a monk, nor yet a layman; he was just himself. He found a bosom friend in the person of Shih-te, who served in the kitchen of Kuo-ch'ing Temple. After every meal Han-shan would come to the kitchen to feed upon the leftovers. Then the two inseparable friends would chat and laugh. To the monks of the temple, they were just two fools. One day, as Shih-te was sweeping the ground, an old monk said to him, "You were named 'Shih-te' [literally 'picked up'], because you were picked up by Feng-kan. But tell me what is your real family name?" Shih-te laid down his sweeper and stood quietly with his hands crossed. When the old monk repeated his question, Shih-te took up his sweeper and went away sweeping. Han-shan struck his breast, saying, "Heaven, heaven!" Shih-te asked what he was doing. Han-shan said, "Don't you know that when the eastern neighbor has died, the western neighbor must attend his funeral?"

Then the two danced together, laughing and weeping as they went out of the temple.

At a mid-monthly renewal of vows, Shih-te suddenly clapped his hands, saying, "You are gathered here for meditation. What about *that thing?*" The leader of the community angrily told him to shut up. Shih-te said, "Please control yourself and listen to me:

> *The elimination of anger is true śīla.*
> *Purity of heart is true homelessness.*
> *My self-nature and yours are one,*
> *The fountain of all the right dharmas!*

Both Han-shan and Shih-te were poets. I will give a sample of Shih-te's poetry here:

> *I was from the beginning a "pickup,"*
> *It is not by accident that I am called "Shih-te."*
> *I have no kith and kin, only Han-shan*
> *Is my elder brother.*
> *We are one in heart and mind:*
> *How can we compromise with the world?*
> *Do you wish to know our age? More than once*
> *Have we seen the Yellow River in its pure limpidity!*

Everybody knows that the Yellow River had never been limpid since the beginning of history. So the last two lines were meant to convey that they were older than the world! Another noteworthy point in this poem is that even hermits—and Han-shan and Shih-te are among the greatest hermits of China—have need of like-minded friends for mutual encouragement and consolation. This is what keeps them so perfectly human.

From the poems of Han-shan, you will see that he is even more human than Shih-te. There were moments when he felt intensely lonely and homesick. As he so candidly confessed:

> *Sitting alone I am sometimes overcome*
> *By vague feelings of sadness and unrest.*

Sometimes he thought nostalgically of his brothers:

> *Last year, when I heard the spring birds sing,*
> *I thought of my brothers at home.*
> *This year when I see the autumn chrysanthemums fade,*

*The same thought comes back to me.*
*Green waters sob in a thousand streams,*
*Dark clouds hang on every side.*
*Up to the end of my life, though I live a hundred years,*
*It will break my heart to think of Ch'ang-an.*

This is not the voice of a man without human affection. If he preferred to live as a hermit, it was because he was driven by a mysterious impulse to find something infinitely more precious than the world could give. Here is his poem on "The Priceless Pearl":

*Formerly I was extremely poor and miserable.*
*Every night I counted the treasures of others.*
*But today I have thought the matter over,*
*And decided to build a house of my own.*
*Digging at the ground I have found a hidden treasure—*
*A pearl as pure and clear as crystal!*
*A number of blue-eyed traders from the West*
*Have conspired together to buy the pearl from me.*
*In reply I have said to them,*
*"This pearl is without a price!"*

His interior landscape can be glimpsed from a well-known gāthā of his:

*My mind is like the autumn moon, under which*
*The green pond appears so limpid, bright, and pure.*
*In fact, all analogies and comparisons are inapt.*
*In what words can I describe it?*

With such interior landscape, it is little wonder that he should be so intensely in love with nature, for nature alone could reflect the inner vision with a certain adequacy. Some of his nature poems shed a spirit of ethereal delight. For example, this:

*The winter has gone and with it a dismal year.*
*Spring has come bringing fresh colors to all things.*
*Mountain flowers smile in the clear pools.*
*Perennial trees dance in the blue mist.*
*Bees and butterflies are alive with pleasure.*
*Birds and fishes delight me with their happiness.*

*Oh the wondrous joy of endless comradeship!*
*From dusk to dawn I could not close my eyes.*

Only the man of Tao, the truly detached man, can enjoy the beauties of nature as they are meant to be enjoyed. As to the others, they are too preoccupied with their own interests and purposes to enjoy the landscape of nature. As an old lay woman called Dame Chen said, in a gāthā she composed on seeing a crowd of woodcutters:

*On the high slope and low plane,*
*You see none but woodcutters.*
*Everyone carries in his bosom*
*The idea of knife and axe;*
*How can he see the mountain flowers*
*Tinting the waters with patches of glorious red?*

## 27. "WHO IS THAT PERSON?"

Yung-an Chuan-teng said to his assembly, "There is a certain person, who avers, 'I do not depend on the blessing and help of the Buddha, I do not live in any of the three realms, I do not belong to the world of the five elements. The patriarchs have not dared to pin me down, nor have the Buddhas dared to give me a definite name.' Can you tell me who is that person?"

Wu-hsieh Ling-meh, a disciple of Shih-t'ou as well as of Ma-tsu, was once asked by a monk, "What is greater than the heaven-and-earth?" He replied, "No man can know *him!*"

Although Ling-meh is usually listed as a disciple of Ma-tsu, he was actually enlightened at his encounter with Shih-t'ou. We are told that when he visited Shih-t'ou, he found him seated without paying any attention to him. So he started to go away. Shih-t'ou called after him, "Acarya!" As Ling-meh turned his head backward to the master, the latter scolded him, "How is it that from birth to death you have been doing nothing but turning your head and twisting your brains?" At these words, Ling-meh was thoroughly awakened to his self-nature, and stayed with Shih-t'ou.

The masters of Zen have referred to this self-nature by a great variety of names, such as "this one," "that one," "he," "the original face," "the true man of no title," "the independent man of Tao," "the self," and so forth. Some have even called him "the family thief."

The whole meaning of Zen lies in the most intimate possible experiential recognition of "That Person" as your real self. As to how does this real self relate itself to God, I simply do not know. I know that the real self *is* and that God *is*. But they are both inconceivable, and who can speak of their relation? In dealing with the things of God, all human words are, as Leon Bloy has so graphically put it, "like so many blind lions seeking desperately to find a watering place in the desert." The Divine Word himself is compelled to resort to parables and analogies. He speaks of the relation in organic terms as the vine and its branches. The whole living tree is one-in-many and many-in-one. It is at once nondualistic and nonmonistic. If the Zen masters insist on nonduality, they do not thereby commit themselves to monism, as some Western students of Zen tend to think. This is all that I can say. Let me therefore stop here, remembering what Lao-tzu is reported to have said:

> To know when to stop
> To know when you can get no further
> By your own action,
> This is the right beginning!

## 28. A BUDDHIST INTERPRETATION OF A CONFUCIAN TEXT

The *Chung-yung* or the *Golden Mean* says: "What is ordained of heaven is called the nature. The following of this nature is called Tao. The refinement of Tao is called teaching." According to Ta-hui Tsung-kao, the first sentence corresponds to the pure dharmakāya. The second sentence corresponds to the consummated saṃbhogakāya. The third corresponds to the endlessly variable nirmāṇakāya. If you can pierce through the barriers of words, you will find that this interpretation is not a far-fetched one.

## 29. OCCASIONS OF ENLIGHTENMENT

It is not possible to describe satori; but to study the occasions of satori is not only possible but extremely fascinating.

The upāsaka Chang Chiu-ch'en was pondering a kōan when he was in the toilet. Suddenly he heard the croak of a frog, and he was awakened, as evidenced by the following lines:

> In a moonlit night on a spring day,
>    The croak of a frog
> Pierces through the whole cosmos and turns it into a single family!

An ancient monk was studying the *Lotus Sūtra*. When he came upon the passage that "all the dharmas are originally and essentially silent and void," he was beset with doubts. He pondered on it day and night, whether he was walking, resting, sitting, or lying in bed. But the more he pondered, the more confused he became. On a certain spring day, an oriole suddenly burst into song, and just as suddenly the monk's mind was opened to the light. He composed a gāthā on the spot:

> All the dharmas are from the very beginning
> Essentially silent and void.
> When spring comes and the hundred flowers bloom,
> The yellow oriole sings on the willow.

The sudden burst of song of the new oriole reminded him of the eternal silence.

Not only sounds, but also colors can be an occasion of enlightenment. One master came to his enlightenment on seeing the peach blossoms. "Ever since I saw the peach blossoms, I have had no more doubts," he used to say. Of course, he had seen peach blossoms previously to that happy occasion. But it was only on that occasion that he *really* saw them as they should be seen, that is, he saw them for the first time against the background of the eternal Void, as though they had just emerged from Creative Mind. On previous occasions, he had seen them vaguely as in a dream. But this time, as his inner spirit happened to be happily conditioned for enlightenment, the sight of peach blossoms opened his eyes to the source of their beauty, so that he saw them not as isolated objects, but as lively spurts from the source of the whole universe.

This reminds me of an interesting chat between Nan-ch'üan and his lay disciple Lu Hsüan. Lu was reciting Seng-chao's saying:

> Heaven and earth come from the same root as myself:
>    All things and I belong to one Whole.

However, he did not really understand the full purport of it. Nan-ch'üan pointed at the peonies in the courtyard, saying, "The worldlings look at this bush of flowers as in a dream." Lu did not see the point.

If Lu Hsüan had comprehended the truth of Seng-chao's saying (which, by the way, was a quotation from Chuang-tzu), he would have seen Nan-ch'üan's point. Only when you have realized that the cosmos and your self come from the same root, and all things and your self belong to one Whole, will you awake from your dream and see the peonies with wide-open eyes.

If we can think of God, not merely as the Supreme Engineer, but also as the Supreme Artist and Poet, nature will reveal entirely new aspects to our eyes and regale our spirits with such enchanting beauty that we will feel as though we were living in the Garden of Delights. As the Sufi poet Sadi has put it:

> *Those who indulge in God-worship*
> *Get into ecstasy from the creaking of a waterwheel.*

Some Zen masters have said that when a man is fully awakened, he can hear by his eye. The psalmist was certainly such a man, who sang:

> *The heavens declare the glory of God,*
> *And the firmament displays his art.*
> *Day to day utters speech,*
> *Night to night transmits knowledge.*

## 30. EVERY DAY A GOOD DAY

Yün-men once put a question to his assembly: "I am not asking you about the days before the fifteenth [the full moon]. I want you to tell me something about the days after." Getting no word from the audience, he gave his own answer, "Every day is a good day."

The full moon symbolizes enlightenment. The enlightened man is the free man. Being dead, nothing worse can happen to him. Being truly alive, nothing can be better. Not that he is immune to the buffets of fortune, but he knows that they cannot injure him any more.

Wu-men, the author of *Wu-men kuan* (The Gateless Gate), commenting on Nan-ch'üan's aphorism that "Tao is nothing else than your ordinary mind, your everyday life," produced a lovely poem:

> *Spring has its hundred flowers,*
> > *Autumn its moon.*
> *Summer has its cooling breezes,*

*Winter its snow.*
*If you allow no idle concerns*
        *To weigh on your heart,*
    *Your whole life will be one*
        *Perennial good season.*

The great paradox is that only a man who has no concern for his life can truly taste the joy of life, and only the carefree can really take care of others.

This reminds me of Pope John. What makes him so charming and so great? Is it not because he has lost himself in God? To him, "All days, like all months, equally belong to the Lord. Thus they are all equally beautiful." On Christmas 1962, he said, "I am entering my eighty-second year. Shall I finish it? Every day is a good day to be born, and every day is a good day to die." On the eve of his death, when he saw his friends weeping, he asked that the Magnificat be chanted, saying, "Take courage! This is not the moment to weep; this is a moment of joy and glory." Comforting his doctor, he said, "Dear Professor, don't be disturbed. My bags are always packed. When the moment to depart arrives, I won't lose any time."

True goodness is always beautiful and cheerful, even when one is on the brink of death. I can no longer doubt this after I have witnessed with my own eyes the deathbed scene of my dear wife, Teresa (d. Nov. 30, 1959). She was cheerful and thoughtful up to the very end. About two hours before her death, she whispered to our son Vincent, who was in her room together with Dr. Francis Jani saying, "The doctor has been standing so long that he must be greatly fatigued. Go bring a chair for him to sit down." Dr. Jani thought that she was asking for something. So he asked Vincent what was her desire. When Vincent told him what she had said, the doctor was so moved that he went out immediately and wept. Later he told me that it was the first time in his thirty years of practice to find a dying person still so thoughtful of others. About an hour later, the doctor called us all in for the final farewell. She was in smiles, speaking to all our children one by one and blessing them and promising to pray for them in heaven. I was simply dazed with wonder. Lowering my head, I prayed and offered her to Christ in the words of John the Baptist: "He who has the bride is the Bridegroom; but the friend of the Bridegroom, who stands and hears him, rejoices exceedingly at the voice of the Bridegroom. This my joy, therefore, is made full. He must increase, but I must decrease." Suddenly I heard our children call me, "Dad, Mommy wants to speak to you!" No sooner had I turned my eyes to her than she leaned forward and, holding my hands in hers, said cordially, "Till our reunion in heaven!" This lifted my spirit to such a height that I forgot my sorrow!

# My Reminiscences of Dr. Daisetz T. Suzuki

During the years 1949–1951, I was a visiting professor of Chinese philosophy and literature at the University of Hawaii. The outstanding student in my classes was Richard De Martino, who was at the same time pursuing his studies in Zen Buddhism under the private tutorship of Dr. Daisetz Suzuki. It was through the introduction of Richard that I had the pleasure of meeting Dr. Suzuki. From the very beginning he impressed me as one who not merely taught philosophy but actually lived it.

It was in those days that his *Living by Zen* made its appearance. I was simply fascinated by his presentation of the subtle insights of great Zen masters like Ma-tsu, Chao-chou, Lin-chi, and Yün-men. Hitherto my acquaintance with Zen was based mainly upon the Sixth Patriarch Hui-neng's *Platform Sūtra*, which I had read several years before and had come to regard as one of the three books of supreme wisdom in the history of China, the other two being *The Analects of Confucius* and Lao-tzu's *Tao-te ching*. But it was through the reading of *Living by Zen* that I began to realize the far-reaching influence of Hui-neng's insights and, what is more, to get a taste of the special flavor of Zen as it was developed in the teachings of his great successors. Ever since then, Zen literature has been my great hobby and its ineffable charm has been growing on me.

My second contact with Dr. Suzuki happened again in Honolulu. It was in the summer of 1959, when the University of Hawaii was holding its third East-West Philosophers' Conference. We were both on the panel. One evening, as he was reporting on the Japanese philosophy of life, I heard him say, "The Japanese live by Confucianism and die by Buddhism." I was struck by this remarkable statement. Of course, I understood what he meant, for this is more or less true also of the Chinese. All the same, I thought that it was an exaggeration, which stood in need of some amendment and clarification for the sake of our western colleagues. So, as soon as he had done with the report, I asked the chairman's permission to put a question to Dr. Suzuki. Having got the green light, I proceeded, "I was very much struck by Dr. Suzuki's observation that the Japanese live by Confucianism and die by Buddhism. Now, a few years ago, I had the pleasure of reading Dr. Suzuki's *Living by Zen*. Is Zen not a school of Buddhism which prevails in Japan? If this is true, there must be many Japanese living by Zen Buddhism. It seems to me, therefore, that the statement that the Japanese die by Buddhism stands in need of some revision." The chairman very carefully relayed my question to Dr. Suzuki (for he was somewhat hard of hearing), and the whole panel was agog for his answer. But no sooner had the chairman presented the question than Dr. Suzuki responded with the suddenness and spontaneity of a true Zen master, "Living is dying!" This set the whole conference table aroar. Everybody was laughing, apparently at my expense. I alone was enlightened. He did not, indeed, answer my question, but he lifted me to a higher plane, a plane beyond logic and reasoning, beyond living and dying. I felt like giving Dr. Suzuki a slap in order to assure him that his utterance had clicked. But after all, must I not still live by Confucianism, especially in the presence of so many respectable professors?

From that interesting experience I came to feel much closer to him. We saw eye-to-eye with each other, although many of our American friends continued to remind me that Dr. Suzuki had not answered my question, and they were quite mystified when I told them that he had more than answered my question. Where two oriental philosophers are in perfect agreement, western philosophers are apt to see nothing but disagreement.

In the summer of 1964, we met each other again at the fourth East-West Philosophers' Conference in Honolulu. We had a happy reunion, and his devoted secretary Miss Mihoko Okamura took some pictures of us. He was delighted to hear that I was writing a book on the golden age of Zen, dealing with the great Zen masters of the T'ang period. He gladly acceded to my request that he would write an introduction to the book when completed. He read over one of the chapters of the contemplated work and encouraged me to continue.

By the winter of 1965, I had practically completed the book mentioned above. I wrote him two letters, of which the second was as follows:

43 Cottage Street
South Orange, N.J. 07079

December 20, 1965

My dear Dr. Suzuki:

I am happy to tell you that I have now completed a book under the title *The Golden Age of Zen*, of which the enclosed forty-four pages are the epilogue. I am mailing the epilogue to you first because it contains something personal. Besides, it is light reading suitable to the holiday season.

The other chapters are as follows:

1. Introductory: From Bodhidharma to Hung-jen
2. The Sixth Patriarch Hui-neng: His Life and His Outstanding Disciples
3. Hui-neng's Fundamental Insights (This is the only chapter presented to you last summer)
4. Ma-tsu Tao-i
5. Pai-chang and Huang-po
6. Chao-chou Ts'ung-shen
7. Outstanding Masters in the Lineage of Shih-t'ou
8. Kuei-shan: Founder of the House of Kuei-yang
9. Lin-chi I-hsüan: Founder of the House of Lin-chi
10. Tung-shan: Founder of the House of Ts'ao-tung.
11. Yün-men Wen-yen: Founder of the House of Yün-men
12. Fa-yen Wen-i: Founder of the House of Fa-yen

Epilogue (enclosed herewith)

I had intended to cover the later periods. But Zen literature is so rich that it will take at least five more years of intensive study before I can produce an adequate history of Zen in China. Even as it is—an account of the masters of T'ang—it is already three hundred pages.

All the above listed chapters have been mimeographed, except the first chapter which is still being written. I am rereading your two authoritative works on the

*Laṅkāvatāra Sūtra.* In fact, your profound insights have been my guide in writing all the chapters. But for the writing of the first chapter, your painstaking research must be painstakingly studied.

I have followed your great insights, not in a slavish spirit, but because after an intensive study of the original material in Chinese, I cannot but see eye-to-eye with you on almost every point. For instance, what you have said about the intrinsic affinity between the Taoism of Lao and Chuang and Zen, in your introduction to James Legge's translation of Chuang-tzu, is so profoundly true that no original spirits can disagree. The truth is that the school of Zen was very much influenced by Seng-chao's book, and to my mind Seng-chao was a true knower of Chuang-tzu.

As soon as I hear from you, I shall mail all the chapters. I hope you will favor me with a foreword, as you so generously promised last summer.

I have been asked by my friends in Formosa to write an English biography of Dr. Sun Yat-sen. In the spring I shall have to go to Taipei. But I want very much to stay a few days in Japan on my way to Taiwan. I wish to visit you. May I? Shall we see the cherry blossoms together?

In the epilogue (pp. 11ff.) you will find a personal account of "A Taste of Suzuki's Zen." Last summer, some old members of the Conference were still speaking as though you had not answered my question! So I think it is time for me to break my silence.

You will note that in the epilogue I have drawn my materials mostly from sources after T'ang. This relieves my mind to some extent. I hope that what I have written about Ta-hui Tsung-kao (pp. 30–31) is not too harsh. I might have a more favorable impression of him, if I knew him better. What do you think of him?

Father Thomas Merton is a very dear friend of mine. Recently, he has published a book called *The Way of Chuang-tzu.* I am happy to see that he confirms your insight about Chuang-tzu and Zen. "The true inheritors of the thought and spirit of Chuang-tzu are the Zen Buddhists of the T'ang period," he writes (p. 15).

Wishing you every happiness and a life at least as long as Chao-chou the Ancient Buddha. I am, Doctor,

A humble pupil of yours,
John C. H. Wu

Kindly convey my best Christmas and New Year wishes to Miss Okamura. I have inclosed here a Chinese translation of Basho's haiku. Do you like it? I may translate more haikus into Chinese.

I wish I could describe the thrill of joy I felt on receiving his answer in February of this year. It is such an invaluable treasure to me that I wish to share it with my reader:

Matsugaoka Bunko
1375 Yamanouchi
Kamakura, Japan

January 30, 1966

Dear Dr. Wu,

Thank you very much for your two letters. They were duly received, but I was away from home for some time. Besides, my eyesight is failing recently and I find it difficult even to read letters and manuscripts, not to say anything about books printed in small types. Hence this delay. Kindly excuse my negligence.

Your manuscript "Epilogue" is extremely interesting. Your interpretation of Basho's poem on the frog hits the essence of all genuine religious experience. I would like to see you in Japan when you go to Formosa. Please try by all means to come to Kamakura and let me talk personally with you on the subjects that concern us both. I am afraid writing takes too much time. Let me know about when you are planning to come this way.

Hoping to see you before long and wishing you everything good and happy.

Sincerely yours,
Daisetz T. Suzuki

P.S. Please find enclosed a photo which was taken while in Hawaii 1959.

The "Epilogue" mentioned in the above letter is, of course, too long to reproduce here. I want only to reproduce the part relating to Basho's haiku, since it had given him such a delight:

## TIME AND ETERNITY

One of the most frequently reiterated couplets in Chinese Zen literature is:

> An eternity of endless space:
> A day of wind and moon.

This brings us, as it were, to the dawn of creation. And nothing stirs the heart and mind of man more profoundly than to be reminded of the first quivering of time in the womb of eternity. An infinite void, utterly silent and still. In a split second there came life and motion, form and color. No one knows how it happened. It is a mystery of mysteries. But the mere recognition that the mystery exists is enough to send any man of sensitive mind into an ecstasy of joy and wonder.

Herein is the secret of the perennial charm of Basho's haiku:

> An old pond.
> A frog jumps in:
>   Plop!

The old pond corresponds to "An eternity of endless space," while the frog jumping in and causing the water to utter a sound is equivalent to "A day of wind and moon." Can there be a more beautiful and soul-shaking experience than to catch ageless silence breaking for the first time into song? Moreover, every day is the dawn of creation, for every day is unique and comes for the first time and the last. God is not the God of the dead, but of the living.

On May 1 of this year I flew from New York and stopped over in Tokyo for several days in order to pay a visit to Dr. Suzuki in Kamakura. It was on the third that I went to see him with my relative Mr. C. F. Liu and his secretary Mr. Ikeba. Miss Okamura who received us first, told me that Dr. Suzuki had been expecting me for the last few days and valued our friendship so much as to say it made him feel that he had not lived in vain! Then the great man came out wreathed in smiles to greet me and my company. Everyone of us was pleasantly surprised to find him in such good shape. I presented to him my manuscript on *The Golden Age of Zen*, for which he was to write an introduction. He very graciously gave me a number of books, including his painstaking editions of the *Platform Sūtra*, of the collected fragments of Bodhidharma, and of the sayings of Chao-chou. Miss Okamura again took some pictures of us.

Obviously he had a greater esteem for Ta-hui Tsung-kao than I had, for he commented favorably on his writings and advised me to read more of him. I have since followed his advice and my impression of Ta-hui has improved, although, I must confess, I still find him a little too verbose.

We spent the whole afternoon with him, and we found him remarkably vivacious for his age. How could I know that a little over two months later he would have completed the journey of his life. I have seen him only once in a dream, still speaking of Chao-chou. But if, as he said, living is dying, then dying is living.

Suzuki is a true man, who belongs to all time and to the whole world. But it takes a great nation like Japan to have produced a great man like Suzuki. He has returned to eternity, but what a lovely day of wind and moon he meant for all or us!

John C. H. Wu

# INDEX